If You Can Walk With Kings

A View of William Le Queux

If You Can Walk With Kings

A View of William Le Queux

David Ian Chapman

JANUS PUBLISHING COMPANY LTD
Cambridge, England

First published in Great Britain 2016
by Janus Publishing Company Ltd
The Studio
High Green
Great Shelford
Cambridge CB22 5EG

www.januspublishing.co.uk

Copyright © David Ian Chapman 2016
British Library Cataloguing-in-Publication Data
A catalogue record for this book is available from the British Library

ISBN 978-1-85756-858-5

All rights reserved. No part of this publication may be reproduced, stored in a retrieval system or transmitted in any form or by any means, electric, mechanical, photocopying, recording or otherwise, without the prior permission of the publisher.

The right of David Ian Chapman to be identified as the author of this work has been asserted by him in accordance with the Copyright, Designs and Patents Act 1988.

Cover Design: Janus Publishing Company Ltd

Cover Image: Drawn by the Author

Printed and bound in the UK by PublishPoint
from KnowledgePoint Limited, Reading.

Acknowledgements

There are two people I have to thank most for the decision to write this biography who are sadly no longer with us. Tony Angelucci who many years ago first fired my interest in William Le Queux. Had he lived I am certain with his knowledge we would have uncovered many more secrets. The other is Yvonne Vincent, nee Le Queux, whose desire to study her family history developed into starting the William Le Queux Society, and through them many unknown avenues were uncovered.

Unbeknown to them the staff of the British Library have been of the utmost help. Over the years they must have lugged armfuls of books and vast volumes of bound magazines. I also have to thank George Locke for supplying, over many, many years, most of the magazines and letters that form the basis of this account of Le Queux's fascinating life, giving us first-hand evidence to prove that he was far from the fantasist that many people still believe. To Barbara Legg, my editor, who had the unenviable task of trying the follow the various threads. To Janet Whitmore who first read the manuscript, and it was her interest and companionship that resulted in the final draft. It is to her I owe the greatest debt.

Despite lengthy investigations I have been unable to locate the whereabouts of the person whom I strongly believe to be the rightful copyright owner of all the unpublished material. That person is Mabel Elizabeth Chatfield, who may have been the natural or adopted daughter of William Le Queux and who emigrated to Canada. There has since been no trace of either her or her descendants. If anyone has any knowledge that may prove to discover Mabel Le Queux, I would

If You Can Walk With Kings

dearly love to hear from them. Fortunately, Peter Le Queux, the great-grandson of Fred Le Queux, has taken an interest and has kindly given us permission to publish.

Aside from all the help I have received all the errors and omissions are mine and mine alone. My hope is that this book will provoke further investigations into a man who has been dubbed *The Master of Mystery*, with good reason.

David Ian Chapman

Contents

Preface		ix
The French Connection	1864–1880	1
Three Weddings and a Funeral	1881–1902	13
The Invasion	1903–1906	49
Mission to Albania	1906	67
Lapland Expedition	1907	103
Divorce	1908–1909	135
William Kelly	1909–1912	153
The Mummy's Curse	1912–1913	175
The Great War	1914–1919	183
Radio Days	1920–1921	213
Journey's End	1922–1927	219
Loose Ends		233
General Bibliography		241
Bibliography of works by William Le Queux in the order in which they were published		243
Index		293

Unknown

Chevalier William Le Queux

Preface

It seems that William Le Queux has been a very misunderstood man and hardly ever taken seriously. This is partly his own fault as he treated his memoirs so lightly and was over secretive to the point of evasiveness. His cause was not helped by comments made by that doyen of the Spy Story, John le Carré, who, in a newspaper interview, called Le Queux 'a talentless posturer'.[1] Another columnist for the *Daily Telegraph*, Professor Christopher Andrew,[2] called Le Queux the 'worst novelist in British history', even classing him alongside William McGonagall; really! However, Le Queux was the author of over two hundred books and countless short stories, so many publishers and editors seem not to have agreed.

There have been three biographies written about Le Queux. The first was his own somewhat impersonal autobiography, *Things I Know about Kings, Celebrities and Crooks,* published in 1923, when he managed to omit almost all of his family situations. This was followed in 1938 by an oddity of publishing, *The Real Le Queux* by Norman St Barbe Sladen, which is practically the same book transferred from the first to the third person. Yet Sladen should have known better as he was the nephew of Douglas Sladen, the editor of *Who's Who*, the latter at one time a near neighbour of William Le Queux. As editor of *Who's Who*, Douglas Sladen accumulated a vast collection of letters from those listed, including William Le Queux. This archive is today housed in the Richmond Public

---

1. John le Carré, *Sunday Times Review*, 23 March 1986.
2. Professor Christopher Andrew, born 1941, former President of Corpus Christi College, Cambridge and Official Historian of MI5.

If You Can Walk With Kings

Library, but is of limited usefulness. Finally, the only reliable biography was the privately printed *William Le Queux, Master of Mystery* by Chris Patrick and Stephen Baister *c.*2007.

Read his autobiography, or any of the long or brief biographies written about him, and you will find many unanswered questions. Such as where was his father born and was he the descendant of a French count; and did he receive a private education, and if so how could his father, a mere shop assistant, afford it; or, how many times did he marry; and did he write all his own books; or, did he use a pseudonym? What was the personal reason for him to turn down the offer from the King of a knighthood; and intriguingly, what was his connection with the mysterious 'William Kelly'; and was Le Queux the first real spy?

Perhaps at this point I should show Le Queux's own entry specially written, by himself, for *Who's Who*:

William Tufnell Le Queux

Novelist; traveller; Commander of the Orders of St Sava of Serbia; Danilo of Monténégro; Crown of Italy; San Marino Order, etc. Consul of Republic of San Marino, retired; b. London 2nd July 1864; e.s. of William Lequeux of Chateauroux, Indre; Educ: privately in London; Pegli, near Genoa. Studied art in the Latin Quartier; made a tour through France, Germany, and Italy on foot; became a journalist and special correspondent of The *Globe*, 1891; special foreign correspondent of *The Times*; resigned to devote his time to novel writing, 1893. Secretary to British diplomatic mission to San Marino. Has travelled in Russia, Algeria, Morocco, Tunisia, Serbia, the Areg region of the Sahara Desert, Asia Minor, etc.; journeyed through Macedonia, Monténégro, Serbia, Albania on special Government Mission, 1907; Arctic (with Harry de Windt), 1908; Sudan, 1909; Correspondent of the *Daily Mail* in various capitals, and war correspondent in the first Balkan War. Collector of mediaeval manuscripts, codices and monastic seals, of which he possesses a large and valuable

Preface

collection; has intimate knowledge of the Secret Service of other Continental Powers; consulted by the Government in such matters. Forecasted the Great War in his book, *The Invasion*, 1910. Is a keen student of criminology, and also well known in wireless research ...

My interest in William Le Queux dates back to the mid seventies and a chance meeting with Tony Angelucci. Over lunch we discussed crime writers and Tony persuaded me to read Le Queux. As Tony was a travel courier he was, like Le Queux, constantly on the move between European cities. Every time we met he would drop another little tit-bit such as Le Queux being on the Kaiser's death list. Strangely Tony lived in Pegli, where Le Queux is said to have lived at one time, and there was also a facial resemblance between him and William Le Queux. I was on the point of asking if there was any family relationship, when Tony suddenly died of a heart attack. So that avenue closed.

Another door opened when I acquired a collection of letters written by William Le Queux to his closest confidant, George Lord Beeforth. Beeforth was born into a Quaker family in 1823 and brought up in his home town of Scarborough, in the North Riding of Yorkshire, where he became a self-made man, amassing a fortune as a fine-art printer, his most prominent works being engravings by Gustave Doré. He was a Justice of the Peace and became Mayor of Scarborough in 1893, living in a large house, Belvedere, on the south cliff where he laid out a magnificent garden, now maintained by the borough council as pleasure gardens. During Le Queux's time Beeforth was a widower, his late wife, Helen, née Crawford, having been ten years his senior. He shared the house with his elder sister, Elizabeth Lord Beeforth, who had been born in 1821 and died in 1914. The Beeforth household also consisted of two granddaughters – Beatrice May Crawford Beeforth, born in Edinburgh in 1882 and dying in London in 1963, and Gabrielle Marie Louise Beeforth, born in San Remo, Italy in 1888 and British by parentage, dying at St Leonards-on-Sea in 1936. Gabrielle remained a spinster all her life but after her death, her sister Beatrice married William Kidd in 1937. Also living in the house was the girls' old governess, Ernestina Kloss, known as Fraulein, who had been born in Arnsberg, Germany in 1862. George Beeforth died in April 1924, aged 101, from pneumonia. Their correspondence, that which has remained, spanned the time of Le Queux's mission to Albania, the abortive adventure to Lapland, and into the Great War. I should state that the spelling, wording and punctuation reproduced in this work are as the originals.

This book answers some questions for the first time, but there may be still much that needs to be learnt. Le Queux does not give up his secrets lightly.

The French Connection
1864–1880

The earliest mention of the family of William Le Queux is in the London Tax Records held by the London Metropolitan Archives. These show a Will 'Le Keux' living in St George's-in-the-East, Stepney in 1789. In Le Queux's own memoirs he recites a poem on how to pronounce his surname:

> It troubles each sex
> So I put it to you
> Is it William Le Quex
> Or William Le Queux
>
> I give you the cue
> So no longer perplex
> It is William Le Queux
> Not William Le Quex[3]

By 1810 we find the first occurrence of the more familiar spelling of Lequex, although the mispronunciation of the family name continues with 'LeKeux' or 'Lequex' and this carried on through to 1844. From

---

3. William Le Queux, *Things I Know about Kings, Celebrities and Crooks*. London: Eveleigh Nash and Grayson, 1923, p 10.

1791 their address is Old Gravel Lane, Southwark, where once again there is a change in how the name is pronounced, to the more familiar 'Lequeux'. This area is by no means the poorest part of London. Charles Booth, the philanthropist, who's *Life and Labour of the People in London* ran to seventeen volumes, graded the area as 'mixed': some comfortable, others poor.

According to Le Queux's autobiography his father was born in or originated from Chateauroux in Indre in central France yet despite extensive research in the Chateauroux area, no trace of the Lequeux or Le Queux family can be found. As the surname suggests, the family may originally have been Huguenots, and if that were the case then they must have come from much further north, closer to the Belgian border.

Information on William Lequeux, senior, is thin on the ground, but according to the 1841 census he was born circa 1827; in those days the census form did not call for place of birth. Whether or not his father or grandfather was a count is still unproven, but not out of the question.

The young William Lequeux was shown as a boarder at Hill House School in Church Lane, Downham Market in Norfolk, under the tutelage of Isaac Goodrick (1786–1855). Goodrick had been born in Marsham, Norfolk in 1786 and lived with his wife, Martha, and family of five children, their eldest boy being Charles Brutus Goodrick who had been born there in 1820. With their other sons carrying names such as Caysius, Augustus and Octavius, it is pretty obvious that the classics would have been on the curriculum. Hill House was a mixed private school where the ages ranged upwards from nine to fifteen.[4] We do not know at what age William Lequeux was first boarded at Hill House School, but he was fourteen at the time of the 1841 census. Most of his school fellows were younger, Robert Vince being the youngest at only 4 years old. So it may be that Lequeux had been sent to Hill House at a very early age. This could have been because his mother may have died in childbirth or shortly after, leaving his father to cope alone.

---

4. 1841 Census (Lequeux is shown as Legueux).

The French Connection 1864–1880

D I Chapman 2013

Hill House School, Downham Market

Situated on the edge of the fens, Downham Market must have been a sleepy old town for such a young child. We do not know how long he stayed there, but Goodrick appears to have given up Hill House in 1845.

There is a brief mention of Downham Market in two of Le Queux's books, *The Mysterious Three* and *The Invasion of 1910*, which could indicate that at least his son was aware of something about his father's background.

Moving on to the 1851 census, it shows that Lequeux was now living and working in London, where he lodged with his employer, Benjamin Howes. Howes had been born and brought up in Kings Cliffe, Northamptonshire, having being baptised on 1 August 1792. His parents were John Howes and Ann née Groome who lived in Kings Cliffe House in West Street. John Howes was a successful linen draper with a warehouse in St Paul's Churchyard, London. They were a well-respected family who were known for providing jobs for some of Kings

Cliffe's young men.[5] Benjamin Howes was also the nephew of Elizabeth Howes who had married a Matthew Henson in Kings Cliffe in 1765. Like his father, Benjamin Howes was a linen draper by trade, and lived at 60 Fleet Street, London, where apart from Lequeux he also employed two other men, William Flint and James Wyatt. For the first, and only, time in his life Lequeux let it slip on the census form that he had been born in Paris. This was clarified by claiming he was a British citizen.[6]

The unusual surname of 'Lequeux' means that the transcribers of the census may have spelt it in any number of ways and have succeeded in doing so. Throughout his lifetime William Lequeux consistently spelt his surname as one word. The more familiar Le Queux seems to be solely the decision of his son, possibly an act of youthful defiance. To avoid confusion between father and son, as they share both the same Christian names, we will use Lequeux for the father and Le Queux for his son.

In 1859 William Tufnell Lequeux, to give him his full name, married Henrietta Maria Henson on 22 April at St George-the-Martyr Church, Southwark. On the marriage form William is shown as a bachelor living in Mina Road, off the Old Kent Road. His occupation is that of a furniture warehouseman, yet intriguingly, his father is listed on the marriage certificate as 'not known'. But then this would be his stock answer when asked difficult questions. Much later, long after he had died, there is a brief mention of his father being employed in the diplomatic service.[7] Lequeux's wife, Henrietta or Henry, came from a country family from Kings Cliffe in Northamptonshire, where she was born on 23 October 1837, but also gave the same Mina Road address as her husband-to-be. How they met is only conjecture, but with Lequeux's former employer also being a native of Kings Cliffe, this may well have had something to do with it. Amongst the witnesses to their marriage was Charles Goodrick, the son of his old schoolmaster. Lequeux and Goodrick must have struck up a good relationship to have kept in touch

---

5. Memoirs of James Roberts, Kings Cliffe Heritage Collection #2531.
6. 1851 Census.
7. Marriage certificate of Frederick Le Queux and Lilian Norris, 7 November 1918.

for at least the previous twenty years and probably a lot more. Goodrick, too, was conveniently living only a few doors away from the newlyweds at 61 Mina Road.

The 1861 census found Lequeux, still a linen draper, together with his wife Henrietta and brother-in-law, Thomas Henson, then a 13-year-old scholar, lodging with a British & Foreign Schoolmistress, Lucy Nichols, at Chase Side, Enfield. It is difficult to guess why they were here, but one thought is that with the old Enfield Workhouse having been turned into a school by the Edmonton Union, Thomas Henson was being schooled there and lodging with his teacher. Absent-minded Lequeux by now has not only forgotten where he was born, but he has also lost track of his age by answering 'not known' to both questions put to him on the National Census form.[8]

The Henson family originated from Northamptonshire in the small village of Kings Cliffe, where they lived in Clockmaker's Cottage, West Street. Kings Cliffe lies on the Willow Brook, a tributary of the River Neme, just off the Great North Road and a little way north of Fotheringay, where the castle stood in which Mary, Queen of Scots was tried and executed in 1587. In an early magazine story Le Queux draws a picture of the village as he knew it:

> Cosy; old-world village of Kings Cliffe in Northamptonshire. Perhaps you knew the place, quiet, even lethargic, nestling deep in its hollow around its quaint old Gothic church and its ancient windmill which does not work now-a-days … I knew it years ago, in the days of my youth, before I received the kicks and buffets of a wearing world – in fifty years it has changed but little.[9]

---

8. 1861 Census. Henrietta gave her age as 23. Lequeux would have been twelve years older than his wife.
9. William Le Queux, 'Mr Theophilus Dixon tells of his Thrilling Adventures', *Peterborough Advertiser*, 21 December 1901.

If You Can Walk With Kings

Henrietta's father was Thomas Henson, who had been a clock and watch maker since 1847, and was born in Stanion near Corby in about 1807. Her mother was Louise Gilks, from Moreton Pinkney on the other side of the county, and six years his junior; they married on 28 March 1831 at Barnack in Northamptonshire. They had a large family consisting of at least nine children, of whom Henrietta was the second-eldest daughter, following on from two older brothers. Of her many siblings, Henrietta must have been closest to her younger sister, Mary Ann, born two years after her.[10]

Louise Henson died on 3 March 1864, followed by Thomas on 8 December 1867. Both are buried in the parish churchyard.

Mary Ann may have met her future husband, James Bamford, when working as a shop assistant in a drapers in Stamford, Lincolnshire. James was then working as a banker's clerk, and was originally from Gretton,[11] some eight miles west of Kings Cliffe. The couple were married far from home on 15 November 1862 in Southwark, perhaps the reason being that James was considered unsuitable. Their address was shown on the marriage certificate as Mina Terrace, the same as Mary's sister and brother-in-law.

Just two years later, on 2 July 1864, William and Henrietta were presented with a son, the future author, who was named after his father, William Tufnell Lequeux. Their address on the birth certificate was once again given as 5 Mina Terrace, in Mina Road, Southwark and William's occupation as a draper's assistant. The actual house was demolished some years ago, but at the other end of Mina Road similar housing still stands today. Le Queux later described his birthplace as:

> ... a small house in a mean South London street, the address, to be exact, being No. 293 Mina Road, a turning off the Old Kent Road.
>
> The six-roomed, frowzy old house, one of a long terrace ...[12]

---

10. 1851 Census.
11. 1861 Census.
12. William Le Queux, *The Crimes Club*. London: Eveleigh, Nash & Grayson, 1927, p 51.

The French Connection 1864–1880

Although William Lequeux claimed to be a humble shop worker, he probably was also the owner of this property, along with a house in Boyson Road. He would probably also go on to own another house in Boyson Road and also one in Wansey Street, off the Walworth Road, otherwise it will be difficult to account for just how, in his will, he would be able to leave his children over a thousand pounds. By 1870 the family are shown as living at 22 Wansey Street, Walworth Road.[13] One of the few mentions of Wansey Street comes from a much later novel:

> … to the Elephant and Castle, and afterwards proceeding down the populous Walworth Road until suddenly it turned into a short, quiet, obscure thoroughfare, known as Wansey Street. Here all the grimy eight-roomed houses were uniform, with basements, and each with eight front door steps.[14]

Sladen gives us practically the only evidence from this early period regarding William Lequeux, of the part he played during the disastrous Franco-Prussian War, despite having a wife and child as dependants:

> His [WmLQ's] father served in the French Army as a Franctireur against the Germans in 1870. He was captured and sentenced to be shot, but he finally escaped and returned to London.[15]

The Franco-Prussian war ended with the defeat of Napoleon III after the Battle of Sedan and finally the Fall of Paris in early 1871. It would only make sense if Lequeux had been captured during the Battle of Sedan in September 1870, for him to have time to escape and be back in London for the census on 2 April 1871. There is good reason to assume that Lequeux had indeed taken part in this battle as it is mentioned

---

13. *Kelly's Post Office Directory*, 1870.
14. William Le Queux, *Fatal Fingers*. London: Cassell & Co., 1912.
15. Norman St Barbe Sladen, *The Real Le Queux*. London: Nicholson and Watson, 1938, p 2.

by Le Queux in passing in his semi-autobiographical book *Scribes and Pharisees*, when staying along the banks of the Moselle:

> Within sight of the window, in the full moonlight, stood the plain stone cross with a list of names inscribed thereon, the names of those gallant sons of Alf who fell at Sedan in the war with the French in '70.[16]

Had William Lequeux indeed been a freedom fighter, then perhaps this had been inspired by his own father. It is possible that *grand-père* Lequeux may have fought in the Napoleonic wars which included the battle off Cape Trafalgar and the final Battle of Waterloo, for amongst Le Queux's donations given to the Peterborough Museum, some time between 1901 and 1904, was a wooden model of a block house carved by Louis Chatiee, who had been incarcerated along with other prisoners at Norman Cross.[17] The prisoner-of-war camp had been constructed at Norman Cross, which was situated on the Great North Road just south of Peterborough, to hold French prisoners from the Napoleonic wars. Those prisoners of high status were known to have privileges allowing them to live outside the camp. With Kings Cliffe being only about fifteen miles distant it is possible that this is where *grand-père* Lequeux, if he had he been imprisoned, met and married an English girl with the surname of Tufnell. As an ardent Frenchman he would certainly want any son to be born in France to preserve his birthright. More so if he had been a nobleman, and as has been suggested, a count. Whilst this is all supposition it would fill in gaps in the long-held belief that the Lequeuxes were members of the French aristocracy. In *Hidden Hands*,[18] the main character, Seton Darville, claims that his descendants extended from a long line of noblemen dating from the days of King Louis XIV,

---

16. William Le Queux, *Scribes and Pharisees – A Story of Literary London*. London: F. V. White, 1898.
17. Chris Patrick and Stephen Baister, *William Le Queux, Master of Mystery*, privately printed *c.*2007, p 251.
18. William Le Queux, *Hidden Hands*. London: Hodder & Stoughton, nd [1926], p 174.

The French Connection 1864–1880

distinguishing themselves until the days of the First Empire when the head of the family lost his beneath the guillotine, near the Bastille. The last point was reason enough to stay away from France at that time.

By the time of the 1871 census, William and Henrietta, along with their son, were shown as still living at 22 Wansey Street. His occupation is expanded to show it as a 'Linen Draper's Assistant', but his birthplace is simply marked as 'unknown'. Here the mere shop worker is able to keep a general servant in 18-year-old Jane Baldwin, originally from Kings Cliffe, as well as housing two lodgers – John Gardener, a civil engineer from Newcastle-under-Lyme, and Thomas Nash, a merchant's clerk from Bristol – and also Frederick Henson, Henrietta's brother, now a warehouse clerk.[19] From the short story previously quoted it would confirm that the young Le Queux would have visited Kings Cliffe with his mother, perhaps to see his maternal grandfather. He may even have remembered going to attend his grandfather Henson's funeral aged 3½.

Le Queux did recall visiting his uncle William Raven and appears to have stayed with the elderly gentleman on a number of occasions:

> Even my old friend William Raven, of King's Cliffe, for many years one of the most prominent figures in hunting circles in North Northamptonshire, but now of venerable age, white-bearded, and unable to ride to the meet; a thorough hunting man of the old school, who, when the hounds pass his window, rises from his warm armchair, thrusts his hands deep into his pockets, and sighs wistfully because he is no longer agile enough to take part in the sport that he loves.[20]

Although in the novel he refers to 'his friend', William Raven was originally from Norfolk, and had married Le Queux's mother's eldest sister, Louisa, who preferred to be known by her second Christian name of Georgina, in 1859. Raven was a retired excise officer who lived at

---

19. 1871 Census.
20. William Le Queux, *The Devil's Dice*. London: F. V. White, 1896.

If You Can Walk With Kings

The Cross on the corner of Bridge Street, Kings Cliffe.[21] William Raven died in 1910 at nearly 90 years old, his wife a year earlier.

A second son, Frederick Henson Lequeux, was born on 2 August 1873 at 22 Wansey Street, named after his uncle who may still have been living with the Lequeuxes. Two years later, in September 1875, Fred's elder brother William was admitted to St Clement Danes Grammar School in Houghton Street, Holborn. The school had been founded in 1862 and funded by the Holborn Estate Charity. The school moved in 1928 and the site was purchased for the construction of the London School of Economics in 1929. The old grammar school was demolished the following year. However, for some reason William was withdrawn only a year after his admission, in December 1876.[22] Was this because he could not keep up or because he was then being 'privately educated' as mentioned in his *Who's Who* entry? When preparing his *Who's Who* entry Le Queux omits any mention of his early education and skips to the period of studying in Pegli near Genoa.

Was this mention of Genoa anything to do with a silk manufacturer? As we hear later, William Le Queux embarked on a tour throughout Europe, stopping en route at Lyons, a silk centre, and then finally once again at Genoa where he obtained a position in the office of a silk manufacturer. It is well known that the Huguenots settled in east London, especially around Spitalfields, where they carried on their trade as silk weavers. Instead of being simply a draper or linen draper's assistant, albeit in say one of London's more fashionable stores such as Marshall & Snelgrove, was his father, Lequeux, in fact involved at a much higher level, which would account for his personal wealth as shown in his will? Perhaps he held ambitions for his son being apprenticed to the silk trade. If so, his son would not be the first to reject and even resent his father's wishes for his career. However, there is a hint to come that his fortune may have been ill-gotten gains!

---

21. Memoirs of James Roberts, Kings Cliffe Heritage Collection #2531.
22. School Admissions and Discharges, LCC/EO/DIV01/STCL1/AD/001.

The French Connection 1864–1880

There is an interesting passage in *The Count's Chauffeur*.[23] The title character, George Ewart, says he was of cosmopolitan birth and education, as his early youth had been spent on the continent, much the same as the young Le Queux. George Ewart's father was also an agent for a London firm of silk manufacturers, in Lyons. Later he and his father quarrelled and he left home. All these threads do support the theory of Lequeux being engaged in the silk trade rather than just occupied as a simple draper.

For the next few years William and Henrietta, along with Frederick, are shown as living at 175 Boyson Road, although official documents show them as also occupying 183 Boyson Road, later described by their son as 'a terrace of smoke-begrimed houses in Boyson Road, Camberwell'.[24]

By the time of the 1881 Census, whilst the family are still living in 175 Boyson Road there is still no sign of the young William, who is possibly abroad. Then on 27 May 1883 Henrietta died at her Boyson Road home of lung and liver cancer; she was just 45 years old.

William Lequeux lived on with his youngest son Fred until he died at the age of sixty-seven on 16 November 1890 at 14 Croydon Road, Penge of phthisis, the old name for pulmonary tuberculosis (TB). TB was thought to be a disease that mainly affected the poor, which Lequeux was clearly not, so was it an occupational disease? There was no indication as to whether his eldest son attended the funeral or was even in the country. In his will he left just over £1,110, quite a fortune, most of which went to Fred. This may have been because Fred was now effectively orphaned and almost alone in the world at 17 years old. The only mention of his father by his brother William is in a later letter to George Lord Beeforth: 'I have as much regard, esteem and love for you as ever I had from my own father.'[25]

---

23. William Le Queux, *The Count's Chauffeur*. London: Eveleigh Nash, 1907, p 7.
24. William Le Queux, *The Temptress*. London: Tower Publishing Company, 1895.
25. WmLQ, letter to George Beeforth, from Hotel Cecil, Strand, London, 'Sunday night' circa September 1906.

If You Can Walk With Kings

This simple statement explains why we know so little of his childhood. Yet despite this, father and son must have spent considerable time in each other's company as he endeavoured to teach his son the French language. It was also said that Le Queux could speak a number of foreign languages, including being fluent in Italian. An early grounding in French would have been the catalyst he needed for him to want to travel.

Three Weddings and a Funeral
1881–1902

Lacking any official proof that Le Queux studied in Italy at Pegli, we turn to his fiction for clues, and I am surprised by the lack of references to his studying in this area considering it may have been the first time he had travelled abroad.

He certainly knew the area from later travels. The first mention of Pegli comes from an early book:

> If you have ever been misguided as to take the tram from Genoa to Pegli, then you have a faint idea of the noisy, dirty thoroughfare between the City of the Lily and industrious Brozzi.[26]

Following the lead given in *Who's Who*, we find the young Le Queux arrived in Paris from Italy to study art in the Latin Quarter on the Left Bank. Where or under whom he studied is uncertain. In the evenings he seems to have dined most nights at the Café Vachette in the Boulevard St Michel, on the corner of Rue des Ecoles.

---

26. William Le Queux, *A Madonna of the Music Halls*. London: F. V. White, 1897.

If You Can Walk With Kings

Amongst his follow diners were Paul Deschanel, the future President of France, and the artist Ignace Spiridon, whom he may have tried to emulate. Was his failure to do so the reason for his giving up art and turning to literature?

Another turning off the Boulevard St Michel was Rue St Severin. Here was the humble room '*au troisième*' in which Le Queux slept, having imbibed too much framboise or cognac every evening.

> I had been recounting those happy, ever-to-be-remembered days when I lived four storeys up in the Rue St Severin; when, careless Bohemian that I was, the sonnets of Musset thrilled me, the quips of Droz convulsed me, the romances of Sue held me breathless, and the pathos of Murger caused me to weep. An unsuccessful art student, a persistent hanger-on to the skirts of journalism, I lived the life of the Quartier Latin, and though I oft-times trod the Pont Neuf without a sou, yet I was, nevertheless, supremely happy and content.[27]

The Rue St Severin is mentioned in another of his novels, *Scribes and Pharisees*, which is subtitled 'A Story of Literary London', yet it begins in Paris, where the main character, Bertram Rosmead, is Le Queux thinly disguised, and is based on his early life. Perhaps it should have been called *A Tale of Two Cities*, especially as Charles Dickens is mentioned so often. It is a strange book in so many ways as it is an early attempt at a biography, yet trying to be a novel, and failing to be either. There were several incidents which actually happened in real life such as the trip to see the Coat at Treves, the reported death of Queen Victoria's coachman and the collapse of the Tower Publishing Company, although not named. Its main purpose seems to be to set the record straight, as Le Queux sees it, regarding his first unhappy marriage, which is how it turned out.

---

27. William Le Queux, *Zoraida*. London: Tower Publishing Company, 1895.

Three Weddings and a Funeral 1881–1902

> ... (a) little wine-shop in the Rue St Severin, a low-ceilinged, smoke-begrimed place much frequented by students, its speciality being the wine at four sous ... As he sat with his worn-out, baggy-kneed trousers turned up over cracked boots, a coat which had once been dark blue, but was now rapidly assuming a shade of stone grey, a soft, round felt hat stuck on the back of his head, a handkerchief knotted around his throat, and a long, thin, and terribly rank cigar between his teeth, he looked the very picture of laziness and carelessness.[28]

One of the difficult paths of the biographer is in deciding how to unravel fact from fiction. In Le Queux's first published novel, *Guilty Bonds*, there is an interesting paragraph:

> In the choice of profession I had not altogether pleased my father, the result being that the old gentleman was somewhat niggardly regarding my allowance and in consequence of this I had lived a devil-may-care Bohemian life, earning a moderate living by my pen.[29]

He goes on to say how this was all to change upon his own father's death. This does have a ring of truth, as it could indicate the reason why he was left only a small share of his father's estate. Did Lequeux consider that his eldest son had already received his share in allowances?

Said to be disillusioned with his art studies, he decided to leave Paris. An alternative reason suggested by his novel *Scribes and Pharisees* was that it followed a broken love affair. Writing in his autobiography at this point about his early life, Le Queux is once again economical with the facts by referring to his *Who's Who* entry regarding a tour on foot through France, Germany and Italy, beginning one August morning.

---

28. William Le Queux, *Scribes and Pharisees*.
29. William Le Queux, *Guilty Bonds*. London: George Routledge & Sons, 1891, pp 10–11. Dedicated to William Huggett: 'The Author dedicates this story in sincere acknowledgement of a literary diet.'

The only facts coming are those from an account of his early life syndicated to a number of newspapers:

> I threw everything to the winds, and without saying good-bye to a soul, and with only a few francs in my pocket, I set out before dawn one summer's morning to tramp that long, wide, dusty highway to Lyons.[30]

No doubt many other young men had done a similar journey before and since. This same journey is described in his novel *Scribes and Pharisees*:

> He had left Paris the day after, and with scarce a franc in his pocket, had tramped the long dusty highroads into Germany, existing as best he could by performing various kinds of menial labour, but often trudging far on an empty stomach, his heart heavy with its burden of sorrow.[31]

His 'Grand Tour' would occupy his time for close on a year. From Lyons he travelled to Nancy, Metz and on to Strasbourg, where he crossed the Rhine to Cologne and on via Berlin to Breslau. Turning south he set off for northern Italy where Sladen claims he found a job as a clerk in the office of a silk-weaving manufacturer in Genoa. With his wanderlust he could not settle and was once again on his way, returning to France by way of the port of Marseilles and hence to Paris.

Back in the French capital, for several months he continued to write short stories, with little success. Then by good fortune, Le Queux met M Lemaire, who was on the staff of the English *Paris Morning News*, in a cafe in the Boul' Mich'. He was given a chance as an occasional reporter on a low salary which barely kept him alive. This induced him to write a sensational story of fifteen hundred words, entitled *La Pipe Cassée*,

---

30. William Le Queux, 'In the Days of my Youth', *Otago Witness*, 24 April 1907.
31. William Le Queux, *Scribes and Pharisees*.

which duly appeared in *Le Petit Journal*. It was picked up and read by Emile Zola who encouraged him to persevere with journalism. It was Zola's advice that directly led Le Queux to become a novelist.

As far as we can judge, Le Queux was back in England by late 1884 when he embarked on his first career as a journalist on a local paper in the south London suburb of Sydenham. However, after only a few weeks he met Arthur Beckett, the publisher of the *Eastbourne Gazette*, who asked if he cared to join them as a reporter. Here he joined the editorial staff and was not, as has been suggested, confined just to police court reporting, as some of his earliest short stories appeared in its pages. Le Queux and Beckett remained friends for the rest of his life, although they only met infrequently. When they did meet it was usually at Beckett's father's home, Lockwood Grange, in Eastbourne.[32]

According to the evidence of Norman Sladen, following the death of Le Queux's mother in 1883, his father called him a ne'er-do-well and cut him off as utterly incorrigible. Perhaps he was right as Norman Sladen recalls a story which took place after Le Queux's return to London of him riding a 'penny-farthing' bicycle all the way from Westminster Bridge to Manchester, when he was about 21 years of age. It is said that his relations in Manchester did not approve of his escapade and on arrival they promptly sent him and his machine back down to London. This seems almost too tall a story even for Le Queux, although Le Queux did have relations living in Manchester, namely his uncle George Henson,[33] who was then living in Market Street. Le Queux himself is silent on this point.

Le Queux soon moved back towards London where in 1885 he joined the *Middlesex Chronicle* based at Hounslow. He was to remain at the *Chronicle* for the next five years, and when he left he was replaced as editor by John Whall. Whall, despite being blind, remarkably edited

---

32. Arthur Beckett, *Eastbourne Gazette*, 15 June 1938.
33. Le Queux presented his uncle with a copy of *The Temptress*, dated 7 November 1895. Offered for sale by Sumner & Stillman of Yarmouth, Maine, USA.

the paper for the next forty years. Le Queux gives us what must be an accurate account of the office:

> ... by a lucky chance, he answered an advertisement which appeared in that journalistic medium, the *Daily News*, headed 'Reporter Wanted', and a week later found himself in a very curious and embarrassing position. He had not been unwise enough to admit himself utterly unacquainted with journalism, and therefore the position which had been given him was the sole charge of a small, obscure, but old-established journal called the *Hounslow Standard*. The staff of this influential weekly organ, whose destinies he was to control, was not a large one. It consisted of himself alone. He was editor, sub-editor, reporter, and reader, and was expected to keep up a good personal appearance upon the sum of thirty shillings weekly. The office of that journal was, like himself, a little bizarre. It consisted of a small, mouldy-smelling shop in a bad state of repair, half-way up the long, dreary, straggling High Street of the dull, uninteresting suburban town, and behind in the garden was a shed in which half-a-dozen youths set type, while further on was a small out-house, originally built for a stable, but now euphemistically termed the 'machine-room', containing, as it did, an old-fashioned press worked by a grunting gas-engine, which very often failed and had to be turned by hand. This interesting piece of machinery was broken in places, and had been repaired with string.[34]

This period in Le Queux's life has been well researched by Chris Patrick and Stephen Baister, establishing that his first article was a kind of sketch – 'A Temple of Justice' – which appeared under the byline of 'Q' in the edition of Saturday 31 October 1885. Further pieces followed in the months to come, including *Sinned Against*, printed over several weeks

---

34. William Le Queux, *Scribes and Pharisees*.

at the end of 1886 and early 1887. This story would be listed amongst his previous works when his first novel was published in 1890.

So began Le Queux's writing career, starting simply as a journalist and continuing as a novelist, playwright, an inveterate letter writer and lastly as a screenwriter. He even wrote a little poetry. However, he kept no diary. How good a playwright he was is open to some dispute. Le Queux wrote, or co-wrote, at least three scripts during this period, two of which were performed by a provincial repertory company. His first was a burlesque, *Tootsie's Lovers*, which was performed in Brentford at Beach's Theatre of Varieties on 19 April 1886.[35] T. W. Beach was a strawberry grower who ran a jam factory to which was attached a theatre providing entertainment for his workers. The theatre ran from 1886 until about 1930. Le Queux's second play was a comedietta, *Gem of a Girl,* which played the same venue two months later on 24 June 1886.[36] His budding career in the theatre world came to a sudden ending in 1887. Le Queux and W. T. Field had just completed a drama entitled *Just in Time* and a notice to this effect had appeared in the *Era*. The following edition carried a stiff letter from an irate playwright, Auguste Creamer, who claimed that the title was identical to a 'successful play' of his which had been performed in Doncaster earlier in the year.[37] Creamer was described as a performer of 'low Irish comedy'!

As has been said, Le Queux's autobiography completely omits any mention of his family life, bar one small reference which belonged to a much later date. So it is some surprise to find that William Le Queux is suddenly married to Florence Alice Dorsett, the wedding having taken place on 23 November 1887 at the Registry Office of Saint Saviour, Southwark, according to the marriage certificate. The fact that it was held in a registry office reinforces the belief that Le Queux was a non-conformist. Nothing, of course, is as it should be, as firstly the groom is stated as being 26 years old, making him a year older than his bride, when on paper he should have been a couple of years younger.

---

35. *The Era*, 1 May 1886.
36. *The Era*, 3 July 1886.
37. *The Era*, 27 August 1887.

Florence on the other hand has lied not only about her age, being almost 27 years old, but has also changed her Christian name. However, she had good reason to lie about her age.

Alice Jane Dorsett is shown on her birth certificate as having been born on 8 December 1860 at 3 Bells Buildings, Fleet Street.[38] Her parents were Alfred Thomas Dorsett, a house decorator, originally from Hackney, and Maria Ann formerly Wright from the parish of St Bride's, also in Fleet Street. Both parents were widowed and there were children from their previous marriages, Frederick and Emma Dorsett and Ann Wright. Alice is shown on the baptism certificate as having eventually been baptised on 13 November 1864 along with her baby sister, Ellen Sarah, who had been born on 4 October of that year. The reason for the delaying the baptism was that Alfred and Maria had only just celebrated their own marriage themselves on 19 August 1860,[39] less than four months before Alice's birth. By the time of the 1871 census Alice Jane had become Alice Florence and her mother was once again without a husband as Alfred has moved out of the family home. By 1881 Alfred was hospitalised in the City of London Infirmary,[40] and he presumably died there.

Whether Le Queux was aware of the original deception is difficult to say but it appears so. We are left wondering just what was the attraction and how did the couple first meet? He was an impulsive man who lived not just for the day but by the hour, if these paragraphs taken from *Scribes and Pharisees* can be believed:

> It was at this juncture, when one night, having treated himself to a little mild dissipation in the form of a visit to London, he was passing along Fleet Street, gazing up wistfully at the brilliantly-lighted newspaper offices, and wondering whether some day he, too, might not spend his nights in one of those great establishments, where the work was light and the pay

---

38. Bells Buildings is shown as being in Salisbury Square, a turning out of Dorset Street!
39. Marriage Certificate.
40. 1881 Census.

handsome, when suddenly, at the corner of Chancery Lane, a face, passing beneath the electric light, attracted him – a face more pure, more regular in outline than he had ever before witnessed.

The face was the face of a heroine of romance; a trifle pale and wistful, perhaps, but eminently beautiful. Was he not seeking local colour for the romance he intended, ere long, to write; was he not wandering, aimlessly, that night, in the great world of London, seeking material for the book which, some day, would make his name world-famous?

For an instant he hesitated. Then he turned and followed her.

Alone, she was walking quickly in the direction of Charing Cross, a neat, erect figure in black, a trifle petite, but essentially dainty. Already she had gained the Law Courts before he drew up behind her, and then he saw how slim-waisted and neat-attired she was, how gracefully she walked, how well her little black, jet-trimmed bonnet, with its tiny white bird, suited her dark beauty.

Since Fosca had gone out of his life, he had gazed upon no other woman with admiration until that moment. He was not a man to wear his heart on his sleeve. Literature was his mistress, and he cared for little else beside his books and the old littered table whereat he spent the silent watches of the night. He was not one to be easily fascinated by a woman, more especially now that Fosca had shattered all his belief in woman's honesty and affection. Even though studiously polite, and essentially chivalrous, he was inclined to treat the fair sex with calm indifference, and never sought their society. During the past three years, he had lived only with his books, and with that Bohemian instinct, in him inborn, cared for nothing outside the range of his own studies.

If You Can Walk With Kings

He passed her, pretending to hurry on without noticing her, but, nevertheless, casting a covert glance at her face. At that instant, however, she raised her eyes and peered into his, with a glance, half of inquiry, half of annoyance.

She was about twenty-one, as far as he could judge, with a pair of dimpled cheeks, eyes dark and luminous, a small, delicate nose that denoted considerable self-will, and a high brow shaded by a mass of fluffy nut-brown hair. Her black cloth jacket, short and smartly made, fitted her without a crease; her skirt hung straight in graceful folds without dragging at the back, as London skirts will; and pinned to her coquettish little muff of quilted black satin was a bunch of violets.

Her face, among all others, had attracted him, because it was such a face as he had imagined his heroine should possess. He decided to study her character, her virtues, and her weaknesses, and reproduce her in his pages with the fidelity of a photograph from the life.

He raised his hat and spoke to her. It never occurred to him, accustomed as he was to the free manners of the Quai Montebello, that he was doing anything extraordinary in thus accosting her, or seeking to force himself upon her without an introduction. She glanced at him for an instant, in haughty contempt, then lowered her eyes modestly, and slightly quickened her pace. Again he spoke, but without heeding him, she turned almost at right angles and crossed the road. Undaunted by this rebuff, he followed her, and a few minutes later, advancing again to her side, expressed a hope that he had caused her no annoyance.[41]

Le Queux was obviously not put off by Lena's manner. So, is this how Le Queux saw Alice, described her in the character of Lena, at the time

---

41. William Le Queux, *Scribes and Pharisees*.

or with hindsight? He even seems to have been prepared to put up with the living conditions:

> [Lena] 'We live in Gough Square, at the back of Fleet Street. Mother has lived there for twenty years.'
> 'Gough Square!' he exclaimed, surprised. He knew the spot, a small paved square, approached by one of the dark, narrow courts off Fleet Street, and surrounded by great printing establishments, book-binders, paper warehouses, type-founders, and kindred trades. The trees under which Dr Johnson loved to walk have disappeared long ago. In that vicinity there were no residents, the old, red, dirt-grimed houses, of notable proportions a century ago, being now let out as offices to engravers, agents, and unimportant journals, for it was the very heart of newspaper London, hemmed in on every side by great, high buildings, excluding light and air. Truly it was not by any means a salubrious spot, the atmosphere thick with the soot of a myriad chimneys, and the odour of printing ink, and crowded at mid-day with 'comps.' and apprentices, who smoked, swore, and idled away their dinner hour. In these meagre, sordid, unhealthy surroundings, Lena had been bred and born. Was it, then, any wonder that her growth should be stunted, her limbs thin and fragile, or her speech should savour of the dialect of Farringdon Market; that she forgot to aspirate her 'h's', or that her education had progressed no further than what had been imparted to her at the Board School round in Fetter Lane?[42]

Lena goes on to explain to Bertram that she is planning to leave home as she does not get on with her stepsister, whose name we later learn is coincidentally Annie, who is making her life unbearable. It transpires that Lena's mother was previously married and the stepsister,

---

42. Ibid.

who is said to be 35 years old, is several years older than Lena. In real life Alice's own stepsister, Anne Wright, would have been about the same age in 1887, the year of Alice's marriage to Le Queux. But, if you believe the census for 1881, then Anne Wright is only 27 years old, having aged just four years since the previous census. It seems the Dorsett family showed little or no respect for authority.

Le Queux is at pains to stress that Bertram does not love Lena nor could he ever do so. A point made with hindsight, one would guess.

At the time of their marriage Alice, then Florence Alice, was shown as living with her mother at 9 East Harding Street, Fleet Street, just yards from Gough Square, and William could be found living at 175 Boyson Road with his elderly father and brother, Fred.

> Lena's marriage was not long delayed. She packed a trunk a week later and left home, telling her mother she could not remain there any longer on account of Annie's continual ill-temper. An hour later she met Bertram at Ludgate Hill station, and drove with him to the registry office in the Blackfriars Road, where they were made man and wife, two cabmen acting as witnesses, and receiving five shillings as their reward.
>
> Three days were spent at Brighton, the longest absence he could take from his journalistic duties; then they returned to Hounslow, taking up their quarters in two furnished rooms in a tiny cottage, one of a row inhabited mostly by railway porters and employees at the neighbouring gunpowder-mills. Bertram's salary as editor was still, as it had been from the first, thirty shillings weekly.[43]

On the marriage form Alice's father is said to be deceased, but no death certificate can be traced and it did not agree with the census forms for 1891. What makes the above quotation all the more believable is that the two witnesses are shown as John Meeds and James Butler, neither name known to have any other association with Le Queux. On

---

43. Ibid.

return from their short honeymoon the newly married couple moved to be closer to William's work, which was described unkindly as:

> Hounslow is a mean and meagre town, notable for three things, – its barracks, its great gunpowder factory, and the number and variety of its lower-class public-houses.[44]

It was into this mean little town that William and Alice moved, taking up residence in a house, Oakleigh, St Stephen's Road, Hounslow.[45]

Apart from articles that continued to appear in the *Middlesex Chronicle*, Le Queux also began contributing to other magazines and on the final day of 1887 there appeared 'The Old Musician'. It was the first of a handful of short stories that would eventually find themselves in the pages of the *Penny Illustrated*. It is set in the old Drury Lane Theatre and is about an old man, Andrew Carter, the old musician, and his young adopted daughter. Despite his living south of the river, in a small attic room, his instrument is a Stradivarius. It is a nice story with the inevitable happy ending. This was followed in June 1888 by 'The Small Packet' with the byline 'W. T. Q', which appeared in the ha'penny *Every Week* magazine. It again features a chance meeting at the old Drury Lane Theatre which leads to Paris and contact with the Russian Nihilists. It is pure Le Queux. Both these stories indicate how close Le Queux could have been to becoming a dramatist rather than a novelist.

Being domiciled in the west of London, readers of the *Middlesex Chronicle* were probably, at first, not overly concerned with events unfolding further east. At the very end of August 1888 the first in a series of murders was reported from Whitechapel, which soon became known as the Jack the Ripper murders. Even today it is far from certain just how many victims there were. Most agree with five, some seven, and some as many as twelve. This last number is less than half the so-called suspects. I doubt if Le Queux had any first-hand involvement with the investigations, despite what he might say in his autobiography, and any

---

44. Ibid.
45. Heston Polling District, 1890.

reports for the *Chronicle* would have been cobbled together from the national dailies. In his autobiography, written many years later, he felt able to put forward his own suspect, Dr Alexander Pedachenko,[46] who he claimed had been unmasked for the first time. His 'evidence' was discovered amongst papers and documents discovered in the cellar of Rasputin, the Mad Monk. Le Queux explains why he did not publish the fact when preparing his own book on Rasputin which he published in 1917,[47] as he had been unable until then to verify his facts. According to Le Queux, Dr Pedachenko had lived in Westmorland Road, boarding with his sister, from where he would nightly visit Whitechapel in search of further victims. Dr Pedachenko was eventually smuggled out of London by the Russian secret police and taken back to Moscow. Here he was caught red-handed in an attempted murder and sent to an asylum where he died in 1908. In those days Westmorland Road ran adjacent to Boyson Road, Le Queux's childhood home. As with all the Ripper claims and counterclaims, there seems no actual evidence to support the allegation.

Le Queux and his wife were certainly still living in Hounslow in the same year in which his father died at Penge in 1890. Despite most of his father's legacy going to brother Fred, it must have left enough for the Le Queuxes to consider moving. Fortunately around the same time he met William Thomas Madge who was then on the *Globe*, London's oldest and most well-respected evening newspaper, who offered him a job on the parliamentary staff, which he accepted. At first his tasks involved attending the Houses of Parliament where he took his seat in the Reporters' Gallery. These were the days when William Ewart Gladstone was Britain's Prime Minister for an historic fourth time from 1892 to 1894. Le Queux was shortly transferred to the sub-editorial staff under E. Garrish, finally becoming Foreign Editor between the years 1891 and 1893. His hours involved an early start at 07.30 where he was at his desk until 14.00. It being too inconvenient to travel in from Hounslow each morning, he had secured rooms in Dane's Inn.

---

46. Alexander Pedachenko (1857–1908), later also identified by Donald McCormick.
47. William Le Queux, *Rasputin the Rascal Monk*. London: Hurst & Blackett, 1917.

Three Weddings and a Funeral 1881–1902

Chris Patrick and Stephen Baister confirmed that these rooms were at 1 Dane's Inn, Strand,[48] an area that Le Queux knew well as this was close to his old school in nearby Houghton Street. The whole area was swept away in the early part of the 20th century for the construction of The Aldwych. Once again this period in Le Queux's own life is repeated in *Scribes and Pharisees*:

> Bertram Rosmead quickly discovered that, while his salary was doubled, his duties were mere child's play in comparison with those at Hounslow. He had taken a set of chambers in Dane's Inn, that chilling, dismal little paved court off the Strand, at the back of St Clement Danes church, a change which caused Lena the most profound satisfaction. The rooms, being situated at the back, were gloomy and prison-like, with ground-glass windows to hide the squalid outlook, and constituted as frowsy an abode as even the most dry-as-dust barrister could have wished for. It consisted solely of a small entrance hall, a living-room, and one bedroom, and there being no room for a servant, Lena declared her intention to manage by herself rather than live in any part less central or further removed from that thoroughfare by her beloved, the Strand. Therefore they were compelled to cook, eat, and live in that one close back room, the faded carpet of which was worn into holes, with shabby, dirt-grimed furniture whence the stuffing escaped, the two book-cases at either end being filled with musty leather-covered tomes of the law.[49]

Moving into 1891, we find that William and Alice had moved up in the world on the back of his literary success and journalism. They had left the gloomy Dane's Inn and taken a suite of rooms at 27 Abingdon Mansions, Warwick Street, Kensington. Described by Charles Booth as 'five floors and basement, better class than those opposite', this change

---

48. Chris Patrick and Stephen Baister, *William Le Queux*, p 31.
49. William Le Queux, *Scribes and Pharisees*.

of address is possibly why they cannot be traced in the census. However, Fred Le Queux is found living with his brother's sister-in-law, Annie Bamford, and husband, Joseph, at 2 St Paul's Street, Stamford. Joseph is described as a 'draper' and Fred as a 'draper's assistant',[50] a term we have met before.

According to Sladen, Le Queux would sit up writing fiction until the early hours, never getting more than four hours' sleep a night. This culminated in what he would call the 'proudest day of my life' when Messrs George Routledge & Sons published his first novel in 1891, entitled *Guilty Bonds*. This was a novel that involved the hero travelling to St Petersburg, where he was imprisoned following a sham trial and sentenced to hard labour in a Siberian silver mine. Russia was a country he claims to have 'visited and knew well', presumably when contributing a series of articles for *The Times*, although this is very doubtful. Chris Patrick and Stephen Baister established that Le Queux wrote only three articles for *The Times*, two in October and one in November 1890, just a few days before the loss of his father. So with no collaboration either way it is difficult to decide if he travelled through to Russia or not. It was a winning formula and this book did set the pattern for the rest of his life, with him going on to produce on average six new titles for every year.

What made the book ultimately successful was its becoming known that it was banned in Russia. Copies of his book had been ordered by booksellers in St Petersburg, Moscow and Odessa and these were duly dispatched.[51] For several months nothing was heard and then it was reported in the *Pall Mall Gazette* that an emissary of the Tzar's government sought out Le Queux at his new Kensington residence. This was with the intention to serve upon him a proclamation from the Press Bureau in St Petersburg stating that the novel *Guilty Bonds* contravened Russian censorship and any further copies entering the country would be seized and destroyed.[52] A few months later Le Queux received a copy of *Guilty Bonds* from the Russian embassy. It had been heavily censored

---

50. 1891 Census.
51. *The Star*, 24 November 1891.
52. *Pall Mall Gazette*, 21 November 1891.

with about a third of the pages removed. Quite what the Russians felt they would get out of it is unclear. The outcome was the printing of his next book, *The Strange Tales of a Nihilist*.[53]

It was whilst on the staff of the *Globe*, that one morning in late summer of 1891 Le Queux was sent as a:

> ... special correspondent to witness the unveiling of the Holy Coat at Treves, in Germany, a ceremonial performed once every fifty years. The sacred relic is kept walled up in the church, and only exposed for adoration during five days twice every century.[54]

Although the above comes directly from his novel, the incident was also repeated in his autobiography. Le Queux recalls that having reached Brussels, he bumped into George Augustus Sala, a correspondent with the *Daily Telegraph*. They continued together on to Treves[55] where they were lucky to find accommodation. Unfortunately the following day they were prevented from seeing the relic on orders of the Bishop, who only allowed pilgrims to enter. So Sala and Le Queux obtained peasant costumes and managed to gain entrance. Le Queux recalls that his article printed in the *Globe* was headed: 'The Holy Coat at Treves: By an Amateur Pilgrim'.[56]

Another story recalled in his autobiography and featuring in his novel *Scribes and Pharisees* was the near disaster of the *Globe* printing an obituary of Queen Victoria. The ticker-tape had become tangled and the piece rushed to the news desk stated that the Queen had died at Windsor. As it was lunchtime most of the reporters and editors were away so the presses were readied to carry the solemn headline. By chance an inspector of the Exchange Telegraph Company arrived only to be challenged by Le Queux about the above report sent out by his

---

53. *Sheffield Telegraph*, 19 January 1892.
54. William Le Queux, *Scribes and Pharisees*.
55. Now Trier.
56. William Le Queux, *Things I Know about Kings*, p 180.

company. Within a few moments the electrician had fished out of the waste paper basket the remainder of the message which had referred to it being John Frayling, the Queen's coachman, who had died! Had they gone to press, the Queen would certainly not have been amused.

Alice Le Queux gave birth to a daughter, Vera Gladys Alice, just before Christmas on 21 December 1891 at their Kensington home. Sadly little Vera died six months later of marasmus, a form of malnutrition, caused by the lack of mother's milk. Her death occurred on 16 August 1892 at Beacon Place, Littleham, near Exmouth in Devon, where possibly the family were holidaying. In spite of its dreadful memories Littleham is recalled in one of his novels:

> Behind me stood the great white facade of Denbury; before, a little to the right, lay a small village with its white cottages – the villages of Littleham I afterwards discovered – and to the left white cliffs and the blue stretch of the English Channel gleaming through the greenery.
>
> From the avenue I turned and wandered down a by-path to a stile, and there I rested, in full uninterrupted view of the open sea. Deep below was a cove – Littleham Cove, it proved to be – and there, under shelter of the cliffs, a couple of yachts were riding gaily at anchor, while far away upon the clear horizon a dark smoke-trail showed the track of a steamer outward bound.[57]

The informant to the registrar was neither of the parents, so you wonder if Alice was unable to cope with a child. If so, this does seem to have had an effect on her for the rest of her life. Certainly if Le Queux found the death of his only child hard to bear, he kept the sorrow to himself and never mentioned her again.

Their marriage seems to have gone downhill after the devastating death of their daughter as, if *Scribes and Pharisees* is to be believed, it is when Alice started drinking.

---

57. William Le Queux, *Wiles of the Wicked*. London: F. V. White, 1900.

I loved you until, by your ill-temper, selfishness, and utter disregard for my welfare, you crushed every spark of affection or respect from my soul. And now you have taken to drink and music-halls.[58]

In the same novel Le Queux also makes the point that his wife had taken no interest in his writing nor shown any sympathy with his work, their early relationship being part of the ongoing story of *Scribes and Pharisees*. Le Queux was beginning to make his way with his fiction writing to the point where he could not manage his full-time work on the evening newspaper and produce articles and agree to a book contract. His home life was also at breaking point. His wife is savagely portrayed as a drunken lush:

Lena, in a soiled pink wrapper, her hair undressed, although it was one o'clock, and her slippers down at heel, was cooking a chop when he entered. A tumbler of whiskey and water stood on the table, and the room retained a stale odour of spirits emitted from a dirty glass on the mantelshelf. Her eyes were bright, her face slightly flushed, and the witching of her mouth and eyebrows were sufficient signs that she had been drinking already that morning. When he related to her what young Mr. Howden had said, she turned quickly, asking —
'Then you intend to give up the *Evening Telegraph*?'
'Certainly. I shall leave as soon as possible after signing the contracts.[59]

Before finally giving up on journalism Le Queux took a short lease on a house in Sussex. It is unlikely to have been the same house as The Firs at Warnham near Horsham – from which he later wrote to Douglas Sladen in 1896 – as in *Scribes and Pharisees* the maid explains that

---

58. William Le Queux, *Scribes and Pharisees*.
59. Ibid.

her mistress left for London by train from East Grinstead. He gives a good description of the property:

> The September afternoon was hot, but the windows of his pleasant little study opened out upon a pretty lawn flanked by a high privet hedge, with a large apple orchard beyond. From outside was wafted in the sweet scent of roses and heliotrope, and the distant sound of children's voices told him that it was already four o'clock, and the village school was over. The room was not large, but was well filled with books, while on the walls were many framed originals of illustrations of his stories in the magazines, together with a copy of a large picture-poster which at that moment was on half the hoardings in London and the provincial towns, advertising one of his serial stories in a Sunday paper. His writing-table was placed in the embrasure of the window, and from where he sat his eyes rested upon a level expanse of lawn, fresh and green after the rain of the previous night.
>
> The house was a good-sized, old-fashioned one, standing at the end of the pretty village of Malstead, in Sussex, a remote little place, scarcely more than a hamlet, three miles from the rail, and about forty from London. Its surroundings were most picturesque, the views of the Downs from his windows were fine and extensive, and the air was fresh and delightful after those dingy chambers wherein he had been cramped and stifled for so long.

We only have Le Queux's side of the story, but he contests that it was his wife who left him, taking only her jewellery, which she intended to pawn. Having followed her to London, Le Queux persuades her to join him as he has decided to move from London to the continent and firstly to the French Riviera.

The move to Nice did not appear to have a lasting good effect on Alice and they soon moved across the frontier to Florence, the Lily

City. As Florence also did not suit her, they returned to London. Finally matters came to head when Le Queux declared the marriage over. He made arrangements for Alice to receive an allowance and then departed alone for Harwich to board the steamer for Belgium. Here we can no longer turn to fiction as *Scribes and Pharisees* ends with the death of Lena. With Alice now being estranged and living in London there is little word from Le Queux of her, her life and her whereabouts.

One of Le Queux's earliest magazine articles appeared in *Chamber's Journal* in 1892, with a report on the Italian Mafia. I always understood that the Mafia were concentrated in Sicily and the south of Italy, but Le Queux tells us they originated in Florence and Genoa. Unlike the Nihilists, the Mafia are not altogether a secret society, nor are they politically minded. One wonders how close Le Queux got to the truth, as anyone on the outside can only guess at it. I did like the line which could have come direct from *The Godfather*: 'If I die, I will be buried; if I live, you will be.'[60]

Le Queux's second book to be published was *Strange Tales of a Nihilist*,[61] in 1892; this was also reprinted as *A Secret Service* in 1896. It was a collection of connected short stories involving Russia, a place he may still have never visited. The Russian theme continued with 'The Siren of St Petersburg' in the *Penny Illustrated*, published on the last day of 1892. Towards the end of 1893 Le Queux edited a soon-to-be-defunct society paper called the *Piccadilly*, which appeared weekly on Thursdays, and in its pages he published a few short stories, none of which, I believe, have ever been collected.

One of the features of any Le Queux novel is the attention to detail, especially of foreign parts. In the midsummer of 1893 it was reported that Le Queux was just then travelling to Kabylia in Algeria in search of local colour.[62] He crossed the Sahara desert when he accompanied a French

---

60. 'The Mafiosi', *Chambers's Journal of Popular Literature, Science, and Art*, 18 June 1892. The article is unsigned.
61. William Le Queux, *Strange Tales of Nihilist*. London: Ward, Lock & Co., 1892. Ward Lock would also be the publisher of his last book in 1931.
62. *Lincolnshire Echo*, 1 September 1893.

military expedition, said to be on behalf of the Royal Geographical Society of London, from Algiers to In Salah.[63] His experiences would soon be put to good use in a forthcoming novel, *Zoriada*.

Now Le Queux partly turned his attention away from the Nihilists to concentrate on the threat of invasion from the French backed by the Russians. The result was the first appearance of a serial entitled *The Poisoned Bullet*. The first instalment was printed in Alfred Harmsworth's *Answers*[64] for 23 December 1893.[65] According to Roger Stern, Harmsworth wanted to emulate a rival weekly publication, *Black & White*, which, in the previous year, had printed *the Great War of 189–*,[66] and Harmsworth knew just the right man for the job. Whilst it may be fiction, it was meant to galvanise an ever-slumbering Britain, to awaken them to the build-up of the opposing armed forces. The *Daily Telegraph* spoke of the state of affairs as being the dark times coming for Great Britain. Harmsworth took over the London *Evening News* the following year. As a newspaper man he knew what effect a sensational story would have on the British public. In effect he was stoking the fears of Britain's unpreparedness. How far he was being prompted by higher forces one can only guess at this point.

The story began with the warning that both Russia and France were making extraordinary preparations with a view to an invasion of the United Kingdom. This imaginary war would begin in August 1897. Yet even then Le Queux is referring to the threat as the 'Great War'. Until now stories of this type had never been attempted and it read like a newspaper report with war correspondents reporting from the frontline. The action is as thrilling, authentic, and totally absorbing now as it was then. The reader, unlike today's audiences who have access to 24-hour

---

63. William Le Queux, 'In the Days of my Youth'.
64. Founded by Alfred Charles William Harmsworth who was raised to the peerage as Baron Northcliffe and later elevated to Viscount Northcliffe in 1918.
65. Roger Stearn referred to *Answers* as being printed on 'Golden Orange' cheap paper pages. My own copy came from the well-known book stalls that used to be in Farringdon Road, sadly now gone.
66. Colomb, Rear Admiral P. et al., *The Great War of 189–*. London: William Heinemann, 1895.

rolling news channels, would perhaps not realise that this was not for real. The places mentioned by Le Queux, which he seems to know well, and the names of the ships involved, all existed. Le Queux had done his homework or was being fed information from other sources.

Answers was ratcheting up the excitement with their headline for the final episode of 1893 being: 'GREAT BRITAIN UNDER FIRE. THE INVADERS' FIRST SHOT!'[67]

A letter from General Lord Roberts, which appears as the preface of the first book version, appeared in the issue of *Answers* for 21 April 1894. As the final instalments were being published, the first book edition under the title *The Great War in England in 1897* was being printed by the Tower Publishing Company for publication in July 1894. By the end of the same year the book had gone through some eight editions. The publishers included quotes from a number of authorities such as Prince George, The Duke of Cambridge, Commander-in-Chief of the British Army; Field Marshall Lord Wolseley; and the Marquis of Salisbury, the former Prime Minister.

The dating of *The Great War in England in 1897* is significant. The Franco-Russian Alliance had only been recently ratified and signed in the January of 1894. It was known that Germany wanted to form closer ties with Britain at this time. Had they done so then, would this still have led to the Great War some twenty years later?

Having reached the age of 30, Le Queux was a successful journalist and promising novelist. His heavy workload may have contributed to the breakdown of his marriage, although the death of his child must have hit him hard. At the time he was a gay man about town who sought the company of women and he did not appear to have many men friends apart from work colleagues. What is remarkable is that among his widening circle of acquaintances there were many who were seemingly way above his more humble beginnings.

At some point in 1894 Le Queux left the former marital home of Abingdon Mansions and moved to a bachelor apartment in Talbot House, on the east side of St Martin's Lane in Westminster. In October

---

67. *Answers*, 30 December 1893, p 91.

If You Can Walk With Kings

1894 a short story of Le Queux's entitled *My Skeleton* appeared in a little-known magazine, *In Town*, edited by T. H. Roberts. This story was later to be published in book form, and renamed as 'Vogue la Galere!', in a collection of shorts which made up *Stolen Souls*, published by the Tower Publishing Company. Another chapter entitled 'The Man with the Fatal Finger'[68] had been printed in *Beeton's Christmas Annual* for 1892. And several of the other stories which completed the collection appeared in various other magazines such as the *Windsor Magazine* and the *Wave*. The rest must have appeared in similar long-forgotten magazines or newspapers of the time.

The marriage of William's brother Fred to 17-year-old Julia Amelia Foskett took place on 28 January 1895 at the Christ Church in Penge. There is no indication as to whether the day was shared with his closest family, or his brother William, whose name does not appear as a witness. On the marriage certificate Fred's occupation is shown as that of 'gentleman', or living off private means. This would have been as a result of the legacy left to him on his father's death five years earlier. It would be for Fred the first of his three marriages.

Following the publication of his latest book *Zoriada*, Le Queux found he had another best-seller. Once again the publisher was the Tower Publishing Company who brought out the book in May 1895, and demand was such that it was reprinted three times in as many weeks. Alongside this *The Great War in England in 1897* was now in its ninth edition. A follow-up book, *The Great White Queen, A Tale of Treasure and Treason*, also set in north Africa, contained an interesting dedication. It was addressed to an Arab friend, Hadj Hamoud Ben Abd El-Metkoub, whom he credits with offering Le Queux his first glimpse of that waterless region of the Sahara known as the Areg in Morocco. In *The Great White Queen*, Le Queux mentions that the main character, Richard Scarsmere, boards the SS *Gambia* out of Liverpool, bound by the way of Funchal for Cape Coast Castle on the Gold Coast. Elder Dempster & Co, did indeed

---

68. This had appeared in a collection of stories published by Ward Lock & Bowden in 1893 along with stories by Coulson Kernahan, etc., under the title of *The Spin of the Coin* by L. Galbraith.

operate the SS *Gambia* on this route as the African Steamship Company, although it is very doubtful whether Le Queux actually took this journey as far as west Africa. This book could, therefore, be one of the few of his that were entirely fictitious.

As well as *Stolen Souls*, a fourth novel entitled *The Temptress* was also published by the Tower Publishing Company, again in 1895. The publishers appear to have ceased trading in 1896, just prior to settling their authors' royalties, leaving themselves in debt to Le Queux and other authors. Financially it could have been a problem, but Le Queux was able to pick himself up by having Ward Lock reprint his earlier book of short stories, *The Strange Tales of a Nihilist*, then out of print, under a new title, *A Secret Service*. He also signed a contract with the London firm of F. V. White who, over the next five years, published fifteen novels and short story collections. These books include *The Great White Queen: A Tale of Treasure and Treason in 1896*; *The Eye of Istar: A Romance of the Land of No Return* and *A Madonna of the Music Halls: Being the Story of a Secret Sin*, both in 1897. The first of these three books, *The Great White Queen*, which begins in Eastbourne, is of interest as it includes a favourite walk over Beachy Head and the Seven Sisters past Belle Tout lighthouse and through East Dean to Litlington tea-garden. The tea-gardens are still there today and East Dean is where Sherlock Holmes supposedly retired to, to take up bee-keeping, according to a blue plaque. It is a walk Le Queux must have done many times before. The remainder of the novel is the story of adventure set in darkest west Africa, where Le Queux had certainly not been. I should add that Le Queux's prose reflects the tone that was acceptable in the Victorian age. His autobiographical *Scribes and Pharisees* followed in 1898 and two collections of short stories in *The Veiled Man* and *The Secrets of Monte Carlo* in 1899. The magazine appearances of these two short story collections had appeared in the *Idler* and *Cassell's Magazine* respectively. Several other uncollected stories also appeared around this time in a variety of magazines.

It has to be said that the cover design of the Tower Publishing Company's books must be amongst the most attractive ever produced for a work of fiction. However, this over-elaboration may well have led to Tower's demise.

William Le Queux had returned from north Africa and he was certainly back in London when writing to Douglas Sladen from Talbot House, in March 1895. He was to stay here for some time. Alice was now back in his life and although Le Queux had increasing problems at home he still tried to make his marriage work. With the success of *The Poisoned Bullet*, then appearing in *Answers*, he no longer needed to rely on his journalistic work at the *Globe*, which was becoming onerous to him, involving long mornings at his office desk and the afternoons and evenings at home working.

We lack any real dates for his whereabouts for the next eighteen months or so. He claims to have wandered through Spain, but this could have been on his way back from north Africa. We do know that Le Queux was reported to have explored the vast underground labyrinth at Maastricht in the Netherlands. Unusually for Le Queux, he was accompanied by his wife, Alice, and with them two Belgian officers. The remarkable St Pietersberg Hill galleries are thought to have been first made by the Romans who were quarrying for stone. The site covers a vast area some twelve miles long by seven miles wide. It was stated that even the most experienced guides have never penetrated the innermost galleries.[69]

Back home he seems to have given up his rooms at Talbot House, as a letter to Douglas Sladen in late 1896 was sent from Warnham near Horsham. This was followed shortly in the new year by a postcard, again to Sladen, advising him of another change of address from 8 to 20 Upper Phillimore Place in Kensington. This was certainly a step up in location and reflected his increasing financial independence. However, the next move ultimately involved the separation from Alice as, conveniently for Le Queux, there now arose the opportunity to move away from London completely.

Alfred Harmsworth, on the success of *Answers*, now founded a new national daily newspaper, the London *Daily Mail*, which was marketed

---

69. *Leeds Times*, 8 August 1896.

to undercut the existing papers at just one halfpenny from May 1896. It very quickly exceeded expectations as regards sales and even today is still one of Britain's most popular daily newspapers. Harmsworth was an astute businessman and was not about to forget someone who had helped expand the sales of his first paper, *Answers*.

Le Queux by now had resigned his appointment with the *Globe* and had already stopped writing for *The Times* as he was soon to become a correspondent with the *Daily Mail*,[70] which involved a move to the South of France. In February 1897 we find Le Queux writing to an unknown recipient from Nice on the Riviera,[71] which pinpoints him having taken up his commission with the *Daily Mail.* Here his duties were to be their reporter in the South of France, stationed at Nice on the Riviera. One such report nearly resulted in him being expelled:

> (I) wrote a series of outspoken articles which very nearly resulted in my expulsion from France. I, however, defied the French Government, for, being the son of a Frenchman, I was by law a French citizen, and although the President had actually signed a decree of expulsion against me, the authorities could not put it into execution.[72]

Le Queux's order to leave France was because he had been critical of the bad drainage on the Riviera and this had been reported in the London *Daily Mail.*[73]

Also, according to a later report in the London *Evening Telegraph*, Le Queux had been spending more and more time on the Continent, and he had at last settled in a villa in the Tuscan seaside village of Ardenza. It was at this time that he published his *A Madonna of the Music Halls.*

---

70. William Le Queux, 'In the Days of my Youth'.
71. WmLQ letter from 89 Promenade des Anglais, Nice, 26 February 1897.
72. William Le Queux. 'In the Days of my Youth'.
73. *Bourbon News*, 7 November 1899.

The report also mentions Monty Carmichael,[74] the British Consul,[75] being a close neighbour. In November, he wrote again, this time to Sladen, telling him he was in Italy, staying at 12 Piazza Della Stazione in Milan, and that he would be back in England for Christmas 1897.

Time spent on the Mediterranean coast gave him ample opportunity to watch and gauge the mood of the locals. In a strongly worded private letter, which found its way into the *British Weekly*, he stated that the French all along the coast from Nice, Cannes to Mentone hated the British and that the local paper, the *Petit Nicois*, was strongly Anglophobe. This was the reason behind the mass exodus over to the Italian Riviera, where there was now hardly a single villa left for rent.[76]

His wanderings continued when he visited Tunis and Egypt, Norway, Sweden and Poland, and then Italy. He then started on what he called a strange round of some of Europe's fashionable resorts namely Trouville and Étretat, both in northern France, and then Spanish San Sebastian, before crossing over to Bagneres de Luchon, then well known for its thermal springs. Then he took in the spa towns of Carlsbad or Karlsbad, and Wiesbaden, and returned via Ems. Mentioned next is Monte Carlo, Aix-les-Bains, Vichy and Royat, which were probably visited before the turn of the century, all in a quest to gain local colour for use in his forthcoming novels.

Prior to his next big journey Le Queux was writing to an unnamed correspondent from the Hotel des Anglais in San Remo. It may have been on his way to begin his tour of Russia, where he travelled across Siberia to the town of Tomsk, there seeing the terrible forwarding-prison for exiles similar to that mentioned in *Guilty Bonds*. This tour began in late February 1900 when he was granted permission by the Russian Government to visit all the penal settlements, mines and prisons in Siberia.[77] The initial intention was to travel by the Trans-Siberian

---

74. Montgomery Carmichael was the British Consul in Leghorn (now Livorno) from 1908 to 1922. He died in 1936 and is buried in the Old British Cemetery.
75. *Evening Telegraph*, 13 July 1897.
76. Quoted in the *York Herald*, 23 October 1899.
77. *Morning Post*, 9 February 1900.

Railway as far as Irkoutsk and then proceed by way of the Great Post Road to Vladivostock. The tour would be expected to take up to six months. It appears that he altered his route and cut short the arduous journey across the Siberian waste, going only as far as Tomsk.

Having returned from Siberia, Le Queux was included as part of a British diplomatic mission sent to sign an extradition treaty with the Republic of San Marino. The mission consisted of Major W. Percy Chapman, Consul General at Florence; Chevalier Linari, the secretary to the Consulate; and Mr Robertson, chief of the Treaty Department at the Foreign Office. William Le Queux travelled with the party as a special attaché and secretary to the mission because of his intimate relations with the Republic.[78] The signing took place in the ancient government palace in October 1900.

According to a local Peterborough newspaper report, whilst in Florence on a diplomatic mission Le Queux first met the woman who would shortly become his second wife.[79]

He was briefly back in London by mid October 1900, when writing to the publishers A & C Black. According to Chris Patrick and Stephen Baister, a record held by *The Times* shows that in November 1900 Le Queux was living at Sunny Bank in Godalming, Surrey.[80] If so, it was only a temporary billet as, towards the end of the year, he had returned to Ardenza from where he was in contact with his literary agents, Messrs A. P. Watt of Paternoster Row.

Watt must have served Le Queux well as in 1898 he was described as one of the highest-paid fiction writers around. According to John Lever Tillotson, of the Tillotson Literary Syndicate, and the *Bolton Evening News*, Le Queux's work was worth about twelve guineas per thousand words.[81] Le Queux's work was being syndicated across the country and his novels were quickly reprinted in publishers' cheap series and on sale

---

78. *Morning Post*, 8 October 1900.
79. *Le Q Magazine*, Autumn/Winter 2004, issue 31, p 5.
80. Chris Patrick and Stephen Baister, *William Le Queux*, p 298 (notes).
81. Roger T. Stearn, 'The Mysterious Mr Le Queux: War Novelist, Defence Publicist and Counterspy', *Soldiers of the Queen* 70, September 1992, p 9.

at the railway bookstalls. Yet in spite of his popularity with the middle and lower working classes, Le Queux was said to be Queen Alexandra's, then Princess of Wales, favourite novelist.[82] And according to Douglas Sladen it was said that even members of the usually sedate Athenæum Club quarrelled over every new Le Queux novel that arrived.[83] His books were being sold all within the Empire, the United States and also throughout Europe. On my shelves, I have editions printed in French, Flemish, German, Italian and Danish. This popularity still brought with it resentment from public librarians and commentators alike. It seems you cannot win them all. Neither was Le Queux the idea of a romantic novelist nor a copy of his literary heroes. Le Queux was described by Douglas Sladen as having 'his affable face, with bright, dark eyes, behind pince-nez, and an inscrutable expression'.[84]

Whilst Le Queux was staying at the Villa Teresa, Ardenza, Leghorn he received dreadful news that his estranged wife Alice had accidentally had a fall at her home on 12 January 1901. Her home was 4 Methley Street, Lambeth,[85] off Kennington Park Road and not far from her husband's childhood home. It was an accident from which she would never recover. At the inquest held in Lambeth, after her death at St Thomas' Hospital on 17 January, the coroner, Mr A. Braxton Hicks, heard that just after midnight her landlady, on hearing voices, went to see what it was and found two constables supporting Alice. It appears she had fallen backwards down the small flight of steps leading to the front door. She was taken to the hospital where the injuries were described as a fractured skull and laceration of the brain which, combined with a weakened heart, caused her death. Alice, who had been separated from her husband for three and a half years, was found to have died from an accident. It came out at the inquest that William Le Queux, in correspondence sent to his mother-in-law, Maria Dorsett, expressed concern for his wife's

---

82. Norman St Barbe Sladen, *The Real Le Queux*, p 11.
83. Douglas Sladen, *Twenty Years of My Life*. London: Constable & Co., 1915, pp 294.
84. Ibid.
85. Incidentally, at the opposite end of Methley Street there is today a blue plaque commemorating the fact that Charlie Chaplin lived there from 1898 to 1899.

Three Weddings and a Funeral 1881–1902

welfare and confirmed that he had sent her £13 at the beginning of the year and had made her an allowance of £8 per month There is mention that at the time of the accident Alice had been drinking heavily.[86] It may have been an accident but for Le Queux it removed any obstacle to his remarrying.

As William Le Queux does not appear on the 1901 National Census I believe he remained living in Italy around Leghorn until August 1901, when he took up residence in Castor near Peterborough. His new home was The Cedars,[87] in Church Hill, a charming old Queen Anne house dating from the early 18th century.

D I Chapman 2013
4 Methley Street, Lambeth

During Le Queux's residence at The Cedars he was looked after by William Chapman, who was his groom and gardener, and his wife, Mary, who was the cook and general housekeeper.[88] We have a lavishly detailed description of the interior of The Cedars:

> A veritable museum of paintings, statuary, china, and old furniture, all of which he brought from his villa amid Italy's fair smile which he loves so well.

---

86. *South London Press*, 26 January 1901.
87. Grade II Listed.
88. *Peterborough Evening Telegraph*, 17 February 1968.

43

If You Can Walk With Kings

The old panelled dining room is covered with pictures. There are some fine examples of Italian art of the 11th and 12th centuries; a portrait of St Francis of Assisi by Giotto, declared by experts to be the earliest representation of the saint; an exquisite 'Pietà', also by Giotto, which Le Queux saw cut from the altar piece of the Church of Pietrasanta, in Tuscany; examples of early Bolognese, Tuscan, Flemish and Dutch Schools; a portrait of the Marquis Appiano of Pisa dated 1393; and a very fine collection of old miniatures, one being especially noteworthy as loot from the Versailles collection in the disastrous war of 1870.[89]

In the reposeful drawing room, hall and corridor, many paintings are hung, together with a genuine terra-cotta Madonna by Della Robbia, the celebrated Florentine. The furniture throughout is old-Italian, of the Renaissance ... perhaps the most valuable and unique of Mr Le Queux's collection is his mediaeval manuscripts. His study is lined with them ... a Papal Bull or Twol with the familiar big lead seals attached, grants of Arms to noble families long since extinct, documents signed by Louis XIII, Charles VI of France, and the great Medician Princes of Florence, and a number of treaties made during the war between the Guelphs and the Ghibellines in the early days of Dante.

The earliest of these documents – of which the collection numbers over 600 – is 1098, and the latest is an autograph letter of Queen Anne ...

Few museums possess such a complete collection of illuminated missals, monastic charters, civil charters, ancient music, treaties and quaint books written on vellum. The celebrated 'Golden Book' of Pisa is amongst Mr Le Queux's most cherished treasures – the book wherein the arms of every noble family entitled to bear them have been illuminated

---

89. Interestingly, the war of 1870 mentioned was the one in which William Lequeux is believed to have taken part. Here we find his son in possession of looted treasure!

since the Middle Ages – and there is also a little vellum volume which was one of the treasures of the library of the great Prince Borgheses in Rome, and is the earliest known example of modern Italian, written by a Sannesse Monk in 1326.[90]

Le Queux, who was no expert in Italian works of art, could as easily have been deceived as any unsuspecting buyer. Many of these so-called art treasures may have been 'by the school of'. I can trace no evidence that links Le Queux with the genuine article, many of which are today protected in museums and art galleries. The items of real value would eventually have to be sold to settle forthcoming divorce costs in later years.

Some time in November 1901 Le Queux suffered a serious accident, injuring his knee. The local Stamford newspaper reported it as a 'serious illness' and that Le Queux consulted Dr Cuthbert Hilton Golding-Bird, a surgeon, of Guy's Hospital in London. Dr Golding-Bird would remain a friend for some years. Le Queux remained bedridden for the next three months, unable to walk.[91] His local paper had recently published a Christmas short story by Le Queux and in an extended interview given to them, he mentioned the injury which kept him laid up:

> Amid a billow of bedclothes and of manuscripts – for five weeks more, when it is hoped that his knee injury will be sufficiently restored to enable him to get about once more.[92]

Just a year after Alice's death William Le Queux married for the second time. His wife was Luisa Gemma Cioni, an Italian, who, at 27 years old, was ten years his junior.[93] They were married by special licence on 22 February 1902 at the Kensington Register Office and both

---

90. *Peterborough Evening Telegraph*, 17 February 1968.
91. *Dundee Courier*, 22 January 1902.
92. *Peterborough Advertiser*, December 1901
93. On the marriage certificate her Christian name is spelt without an 'o', but on other official documents the 'o' is included.

gave their addresses as 52 Warwick Gardens, Kensington. It must have been a quiet affair with no family members in attendance, much like his first wedding fifteen years earlier, as the register is witnessed by at least one person from the Register Office. With Luisa being a Catholic, a marriage outside church was almost unthinkable if she was, as believed, coming from a very old and distinguished Florentine family. Le Queux makes reference to the family in one of his novels:

> '... her name is Cioni of the Cionis of Firenze, one of the most ancient houses in Italy the Countess Guilia Cioni.'
> 'A widow?'
> 'No, signore. She is daughter of the late Count Ferdinando Cioni, head of the house. Their palace is on the Lung 'Arno in Firenze.'
> 'Of what age is she?'
> 'Thirty.'
> 'You say she was from Milan.'
> 'They have a palace in Milan in one of those short streets off the Piazza del Duomo.'[94]

At the time of their marriage there was no indication that her father, Ferdinando Cioni, was dead. According to a contemporary newspaper account the official service was followed by a blessing at the Italian Consulate General. The report also stated that the ceremony was strictly private on account of the bride's family being in mourning. None of this adds up as one would expect the ceremony to have been postponed. It is more likely that the bride's family, who were devout Catholics, did not approve, especially as she was marrying a non-Catholic.

Luisa's mother was the Countess Eva Cioni, the only daughter of the Marquis de Frosali. It was said that she was an intimate friend of Queen Margharita, the widow of King Humbert.[95] The noble house of Cioni

---

94. William Le Queux, *Her Royal Highness*. London: Hodder & Stoughton, 1914.
95. *Le Q Magazine*, Autumn/Winter 2004, issue 31, p 5.

Three Weddings and a Funeral 1881–1902

dates back to 1286 and they were Ghibellines who fought on the side of the Holy Roman Empire.

The happy couple left for a brief honeymoon in Paris.[96]

---

96. *Northampton Mercury*, 21 February 1902 (oddly the day before the wedding!).

J Russell & Sons

William Le Queux *c.*1906

The Invasion
1903–1906

The newlyweds began settling into their new life together and, as an Italian, Luisa should have felt at home here at Castor, as it had once been the site of an extensive Roman settlement or prætorium. However, it seems that once again Le Queux had made the wrong choice. Perhaps he was too much of a romantic and too quick to make such decisions as it would be another he would come to rue.

In a letter to Douglas Sladen dated 3 March 1902 written from Castor, in which he is putting off a dinner invitation, there is no mention even of Mrs Le Queux's existence, although we may assume that she was the reason for the dinner invitation. What we are not even sure of is how long Luisa remained at Castor with her new husband having returned from Paris a year ago. Further doubt comes from another letter to Sladen on 30 June 1902, as again Luisa is not mentioned. Le Queux does mention his old friend Monty Carmichael, who was over from Leghorn, and who had been staying with him, casting further doubt on Luisa's whereabouts.

An 'At Home' feature appeared in *Cassell's Magazine* for 1905[97] prior to the serialisation of *The Spider's Eye*. It began by reiterating the same biographical details that were in *Who's Who*. It included a few photographs of both William and Madame Le Queux, as well as the house and study at Castor and his study in Florence. Mention was made

---
97. 'A Master of Mystery', *Cassell's Magazine*, December 1905, pp 691–4.

of 'his' other homes at Florence in the Viale Michelangelo and at Siena on the foothills of the Apennines. We learn that Le Queux's method of writing was always by hand, never using a typewriter or even giving dictation. Towards the end of his life he did resort to a secretary and there exists a number of typewritten replies. In an earlier newspaper interview Le Queux explained that his writing day began by rising at eight and by half past he was in his study, and then working through until one o'clock when he finished for the day. He achieved an average of about a thousand words each day and also still claimed not to have employed a secretary.[98]

This last point was untrue to some extent. There is a letter written in 1903 to a person known only as 'Everett' claiming that his 'secretary' has mislaid the proofs of 'The Treasures of the Sherburns'.[99] As this short story has not been traced, does it mean it was lost for good?

Because of Le Queux's personal interest in anything archaeological, in 1902/3 he participated in the excavations of a Roman bath house made by the curator of Peterborough Museum, which partly extended into his own garden. The breakthrough came on Saturday 13 December 1902 when in a field close to what was the ancient road Ermine Street, a Roman temple was discovered. Believed to be dedicated to the Roman god Jupiter, the red and white tessellated floor measured forty feet by twenty feet and was in perfect condition. In the centre is what was believed to be the base of an altar. Quantities of Roman pottery and glass were also uncovered.[100] What significant finds there were, 'Chevalier Le Queux' presented to the Peterborough Museum in October 1904 shortly before leaving the area and returning to London.

Whilst Le Queux lived at The Cedars he was always willing to join in with village life. There are some notes made in the log book of the local National School, Fitzwilliam, made by the headmaster, George Holmes, which included the fact that Le Queux attended school prize-giving in

---

98. *Peterborough Advertiser*, December 1901.
99. WmLQ letter to Everett, from Cedars, Castor, 25 September 1903 (in the Lilly Library, Indiana University, Bloomington).
100. *Stamford Mercury*, 19 December 1902.

The Invasion 1903–1906

August 1903. The following year in April a visit was made by some of the older boys across the road to see Le Queux's stuffed Himalayan bear and Bengal tiger, with which the boys were 'much impressed'. Even when he had left the area he did drop in at least once after his excursion through the tundra, when he was persuaded to give a talk.[101]

At this point in his life Le Queux was still adding important items to his growing, and important, collection of early incunabula. In a newspaper interview granted to the *Peterborough Advertiser* he mentions a Book of Numbers dating from around 1120:

> It is a complete copy of the Book of Numbers written in the Abbey of Cornu, in France, by the famous Petrus Lombardus, about 1120, and not only is it complete, but it also contains the whole of the comments of St Augustine, the Venerable Bede, Origines, Rabanus Maurus, Gregorius, Josephus, Flavius and other early commentators, The cover itself is in Latin in a bold Gothic hand, on 106 pages of finest vellum, while interlines and in columns on either side are the valuable comments of early writers.[102]

This may have been one of the last treasures to have been obtained by Le Queux. Occasionally items emanating from Le Queux's library do turn up on the international book market. One such manuscript on vellum written by Gianfranco Pico and printed in Bologna in 1497, with Le Queux's own book-plate pasted in, was recently offered for sale for over thirty thousand US dollars. This is an important book of Americana as it was the first book to mention the discovery of America.[103]

The reason that Le Queux was able to use the rather grandiose title of 'Chevalier' is that he had recently been honoured by the Republic of San Marino. The title and Cross of Chevalier had been bestowed upon him at a special sitting of Parliament in recognition of his diplomatic

---

101. From notes sent to me by Kath Henderson, 16 August 2005, for which I am most grateful.
102. *Peterborough Advertiser*, 17 May 1902.
103. Bookseller: Herman H. J. Lynge & Son, Copenhagen, Denmark.

services to San Marino and Italy.[104] It was announced by the Foreign Office that the King's approval for Le Queux to act as consul in the north of England for the Republic of San Marino had been granted on 6 August 1902.[105] This honour was followed by another, of being allowed to wear the insignia of the Order of the Crown of Italy.[106]

References to Le Queux's life can come from all manner of strange places. In a 1923 book catalogue issued by the renowned London antiquarian booksellers, Messrs Maggs and Bros, they offered for sale a small collection of his books, many of which were presentation copies to Charles Dack.[107] In one volume there is an inscription recording a visit that Dack and Le Queux made together to nearby Spalding in Lincolnshire on 14 August 1903. Dack was clearly interested in Le Queux's writing and continued to receive copies from him long after Le Queux had left the area.

His main achievement whilst at Castor was the thrilling novel of lost treasure, *The Tickencote Treasure*. Tickencote village lies just off the Great North Road beyond Stamford and Burghley House where Le Queux himself believed there was a hidden hoard.[108] The story behind the story is that Le Queux had been sent a letter from a well-known palæographist – not named – which led to further research. This produced conclusive evidence – not stated – of buried treasure hidden in either Stamford or Northampton. All that would be needed to track down the buried hoard was an old Latin manuscript – not to hand. All this has the ring of a marketing ploy, except the name of Le Queux's book was never mentioned in a newspaper paragraph which appeared in the *Northampton Mercury*.[109] The book is a real boy's thriller, if you can accept that after several centuries of lying on the seabed, the ship the *Seahorse* suddenly bobbed up and sealed in an airtight deck is

---

104. *Northampton Mercury*, 12 June 1903.
105. *London Gazette*, 15 August 1902, p 5329.
106. *Lichfield Mercury*, 23 September 1904.
107. Charles Dack was the author of *Weather and Folklore of Peterborough and District*.
108. Norman St Barbe Sladen, *The Real Le Queux*, p 35.
109. *Northampton Mercury*, 22 August 1902.

The Invasion 1903–1906

found an old sea dog. As well as a treasure chest, the contents included several old books written in Latin.

Apart from his own novels, Le Queux also began translating a book, *The Stella Polare* or Polar Star, about an Arctic expedition to reach the North Pole, written by Luigi Amedeo of Savoy, the Duke of Abruzzi. The Duke was the grandson of King Victor Emmanuel II of Italy. We know Le Queux wrote *The Closed Book: Concerning the Secret of the Borgias* whilst living in Castor,[110] and also one of the chapters of *The Count's Chauffeur*, namely 'The Lady of the Great North Road',[111] which was also set in this area. This may not seem to be a great output, except that we know that at this period he spent the summer in England and the rest presumably in Italy with Luisa, so it would be in Italy where the bulk of his fiction writing would have been done. In the autumn of 1903 Le Queux purchased an Italian villa, renamed Villa Le Queux, at Lastra a Signa near Florence, where he intended to settle for the winter.[112]

Le Queux's decision to move from The Cedars to settle in Lastra a Signa appears to have been the reason for his generous gift of finds to the Peterborough Museum. For whatever other reasons he had, Le Queux also put up for auction a considerable part of his library. These were sold by Sotheby's in London on 28 and 29 July 1904, catalogued as 'Valuable and rare books and manuscripts from the Library of W. Le Queux Esq'.

Amongst Le Queux's treasured volumes were several *Books of Hours*, all mid to late 15th century, several bibles and other theological works.

One important book he had begun working on was *The Secrets of the Foreign Office: Describing the Doings of Duckworth Drew of the Secret Service*. It is thought by some that the British secret agent Drew was used by Ian Fleming as the model for his James Bond. Was his tongue really in his cheek when Drew says of himself: 'My real name is Dreux, my father having been French and my mother English.'[113]

---

110. Maggs Bros Catalogue, 1923, p 358.
111. William Le Queux, 'The Lady of the Great North Road', *Cassell's Annual*, London, 1904.
112. *Northampton Mercury*, 6 November 1903.
113. William Le Queux, *The Secrets of the Foreign Office*. London: Hutchinson & Co., 1903, p 7.

However, I do not see Le Queux as the suave and urbane James Bond as portrayed in the eponymous films. In *The Secrets of the Foreign Office*, facts and fiction are never far apart. One of the chapters, 'The Secret of the Fashoda Settlement', was inspired by the real Fashoda Incident of 1898 when Britain and France came so close to war over a territorial dispute along the Nile.

The suggestion that Fleming may have borrowed from Le Queux the idea for the creation of James Bond was aired in an article by Geoffrey Levy in the *Daily Mail*.[114] Levy does not claim that he has conclusive proof; in fact there is no evidence that Fleming ever read Le Queux at all. Similarities, yes certainly. Bond, like Le Queux himself, moved in the same social circles and had the impeccable manners of a born gentleman. What must have prompted Levy's article was the striking use of initials. For Duckworth Drew reports to the Marquis of Macclesfield or the Chief, whereas Bond answers only to M. But, was Q a direct reference from Fleming to Bond's real inspiration?

As Professor David Stafford has pointed out,[115] Le Queux would go on to resurrect gentleman Duckworth Drew in a number of guises. Following on was *The Man from Downing Street*, Jack Jardine, with a country estate in Cheshire.[116] Having been in the Cavalry Regiment he moved to the Confidential Department of the Foreign Office. There was also a Wykemist, Cuthbert Croon, of His Majesty's Diplomatic Service,[117] and Hugh Morrice, this time working for the Nameless Department of His Britannic Majesty's Service. Hugh inherited a medieval villa high above the River Arno in Italy,[118] an area that Le Queux knew well. In Edwardian England in the days before the Great War, it would appear that the requirements of a spy were not cunning and intellect, but social mobility and upbringing. Perhaps there were lower- and middle-class spies of whom we are simply unaware.

---

114. *Daily Mail*, 2 November 1995.
115. David A. T. Stafford, 'Spies and Gentlemen: The Birth of the British Spy Novel 1893–1914'. *Victorian Studies* XXIV, 4 (1981).
116. William Le Queux, *The Man from Downing Street*. London: Hurst & Blackett, 1904.
117. William Le Queux, *Confessions of a Ladies' Man*. London: Hutchinson & Co., 1905.
118. William Le Queux, *Revelations of the Secret Service*. London: F. V. White, 1911.

The Invasion 1903–1906

One of very few mentions of Luisa, at this time, comes from a letter to Canon Alderson.[119]

> Hotel Curzon
> Brighton
> Aug 24. 04
>
> Dear Canon Alderson
>
> I find very much to my regret, that we cannot return to Castor to-day as I had arranged. My wife is not at all well, & we are in Brighton for a few days again, in order to see if the air will benefit her. So we are both awfully sorry that we cannot come & lunch with you.
>
> I wanted <u>so much</u> to have an afternoon in the library, & am deeply disappointed. However, I hope we may be able to do it on some future occasion.
>
> With our kindest regards to Mrs Alderson & yourself.
>
> Yours
>
> William Le Queux

Some time in early October 1905 Le Queux travelled to Montenegro. Why, and what Le Queux was doing there, is unknown. It may have been on secret government business, but for whatever reason he would find himself back there in a year's time.

During their married life 'together' Luisa always appeared to be missing for one reason or another. In an interview for *Cassell's Magazine* Le Queux explains that the English climate did not suit his wife and she could not settle to life in England.[120] Two months later Le Queux was about to return to Italy, yet once again, in a letter to an old editor friend, his wife is not mentioned as accompanying him and it is suspected she was there already.

---

119. Frederick Cecil Alderson, Rector of Lutterworth 1894–1907 and Canon of Peterborough Cathedral 1890–1907. He died 3 December 1907.
120. 'A Master of Mystery', *Cassell's Magazine*, December 1905, p 693.

If You Can Walk With Kings

The Clifton Hotel
Welbeck Street
Cavendish Square
Oct 28. 04

Dear Dr Nicoll

Could you see me one day in the present week to have a chat about the serial you so kindly commissioned me to write for the *British Weekly*? I would so much like to have a chat with you about it, if you would give me an appointment. I am here only for few days prior to returning to Florence for the winter.

I trust that you are quite well, & with kindest regards remain

Yours

William Le Queux[121]

The year 1905 proved to be one of the most productive in all of Le Queux's career as it saw the publication of no less than six novels and a collection of short stories. The latter was *Confessions of a Ladies' Man*; one of these stories had appeared in the *Realm* in 1904. We know very little of his movements for this year and can only guess that he was tied to his study chair in 'Villa Le Queux', high above Florence. Successful novelist he may have been, and even greater achievements were about to come his way, yet at the very high point of his career there would be turmoil in his private life.

Le Queux's lengthy correspondence with the man who in time would become his closest confidant, George Beeforth, appears to begin with this letter written after they had recently met socially:

---

121. It is not certain that any such serial appeared in *The British Weekly*.

The Invasion 1903–1906

> Queen Anne's Mansions,
> St James' Park,
> London S. W.
> Dec 3. 05
>
> My Dear Beeforth
>
> I have omitted the 'Mr', so you must do the same.
>
> I got your letter & ought to have written far earlier, but I have been very busy since last Saturday, when I got back to London to give the matter a reply.
>
> My wife has left Florence with Edie Purser to-day & will be in town I expect next Wednesday.
>
> I am sure we shall get on with your guests – they are certain to be a merry lot!
>
> You say when the time comes I am to tell you the train. If the weather is right I shall run up in the car, & so be independent of trains and the Xmas traffic.
>
> London is hateful just now, and I do far prefer the village duck ponds & hedgerows, only for a full fortnight I am tied to my desk.
>
> I hope the young ladies & Fraulein are well.
>
> When my wife arrives she will write to Beatrice.
>
> With all kind remembrances & hoping to help to hang up the mistletoe in the hall!
>
> Yours
> William Le Queux[122]

With Christmas and the New Year spent in Scarborough with Beeforth, it was during this time that Le Queux had already begun work on his next big project. Throughout Europe there was beginning to be felt another period of uncertainty. This time the threat to Britain lay

---

122. The composer Edward Elgar had once been a resident of Queen Anne's Mansions, which were demolished in 1973.

not with France and Russia as Le Queux had argued a decade earlier, but with Germany. An arms race was being stepped up especially on the high seas, when Britain launched the first of her modern Dreadnought class battleships. Once again with the backing of Field Marshall Lord Roberts and Alfred Harmsworth, the then owner of the *Daily Mail*, Le Queux began writing a book which yet again underlined Britain's unpreparedness for conflict. His research would involve driving all over England and Wales in his 40 hp Napier, covering some 5,000 miles,[123] in order to describe the towns and cities mentioned in the new book.

The new book was entitled *The Invasion of 1910*[124] and the first episode appeared in the London *Daily Mail* for 14 March 1906. The completed version appeared in hardback in August 1906 with an endorsement by Lord Roberts. In the preface Le Queux quotes from Earl Roberts' speech made in Parliament in July 1905: a speech in which Roberts stated that Britain had not seemed to have learnt any lessons from the last war and was cutting back on its defence spending, and that history should have taught us that any Empire which cannot safeguard its own possessions will inevitably perish. Le Queux said this state of affairs was the reason behind his publication of the book. In the open letter, printed in facsimile, Lord Roberts refers to his speech he made to the House of Lords on 10 July 1905 in which he publicly supports Mr Le Queux's new book.

The origins of the book came about one day following a conversation between Le Queux and Lord Roberts:

> One afternoon, when I sat with Lord Roberts in his library, I told him that all I had endeavoured to do was without avail; for I was being denounced on every hand as a scaremonger, and told that I was a novelist and should stick to my profession of writing fiction.[125]

---

123. *The Automotor Journal*, 6 January 1906.
124. William Le Queux, *The Invasion of 1910*. London: Eveleigh Nash, 1906.
125. William Le Queux, *Things I Know about Kings*, p 244.

The Invasion 1903–1906

So Roberts urged him to write a description of what would happen if Britain were invaded, and he, Roberts, would work out a scheme of attack. He also suggested asking Lord Northcliffe to publish it.

> The next day I saw my old friend whom the *Daily Mail* staff called 'The Chief'. Within an hour he had given me a commission. I was to write regardless of expense, a forecast of 'The Invasion' for the *Daily Mail*, besides being promised a very handsome price for it.[126]

The fictional invasion by Germany began on Sunday 2 September 1910 and in London the following day was known as Black Monday.[127] The Germans began by cutting the telecommunications from East Anglia and the train lines were disrupted by bridges being destroyed by high explosives, laid by spies. The main aim for the German high command was the capture of London, which came under siege. Yet once again, despite being woefully unprepared, the British come out on top and the Hun are sent packing. The rights to publish the book in Germany were sold by Le Queux's literary agent, Messrs A. P. Watt, for a considerable amount of money. However, much to Le Queux's annoyance, when the book was republished in Germany as *Die Invasion von 1910: Einfall der Deutschen in England*, it had an alternative ending, with the Germans sacking London! The German version does not include Earl Roberts' open letter, but it does correct Le Queux's mistake as the Sunday was in fact 4 September. The Germans can as always be relied upon to be predictable.

In the press and in Parliament *The Invasion of 1910* was both praised and criticised, more the latter than the former it has to be said. Some called it implausible. Oddly, even with the benefit of hindsight, modern-day commentators have also challenged its probability. No one person can predict what will happen in wartime or how events will twist and

---

126. Ibid. pp 244–5.
127. A curious mistake by Le Queux as 3 of September was in fact a Saturday. Germany made a habit of declaring war on Britain on a Sunday, as they were to do in 1939.

turn – real wars rarely follow the script. What would they have said if Le Queux had written of soldiers being ordered to 'go over the top' into certain annihilation – no doubt he would have been told to stick to romantic fiction.

Sales from the book are said to have made a fortune for both Le Queux and Harmsworth. But not all was well with Le Queux.

In a letter written to Beatrice Beeforth by her brother on 10 February 1906, he mentions that the current issue of the *Daily Mail* was chiefly devoted to the forthcoming novel by William Le Queux. The letter goes on to mention that they had seen quite a lot of Le Queux recently. He had attended a couple of their 'musicals' and he had accompanied them to their friends, the Holmans, for dinner. Le Queux, being the 'modest' man he was, appears to have turned up wearing a row of enamel stars and a rose in his buttonhole. They had wanted him to wear a cocked hat but he had refused. Their news on Le Queux ends with how he was worried about his wife as Luisa had not written to him for a fortnight.[128] A month later the *Daily Mail* carried an article by the author giving the background on how his novel was written and also carrying a laudatory recommendation by Lord Roberts.[129]

His worries about Luisa had to be put to one side because the imminent publication of *The Invasion of 1910* required his full attention, as mentioned in a letter prior to the *Daily Mail* serialisation:

Queen Anne's Mansions,
St James' Park,
London S. W.
March 7. 06

My Dear Beeforth

I find that it is impossible for me to get to Scarboro' for the week-end – as much as I want to.

---

128. Letter in the author's collection dated Upper Norwood, 10 February 1906.
129. WmLQ, 'Can England be Invaded?', *Daily Mail*, 17 March 1906.

The Invasion 1903–1906

The 'Invasion' appears in the *Daily Mail* next Wednesday. That see the *Mail* [sic] on Saturday.

I daresay you will also see the flowing advertisements that are being prepared. They are spending £2,000 in advertising in the London papers, & printing two million war-maps & leaflets, a copy of which I will send to you.

So I have to see after the troops, which keeps me a lot at the *Mail* office.

Moreover Lord Roberts & I are guests at the Marines mess at Chatham to-morrow night, & we stay down there on the following day as there is to be a mobilisation of all the troops etc.

I have had absolutely no word from Italy, except that my man Michele writes that Madame sent him home to Rome, & that he intends to come to me in London next week as Madame told him to!

I am terribly upset, for the whole affair is on my nerves. Yet I have told nobody except your kind dear self.

I wonder if I may come down and chat with you at the end of next week? But you won't make company of me, will you. Kindest regards to Miss Lizzie, & all good wishes to yourself.

Yours

William Le Queux

In a telegram to George Beeforth in early March 1906 he says that a 'question' was being asked in the House of Commons that afternoon and to be sure to watch for the morning papers. The then Prime Minister, Sir Henry Campbell-Bannerman[130] stood up in 'the House' and accused Le Queux of being a 'pernicious scaremonger', and saying that this book should never have been written, although it appears that the Prime Minister had not actually read the book himself! Le Queux

---

130. Sir Henry Campbell-Bannerman (1836–1908) was a British Liberal Party politician who served as Prime Minister from 1905 to 1908.

then challenged Campbell-Bannerman in the pages of *The Times*[131] as to why he should condemn a book he has never read. In a private moment Campbell-Bannerman did apologise to Le Queux, explaining it had been a political error. Tactically Campbell-Bannerman knew Le Queux was right to highlight Britain's danger, but at this moment the Prime Minister was clearly 'playing to the gallery'. Yet there was a darker side to events, as Le Queux revealed just a few hours before publication:

Queen Anne's Mansions,
St James' Park,
London S. W.
March 14. 06

My Dear Beeforth

The Government think that I am giving away official secrets, & I understand are seriously considering whether they will not bring me to the bar of the House of Commons!

Rather fun, is it not?

Did you see in 'The Times' to-day, the 14th, my letter to Campbell-Bannerman replying to him.

In these circumstances, because I do not know what is happ going to happen, from day to day I cannot leave London.

May I come to you say <u>next Monday</u> night? Just for a day.

I have had absolutely <u>no word</u> from Italy!

I hope you are well. It is very cold and snowy here.

All kindest regards to Miss Lizzie & yourself.

Yours

William Le Queux

In hardback alone the book sold in excess of a million copies and it is claimed to have been translated into twenty-seven languages.[132]

---

131. *The Times*, 14 March 1906.
132. William Le Queux, *German Spies in England; An Exposure*. London: Stanley Paul, 1915, p 117.

The Invasion 1903–1906

On 24 March 1906 the *Daily Mail* reported that Le Queux had received hundreds of letters on a daily basis, mostly congratulating him and declaring that he had rendered a national service. There were a few of a more abusive nature warning him 'to take care' or 'stay away from Italy' – the one thing he did not want to do.

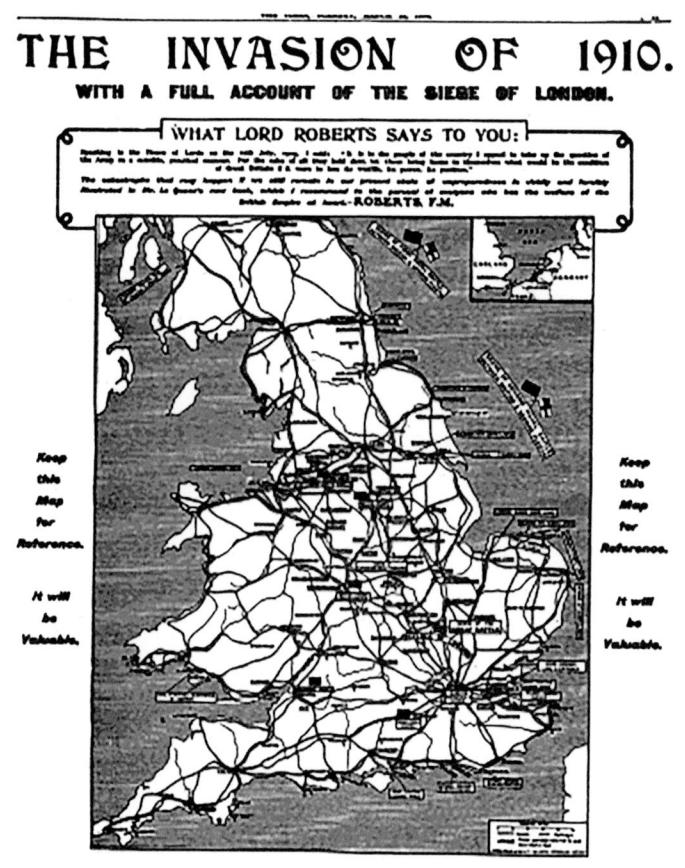

Map used for advertising *The Invasion of 1910* by *Daily Mail*

A memo was sent to London by Reginald Tower,[133] from the British Legation in Munich, in which he reports that Le Queux's novel was receiving much attention in the Bavarian press,[134] as one would have expected.

Despite much carping from many angles, Le Queux still remains relevant to this day. With the centenary of The Great War, the august Bodleian Library produced a new edition to coincide with the centenary, under the title *If England Were Invaded*.

The following month George Beeforth, in a letter to his granddaughter, Beatrice, tells her he has had word from Le Queux. He explains that due to the huge success of *The Invasion* Le Queux needs to expand it and that he is expecting to go motoring to Devon and Cornwall, all at a moment's notice.[135] During the next couple of months Le Queux moved again, this time to the Hotel Cecil[136] in The Strand, which he would call home for the next fourteen years.

Hotel Cecil,
Strand W.C.
August 10. 06

My Dear Beeforth

So many thanks. Newton[137] yesterday sent me an invite to go to Burton to-morrow till Monday. So I'm going.

During Tuesday, Wednesday & Thursday this next week I shall have to be in London. After that I shall be delighted to come down, if you really think that my visits will not be misconstrued.

Thanks for what you say regarding the Normands, for it has much relieved me. I felt all along that they would not

---

133. Sir Reginald Thomas Tower, KCMG, CVO, FSA (1860–1939).
134. National Archives, Kew, FO 371/77/280, 28 March 1906.
135. Letter in the author's collection dated Scarboro, 1 April 1906.
136. The Hotel Cecil was largely demolished in 1930 and the Shell-Mex House built on the site.
137. Frederick Newton Husbands, a stave merchant from Burton-on-Trent.

The Invasion 1903–1906

believe such allegations. Forquats, my man in Florence, has written me some details of Mrs Le Q's goings on there, & I am much troubled.

I was at Brighton yesterday with a motoring party & only just returned this morning

Till Sunday I shall be at Burton.

With all kindest regards to everybody & longing to see you again.

Yours as ever

William Le Queux

PS The King, through Sidney Greville,[138] has written me a letter of congratulations upon 'The Invasion'. I have just this moment received it. He dates it from the Royal Yacht at Cowes.

Unknown

Hotel Cecil, London, from Embankment Garden

---

138. Hon. Sir Sidney Robert Greville, born on 16 November 1866. The son of George Guy Greville, 4th Earl of Warwick. Died 12 June 1927. At the time of his death he was Groom-in-Waiting to King George V.

If You Can Walk With Kings

Regardless of what was being said about Le Queux publicly or what people thought of him, he was held in high regard at the Foreign Office. And he was about to set off on a two-month-long, difficult and dangerous mission into a virtually lawless region of Europe.

His personal life, however, was in turmoil. Buoyed up by the financial success of *The Invasion* and in spite of the support from many readers, his home life was about to fall apart. Facing months away from home, it was not the right time to receive the news that Luisa was filing for divorce. Her petition was placed before the Divorce Court of the Royal Courts of Justice on Tuesday 22 May 1906.[139] A few weeks later the defendant, through his solicitor, dismisses all the allegations and prays that the court will dismiss the petition.[140] The inference is that Le Queux had no intention of divorcing his wife, but for what reason? As they remained separated it must be solely on the grounds of what his liabilities would be in terms of allowances and costs.

---

139. Court minutes, 22 May 1906.
140. Court minutes, 13 June 1906.

Mission to Albania
1906

One of the last outposts of Europe is Albania, once part of the Ottoman Empire until it became a republic in 1912. It is sandwiched between the old Yugoslav countries to the north and ancient Greece to the south. To us now it still seems a strange and forbidding land.

In his autobiography Le Queux recalls travelling from London by way of Trieste and on by steamer to Montenegro. Within hours of arriving in Cettigne he arranged an audience with Crown Prince Nicholas,[141] where he requested permission to visit northern Albania.

'I want, your Majesty, to be allowed to go into Northern Albania and see the mountain tribes of which so much has been said'.

'The Skreli brigands!' he exclaimed in surprise. 'Do you actually contemplate visiting the tribes in what we Montenegrins call "The Accursed Mountain"?'[142]

The advice given was simply – 'Do not go'. Until recently the main problem with his account of his mission had been that it lacked dates which makes it all the less credible. Fortunately Le Queux left his detailed plans of his intended mission and we now know from them

---
141. Nikola I Mirkov Petrović-Njegoš (1841–1921). Became King in 1910.
142. William Le Queux, *Things I Know about Kings*, p 44.

If You Can Walk With Kings

that he had already planned to spend time in Albania. His account of his visit was duly written up and published the following year in 1907 as *An Observer in the Near East*,[143] but anonymously, as he himself says he was engaged in secret-service work.

This is his outlined timetable for the mission which he allowed four weeks to complete:

13 October	Hotel Imperial, Ragusa, Austria[144]
16–19 October	Grand Hotel, Cettigne, Montenegro
20–23 October	Europe Hotel, Scutari, Albania
25 October	Hotel Narenta. Mostar, Herzegovina
26 October	Hotel Europe, Sarajevo, Bosnia
28 October for a week	Hotel Imperial, Belgrad, Servia[145]
Then	Hotel Orient, Nisch, Servia
	Grand Hotel de Bulgarie, Sofia, Bulgaria
	Hotel Continental, Rustchuk, Bulgaria
	Grand Hotel de Boulevard, Bukarest, Roumania
	Grand Hotel & Pera Palace, Pera
	Constantinople, Turkey
	Hotel le Globe, Dede, Turkey
	Hotel Angleterre, Salonica, Turkey
	Hotel Belgrad, Monastir, Macedonia, Turkey
	Hotel Turati, Uskub, Kosovo, Turkey

---

143. William Le Queux, *An Observer in the Near East*. London: Eveleigh Nash, 1907.
144. Better known as Dubrovnik.
145. Servia became Serbia towards the end of 1916.

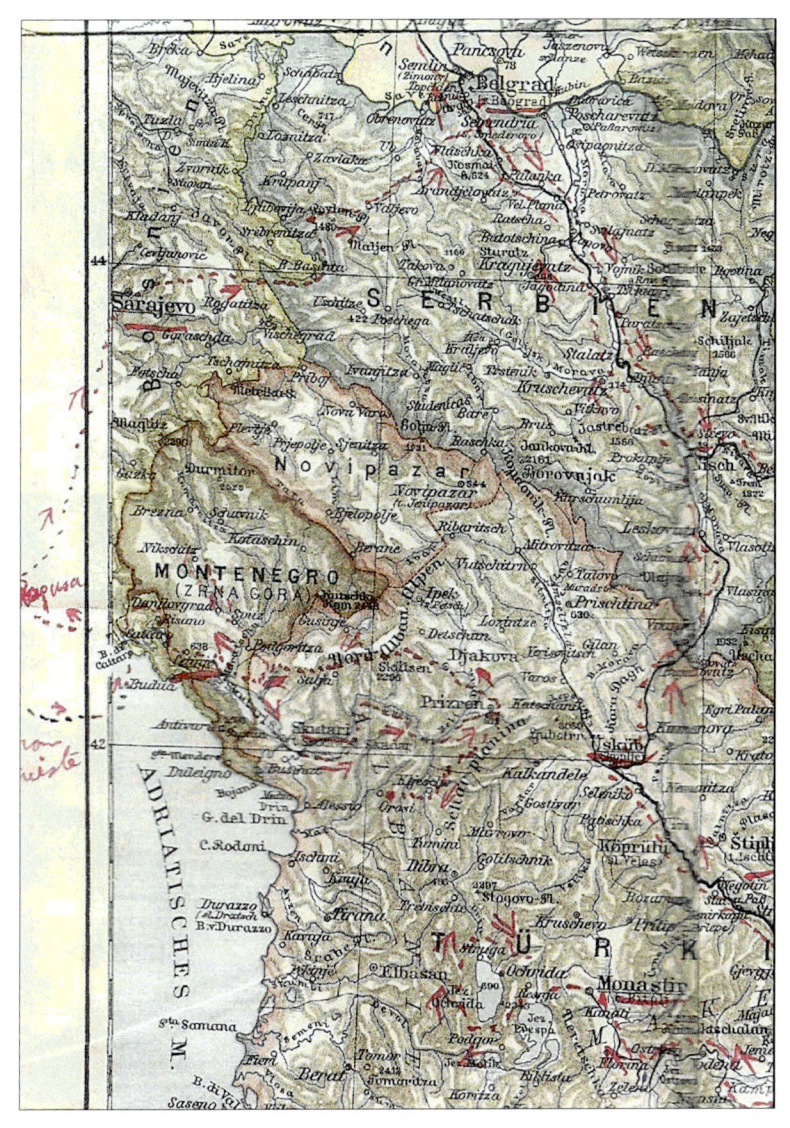

Details from Le Queux's own map of the Balkans
showing his route through Albania

If You Can Walk With Kings

In a final letter to George Beeforth before his departure Le Queux may have slightly exaggerated the risks he was taking, and it reads like the thriller writer he was and not the explorer:

Hotel Cecil,
Strand W.C.
'Sunday Night'

My Dear Old Fellow

I was so very glad to get your kind letter, & to think that at a date in the near future we may be able to go over the colleges together & see their treasures. We ought to do it systematically, writing before hand, so as to get permits.

We will do this!

Well – my dear chap, I have now to bid you <u>*au revoir*</u>. I do not disguise from myself that my journey in some places will be fraught with considerable peril, but I shall try & do my utmost as I have done in the past, for the prestige & honour of our country in Europe. I have a very difficult & very delicate mission – how difficult I will tell you afterwards – and I fear it will require more tact than I possess, & probably more courage. Still I will do my best, & if I fail – well as the French say – *tout pris*!

Towards you my dear old friend I have been drawn so closely that I regret to leave you more than any other of my very few friends. You may not believe it, but I have as much regard, esteem & love for you as ever I had for my own father. I therefore write this to bid you farewell, feeling that you are my <u>best</u> & my most <u>intimate friend</u>, & knowing that, at least, you will sometimes think of me, as I shall think of you.

Remember that – both now & always – when you are in any difficulty a telegram will bring me straight to your side wherever I may chance to be. I know that you are my true friend, while I, on my part, am yours devotedly.

Mission to Albania 1906

Fate has decreed, I suppose, that I shall in future be a wanderer. Domestic happiness seems denied to me. Empty fame is but a poor consolation for the quiet homely comfort for which I have for years been longing. Still, I suppose I must hope, & hope on to the end.

I do not say 'good-bye' to you, my dear old chap, but merely 'au revoir'.

I put my trust in God, & I know He will protect me and let me return in safety. When I get back, my first visit will be to you.

But on my journey I shall often think of you, & I beg of your prayers on my behalf.

May God also bless and comfort you.

I grip your hand in adieu.

Your affectionate friend

William Le Queux

PS I send this to Scarboro in case it misses you at Kentford. A letter posted on Wednesday to Cettigne will catch me up before going into the wild.[146]

The following day Le Queux sent Beeforth a telegram from Charing Cross Road Post Office and his mission was then under way, taking the train from London to the channel port and then on to Trieste, still then a free port. Here he boarded the Austrian Lloyd steamer *Graf von Wurmbrand*, bound for Cattaro[147] where he disembarked at noon in bright sunlight, taking the ladder-like road to Cettigne, described by Le Queux as a quaint little place not much larger than a mountain village with broad streets. Having signed the hotel register he immediately wrote to Beeforth:

---

146. WmLQ letter to George Beeforth, 7 October 1906.
147. Generally known as Kotor in Montenegro.

If You Can Walk With Kings

Grand Hotel,
Cettigne
(Monténégro)
Oct 09, 1906

My Dear Beeforth

On arrival here to-day a huge Montenegrin armed to the teeth, with great ceremony handed me your telegram!

It was awfully kind of you to think of me. I know that at best I have one friend who is watching my movements!

Well, the sea voyage from Trieste to Cattaro is the finest I have ever experienced. The Adriatic is like a lake, & a glass filled with water would not have spilt during the whole trip. The Dalmatian islands are simply superb. You & I <u>will have</u> to do the trip one day, as far as Cattaro.

From Cattaro I journeyed 12 hours in the mountains through a bare desolate country, terribly wild, without even a hut. The road is a marvellous one – said to be the most wonderful engineering feat in the world. And here I am in a wretched miserable so-called hotel in the capital of Monténégro. Myself and the British Minister[148] to Monténégro are the only two people in the hotel, so we are chums, & spend the time yarning. There is no house fit to an Embassy, so he lives in the hotel.

I've just presented my credentials, & to-night – I dine with the Crown Prince[149] & his wife, while to-morrow the reigning prince receives me in audience.

His chamberlain has just been to see me, & so gorgeous was he that I thought he was the prince himself!

Oh! How quaint this place is! The men are all fighters & everyone is fully armed, quite an arsenal of weapons in everyone's belt. I hear rumours that there was a Christian

---

148. Charles Louis des Graz (1879–1940). Attended Harrow School, knighted 1915.
149. Prince Danilo Aleksandar Petrović-Njegoš (1871–1939).

village massacred on the Turkish frontier the night before last, & a whole regiment of soldiers have just passed the window going to avenge it.

Whew! What a blood thirsty lot they are!

Every man stands six feet, and are magnificent fellows.

I shall be here about four or five days, & then I go with an escort out into the wilds. The wilderness I passed through yesterday was bad enough. Heaven knows what wild Albania must be like!

All kindest regards to everyone at the Belvedere & lots of luck to you, my dear old chap.

Yours as ever

William Le Queux

PS Gabrielle will show you the post-card.

Before leaving Montenegro, Le Queux found time to update Beeforth of his audience with Prince Nicholas and on his continuing mission:

Grand Hotel,
Cettigne
(Monténégro)
Oct 15, 1906

My Dear old chap

I expect you wonder how I am getting on. Well I have just completed the first chapter of my rather difficult mission.

To-day at four o'clock I had an audience of Prince Nicholas of Monténégro. His aide-de-camp came for me in a carriage, & my reception by gorgeous servants with wonderful red & gold dress & pistols in their belts was quite warlike. The Palace, plain outside, is very beautiful within. The Prince first received me in the Hall of the Ambassadors, & then took me into an ante-room where coffee & cigarettes were served, & we had a chat for an hour & a half, all of course in confidence. He's a charming man – father of the Queen of Italy – & was very <u>very</u> kind to me. Told me he would send me his photograph tomorrow as souvenir! He told me – & explained to me almost as a father would – the whole situation in the Balkans. He gave me permission to shoot & fish in any part of his 'Dominion', & in parting took both my hands & said in Italian, – remember, my Dear W Le Q., come back again here to Cettigne & you have only to ask audience of me.

Well, I think, & hope – I have gained my Diplomatic point. Monténégro is one of the hard nuts to crack in the Balkans, & while yesterday the British Minister, my friend Des Graz, was received for only five minutes in a <u>formal</u> audience. I have had this long one! Oh! The carefulness with which I had to choose my words! And yet we sat smoking, as in a study after dinner!

To-morrow I go into Albania – the wilds where life isn't worth a month's purchase. My escort are awaiting me – a blackguardly looking lot! I go to Scutari, and thence through Albania. I have wonderful permits written in Turkish, and heaven knows what will happen when we get to the frontier.

Outside, in the bazaar, a crowd are at this moment discussing a raid which took place yesterday upon a village in which 22 men were killed, & a number of women & children slaughtered in cold blood!

By jove! Life seems cheap on the frontier, & now I'm off to see what it all means.

Good bye. I shall turn up at 'The Belvedere' later (D. V.) My escort have just been overhauling my rifle & revolver! The Prince himself told me 'You'll have a rough time. I expect!' All kindest regards

Yours as ever

William Le Queux.[150]

---

150. WmLQ letter to George Beeforth.

Mission to Albania 1906

Details such as the slaughter of women and children were kept out of his book *An Observer in the Near East* and his autobiography for obvious reasons. Now began the trek through the 'Accursed Mountains to Scutari'.[151]

In Camp, Village of Scutari – Albania–Turkey

Oct 19, 1906

My Dear Beeforth

I am writing this by a lantern, so perhaps you will not be able to read it!

We have been for the part of four days in the mountains, and are having a pretty rough time. Here on the frontier we are keeping a sharp look out. Last night there was an alarm – a lot of firing, but nobody hurt. I haven't had a wash for three days! Travelling up in this terrible wilderness of mountains is the hardest I have ever done. Yesterday it rained, so sleeping out is not very pleasant, still up to the present I'm all right, I'm pleased to say. The escort with me seems always dying to have a go at somebody. They sometimes fire simply for the sake of firing. This is very different to our comfortable excursions in Yorkshire! Food is a difficulty & I'm living on my stores, but as I have to give the officer some, I've had some <u>tinned stew</u> and a nip of neat whiskey, as we have no water, but hope to get to a spring to-morrow.

You have no idea what these Albanian mountains are like. But the photographs I'm taking will show you later.

It is a strange scene here – in the lovely Oriental night under the stars, the soldiers singing their national songs in chorus prior to turning in. One seems so far from the world up here, yet in places the Albanians lurk behind every rock. In the province of Turkey there is practically no law or order.

---

151. Now known as Skodra.

If You Can Walk With Kings

There were 19 people murdered in the open streets of the town of Scutari last week!! We hope to get down there tomorrow, or next day. When I will post this. Tell Gabrielle that if there are any postcards in Scutari I'll send her them.

Hope you are all right & fit, old chap. All the best of luck to you from

Yours as ever

William Le Queux.

In his book of his journey through the Near East Le Queux recalls being in the bazaar wearing his recently purchased fez so as to 'blend in', when he heard a pistol shot and saw a man lying dead on the ground. He seemed shocked to realise that no one thought this unusual and no one went to his aid. Life was, as he says, 'cheap'. Apart from this one letter there is no further surviving correspondence whilst Le Queux was in Scutari, nor of his visit to meet Vatt Marashi, the chief of the Skreli tribe. Le Queux does claim that he was the first Englishman to meet Marashi and take his photograph. His visit involved travelling for several days on foot with only his guide, Palok, accompanying him, but he had the reassurance of safe passage. Apart from the many photographs that appear in *An Observer in the Near East*, I have twenty-five or so more, all taken by Le Queux and all described by him in pencil on the reverse. Some of these appear in the text.

His experiences in Scutari were used in Le Queux's collection of short stories *The Lady in the Car*.[152]

Before Le Queux left Scutari he gave a promise to Vatt Marashi that he would one day return with his friend 'who shoots Tigers in India', whom I take to be George Beeforth. Having reached Cettigne he rejoined Charles des Graz for debriefing. After resting overnight Le Queux continued his journey, retracing his steps to Cattaro to catch the same steamer, this time to Gravosa, the port for Ragusa in Dalmatia.

---

152. William Le Queux, *The Lady in the Car*. London: Eveleigh Nash, 1908.

Mission to Albania 1906

In *An Observer in the Near East* Le Queux tells us that he was carrying dispatches in a diplomatic bag for the Foreign Office. He left Dubrovnik early the following morning by train heading for Mostar for his next overnight stay. Soon Le Queux was pushing on to Sarajevo in Bosnia, his every step being followed by spies, on account of his carrying a diplomatic bag which was to be handed over to the King's messenger, before making for Belgrade, where he was expected.

Le Queux arrived in Belgrade on 31 October 1906 and, reaching the Grand Hotel, he immediately wired his friend in Scarborough that he was not staying at the Imperial Hotel as originally planned. The following day Le Queux updated Beeforth on his adventures:

> Grand Hotel, Belgrade
> (Serbia)
> Nov 1, 1906

My Dear Beeforth

I was so pleased to see a letter from you this morning, & to hear that you are well. Also to hear that the Palermo visit is postponed!! I wonder why? I must find out.

Watney was quite right when he said that I was in Ragusa, as I had to go down there to meet the King's messenger, & give him my dispatches. The Foreign Office are now digesting them I expect. You see Monténégro is a most important geographical position, & will play a great part in the future of the Balkans. It is the back-door to the Balkans, & the whole country consists of an impregnable fortress of mountains.

Last night we had a very pleasant dinner at the Embassy. Mr Pashich, the man who now rules Serbia, & who is Prime Minister, was very nice to me, & has promised me an early audience of the King. Madame Pashich is half Italian, so I got on very well with her, & she invited me to dine on Saturday.

If You Can Walk With Kings

This place is externally gay & I have already quite a lot of 'invitations' and, card-leaving. But one wants a lot of hard physique to stand what I've been through there last three weeks or so. The Serbians all seem pleased they got rid of Queen Draga, & King Alexander, & are loud in their praises of the present king. My mission is however, a very delicate one, & will require a lot of careful thought.

This is a place of gay uniforms and pretty women, diplomatic intrigue and spies on every hand. The town is rather ugly, as you will see by the post-cards, but everything is double the price of anywhere else in Europe.

How glad I shall be to be back again, however, I hate making so many new friends, & all this kow towing and strict etiquette, & wearing my uniform. I don't know how long I shall be here, but I want to get on to Sofia & Bucharest. Give my best wishes to the girls & to your sister & Fraulein.

And lots of luck to your dear old self from

Yours as ever

William Le Queux.

Amongst Le Queux's documentation was a request which had been granted for an audience with King Peter of Serbia.[153] He would eventually have a total of three audiences with the Serbian King.

---

153. Peter Karadodević, the last King of Serbia (1844–1921).

William Le Queux
Mes Bridge north-east of Shkoder, built 1780

Sunday in Scutari

Belgrade, le 22 Octobre 1906

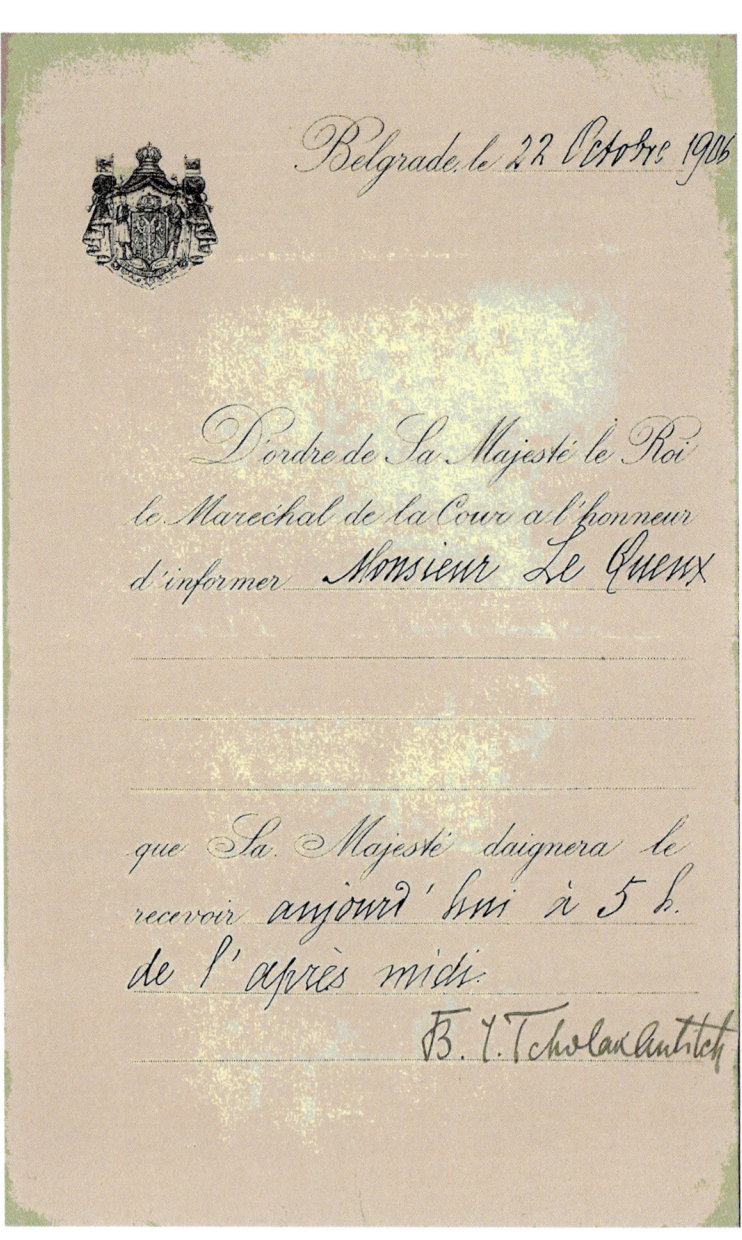

D'ordre de Sa Majesté le Roi le Maréchal de la Cour a l'honneur d'informer *Monsieur Le Queux*

que Sa Majesté daignera le recevoir *aujourd'hui à 5 h.* de l'après midi.

B. J. Tcholak-Antitch

An audience with King Peter of Serbia

Mission to Albania 1906

For the first time in some months Le Queux received word from George Beeforth concerning Luisa:

> Grand Hotel, Belgrade,
> Wednesday

My Dear old chap

It is so very good of you to send the papers – which are a God-send here, as I can't read a line of any of the local papers here. Thanks for the article on Macedonia. I shall be in Macedonia I hope, about the beginning of next month, on my way home, as you will see from the note I sent you.

You ask me for my dates. Since it is impossible to give, as I don't know how long I shall be in each of the towns, or how long my negotations take. I shall, however, write you now & then simply saying where a letter will find me. Though so gay, & so pleasant I have a <u>very worrying</u> time here but I cannot explain in this letter, as most correspondence is opened. Yesterday, however, the Prime Minister told me that the King was very pleased & had made some very complimentary remarks about myself. So I am hoping for complete [unreadable] All tends to show much will be the case. Everyone is externally kind to me here. I am out the whole time. There was a big dinner at the British Legation last night at which the Premier & Ministers were present. I took in the young Princess of Thurn & Taxis, a German Princess about 21, and unmarried.[154] There is a little too much dancing attendance on petticoats here to suit me, but it has of course to be done. But political intrigue is everywhere, & the very walls have ears. I have a lot of photos, documents etc that I want to get rid of before entering Turkey, where all the books etc, are confiscated. May I send them to you to keep for me?

---

154. Princess Helen of Serbia (1884–1962).

If You Can Walk With Kings

Your kind words regarding Mrs Le Q are very sympathetic. I have worried a lot. But I'm ceasing to do so now. A letter from you is so welcome, you can't tell. I look at every post & wonder whether there is news from you, dear old fellow.

I hope you are all right. I shall inspect the new roses very soon, I hope.

As regards the Villa Trollope I <u>should not go</u>. Beatrice hates Mrs Hope, & the latter is just as antagonistic to B. All good luck old chap.

Yours ever

William Le Queux.[155]

His comments about the very walls having ears turned out to be quite profound.

Grand Hotel, Belgrade,
Nov 9 06

My Dear old fellow

I have to-day sent you two packets of photos if you will kindly keep them for me till my return. <u>Open them & look at them</u>. There are Kings, Princes, Ministers etc. May spoil when packed up, so if you don't mind keeping them for me. I'd be so much obliged. Please tell me when they come safely to hand.

Still very gay here. I have an audience with the King [Peter of Serbia] again to-morrow & & I hope on Monday to leave for Nisch & Sofia (Hotel Belgarie). I hope to leave Sofia about 17th or 18th for Rustchuck [sic] & Bucharest. I probably shall not stay at Rustchuck, but go straight to Bucharest. Last night a diplomatic ball, & to-night the King's (Edward's) Birthday. I go to the big dinner at the Embassy. Luncheon to-day at the Minister of Justice's. So you see that special engagements crowd upon me here.

---

155. WmLQ letter to George Beeforth, 7 November 1906.

Mission to Albania 1906

Still I'm worried over certain matters, & shall have to be here again in February. Ah! What intrigue! I'll tell you all when we meet.

I'm glad Beatrice is having such a jolly time. I have heard from her – only once – since I left. Too busy to write I suppose.

I shall be glad to be back & have a quiet smoke with you. This life is very wearing.

The very best of good luck, & with thoughts daily to you & yours, dear old fellow.

Yours friend

William Le Queux.[156]

Le Queux mentions leaving his hotel one evening and driving in through the wide ornamental gates of the Royal Palace or New Konak, how the blue-coated sentries saluted him on his arrival before entering the big entrance hall, whilst liveried servants dressed in blue and gold looked on. Here he was met by the Royal Marshall and conducted into an audience chamber where he was left alone with His Majesty, King Peter. You can hardly imagine how awe-inspiring it must have been in such palatial surroundings, although in which Le Queux seems to be at ease.

Le Queux had been asked by Whitehall that, as he was on friendly terms with King Peter, he should try to arrange for a private chat about political matters. The content of his private talks were to be kept from the Serbian officials, which is one reason why no mention of what transpired appears in his correspondence, which Le Queux knew would be inspected. The reason for his mission to Serbia is mentioned in his autobiography:

> On one of my visits to Belgrade I was charged with a secret mission concerning new armaments for Serbia, in view of the coming war – a mission that had a dramatic dénouement.[157]

---

156. WmLQ letter to George Beeforth, 9 November 1906.
157. William Le Queux, *Things I Know about Kings*, p 77.

If You Can Walk With Kings

This would have been the run-up to the first Balkan War of 1912. Le Queux's secret mission was uncovered by an Austrian spy who listened, from an adjoining room in the Grand Hotel, to a conversation between Le Queux and Alexander Tucker, the London-based Consul General for Serbia. Tucker was acting as Le Queux's secretary as well as representing a group of financiers involved with the proposed arms deal. During the lunch which followed, Dr Vesnitch, the Justice Minister, took a surprise telephone call which confirmed what Le Queux and Tucker had been discussing the night before and the detailed contents of his subsequent telegram to London. Questions were raised in the Serbian Parliament the following day, but it meant that the Serbians had to deny everything and the mission ultimately failed. The arms deal did not go to Germany, as the British feared, but was awarded to the French.

Le Queux dashed off an urgent telegram to George Beeforth telling him he would be leaving Belgrade for Sofia on Wednesday morning (14 November 1906). He also mentioned that King Peter had bestowed upon him the Star of Saint Sava,[158] Serbia's highest order.

Le Queux left Belgrade on the Orient Express in the company of the ex-French Minister of War, M. Etienne. Once out of Serbia, Le Queux could be more open in his next letter to George Beeforth:

> Grand Hotel Bulgarie,
> Sofia Thursday
> [15 November 1906]
>
> My Dear Beeforth
>
> Now that I am out of Serbia I can write to you.
>
> During the past fortnight I've lived in a prefect maelstrom of worry, combined with gaiety. Spies – against the present regime – were everywhere. All my letters were opened & read, & I was followed everywhere by the emissaries of Austria. Life was intolerable. The Ministers apologised to me for it, and

---

158. WmLQ telegram to George Beeforth, from Belgrade, 12 November 1906.

asked what they could do? King could do nothing. Ah! My dear fellow, you have no idea what Diplomacy here in the Balkans means. The Minister for the Interior told me that there were 113 known spies of Austria in Belgrade alone! And Austria fears our Diplomacy? Well, I did my best. I had three audiences of the King & many with the Premier. The King was most gracious, & invited me to the two Court balls. He listened to me, and thanked me for my efforts. After long argument we got in accord, & I believe I've scored well against Turkey. On Monday afternoon, quite unexpectedly he sent his aide-de-camp for me & when I got to the Palace he put the ribbon of the Saint Sava – the highest Servian Order – on my neck with the gold star and in a very nice little speech told me that he had decorated me a friend of Servia, & he wished to acknowledge that friendship. Now that I know the whole thing I see that Servia, & the so-called emissaries of Draza & Alexandra are quite misjudged. Had I been a Servian I think I should have been in the plot. Life in Servia under Alexandra was like Spain at the time of the Inquisition. Now, all is most prosperous, & the whole nation worships the present King.

I think I've been through the most trying fortnight of all the Diplomatic manoeuvring that it has been my lot to do. But His Majesty was most kind. He sent his aide-de-camp to the hotel yesterday half an hour before I started with a message bidding me au revoir, & saying that he hoped to see me again without fail in February!

And how are you, dear old chap?

This is not much of a place – a rather poor undertaking of Brussels.

I am seeing the Prime Minister to-morrow, & I expect to have an audience of Prince Ferdinand[159] on the following day. I will report later.

---

159. Ferdinand Maximilian Karl Leopold Maria of Saxe-Coburg and Gotha-Koháry (1861–1948). Reigned as Prince Regent in Le Queux's time.

If You Can Walk With Kings

Here, it is intensely cold – bare trees, & the very depth of winter. There is slight-snow on the ground.

In this hotel not a soul speaks anything else but Bulga. The Diplomats, of course, speak French. Our Minister, Sir George Buchanan, is a good chap.[160] I lunch with him & Lady Buchanan to-morrow.

I wonder if Beatrice is back?

Reply to Hotel de Boulevard, Bucharest, Roumania.

For as soon as I've seen the Prince I shall clear out from here. The best of good wishes to all at the Belvedere, from

Yours as ever

William Le Queux.

A few years later, in March 1911, the Bulgarian Prime Minister, M Petkoff, was assassinated whilst walking in the Boris Gardens.

Before leaving Sofia, Le Queux in the company of George Buchanan was privileged to attend the Bulgarian Parliament and hear first hand the arguments for a possible war with Turkey over the Macedonia Question. Le Queux left Sofia on 17 November 1906 by road, taking the Shipka Pass through the mountains to Rustchuk, now known as Ruse, then crossed the Danube by steamer to Guirgevo and then caught the train to Bucharest, where he hoped to arrive in three days' time. Seating himself alone in a compartment he was annoyed to be joined by an Austrian spy. Le Queux had first noticed the spy in the streets of Sofia over a week earlier. Worried that an attempt might be made to obtain the dispatch box by his side, Le Queux kept his hand on his revolver which he fully intended to use. When the spy spoke to him, Le Queux said that he was not interested in conversation and that he was aware he was being followed. The spy eventually left the train although their paths were to cross again in Bucharest.

---

160. Sir George William Buchanan (1854–1924) was British Ambassador to Moscow during the Revolution in 1917.

Mission to Albania 1906

Grand Hotel Bulgarie,
Sofia
Saturday morning
[17 November 1906]

My Dear Beeforth

As I wired you this morning, I'm just leaving Sofia to cross the Shipka Pass and get to Rustchuk. Then on to Bucharest. The Prince of Bulgaria is at his villa at Varna, on the Black Sea, so after Bucharest I go there to have audience.

He has just written me through his secretary regretting that he is not in Sofia, & that I have to take such a long journey to see him.

The weather is dry, but intensely cold. The Balkan winter has set in, & the thermometer today is at zero! I have a ride of 90 miles before me – to-day & tomorrow – into the very heart of the Balkans. But the country there is quiet & there is no danger. I want to see the celebrated Shipka Pass where two Russo Turkish battles were fought.[161]

I have no particular news. My address at Constantinople[162] will be the Pera Palace Hotel & not the 'Grand'.

All goes well with me, thank God. I'm a bit fagged, but beyond that am all right.

As you know, I'm used to late hours, & one has to keep up very late amid all the Diplomatic gaiety in the city.

I suppose Beatrice is back. I'm anxious to have a letter from you.

In reply to this letter, write me to <u>Constantinople</u>, – Pera Palace Hotel.

I shall not be long in Bucharest, as I only want to see the Queen, & the Prime Minister. The King is ill and sees nobody.

---

161. 1877–1878.
162. Now Istanbul.

If You Can Walk With Kings

Good-bye old chap. I'm looking forward anxiously to treading the gravel walks of the garden again with you. Scarboro' seems so far away from me. Remember me to Miss Lizzie very kindly, & to all.

Yours as ever

William Le Queux.

Le Queux finally arrived in Bucharest on Friday 23 November 1906. Having exchanged several telegrams with George Beeforth, Le Queux was able to sit down and write in full. There was an artist named Paoletti who lived in Palermo; whether this is the same as the one mentioned below is unclear. Beatrice was twenty-four at the time and probably a heart breaker. Despite the age gap even Le Queux seems to have been infatuated by her.

> Hotel du Boulevard,
> Bucharest (Roumania)
> Sunday
> [25 November 1906]

My Dear Beeforth

I wired you, you got my reply, & wired again. All I know of the Palermo affair is that Paoletti has written me a letter asking for my sympathy & my good offices with Beatrice, for the latter has written saying 'that she does not love him sufficiently to be his wife'!!! The letter is in Italian, so useless to send to you. It is a long screed of 8 pages – very passionate. She has evidently broken it off on account of those abominable inquiries – at least so I understand.

Neither of the girls in 'their' letters have written me a single word about it. Evidently Fraulein is also in the dark about it. Of course you will appear to know nothing, or I shall get in a row for letting Beatrice's secret out! I can imagine what a

Mission to Albania 1906

relief my wire was to you. I cried instantly and then went down & had a drink to congratulate us both, old chap.

I have a lot of difficult diplomacy here. The King[163] is ill, & in bed, & I've been a lot with the Prime Minister[164] & Minister for Foreign Affairs. This evening I had audience with the Queen.[165] She was most charming to me. And tomorrow she is meeting me at her blind institution to show me it & explain its working.

We had an hour & a half's chat over politics & other things, & she was most gracious & a delightful person. She gave me a post card which I have sent to Gabrielle, & she has promised to send me her portrait tomorrow.

I'm very busy with my report (confidential) regarding my Bulgarian negotiations to the Foreign Office, & it goes by messenger to London on Tuesday. I shall, I hope, leave for Constantinople on Thursday, calling at Varna.

This place is very gay socially. I'm out all the time to dinners or receptions or dances, & the people are the very smartest of the smart.

But the city is a veritable den of iniquity. I have never seen such a thing in all my life. The town is like Paris in miniature, but there isn't an honest woman in this whole place. The diplomats will not have their daughters here. In this hotel, the best in the city, there are dozens of girls always at hand. If you want one you simply tell the hall-porter!! Sir Conyngham Greene,[166] our minister here, is living in this hotel with me, & we look over at some of the most amazing sights that would be tolerated in no other city in the world. In society, things are too dreadful. I know from personal experience. Whew!

---

163. Carol I (1839–1914).
164. Gheorghe Grigore Cantacuzino (1833–1913).
165. Elisabeth of Wied (1843–1916).
166. Sir William Conyngham Greene (1854–1934).

The atmosphere here is itself without morals. I'm simply astounded.
Write by return to Pera Palace Hotel Constantinople. The best of good luck from

Yours as ever

William Le Queux.

Le Queux's aim appears to be to gain at first hand an indication of Roumania's political aims and aspirations. This included meetings with the President of the Council, the Minister of War and the Foreign Minister. To be meeting with so many top officials, Le Queux has to have been working under instructions direct from Whitehall. On leaving Bucharest Le Queux caught the Orient Express firstly, via Varna to Constanza, where he boarded the Black Sea steamer, the *King Charles*, bound for Constantinople. On arrival he immediately wrote to George Beeforth.

> Pera Palace & Summer Palace,
> Constantinople
> Saturday Dec 1 1906

My Dear Old Fellow

When I got here today I got your very welcome letter of the 21st. You did not then know the welcome news of the Palermo affair being 'off'. I do hope Beatrice will find someone suitable. We must look around!! I had also today a letter from Fraulein, telling me the news, but have had not a word from either of the girls about it. I expect that after all the inconvenience Beatrice has put you to, she scarcely likes visiting. But I have written to her.

Have I not been a prophet? I told you, all along, to let their matter run on, & it would run out like an hour-glass.

Mission to Albania 1906

Well, I got here all right, after a rough voyage over the Black Sea. I saw Tewfik Pasha[167] this afternoon, & he is getting me an audience of the Sultan.[168] But the latter is not at all well, so the date is uncertain. Instead of wasting time I leave to-morrow for Brusa – in Asia Minor – the ancient Turkish capital. Then back here. I have a wonderful servant from our Embassy – a chap in red & gold with pistols & knives in his belt. One cannot go out here without a guide. Oh! What a city is Constantinople? It is fifteen years ago since I was here, & I think it is just the very same.

The voyage down the Bosphorous through the sweet waters[169] is lovely. Tonight as I write, I have the Golden Horn below my window with the full moon shining upon it, almost a fairy dream, and yet what a disenchantment in the streets, with all their mud & hordes of wild dogs.

How I wish you were with me, my dear old chap.

Here in the Orient, all is so fresh and interesting. There is nothing like it in Europe.

I'm glad you have got the coffee-set all right. It is a good example of Turkish work by the Turks in Bosnia.

My diplomatic affairs are both exciting and worrying. My private affairs are the same. The case is 'stayed' until I return, when Mrs Le Q accepts the terms I first offered.

Oh! How I long for quiet and comfort, & a chat with you. I feel very worn out, but God is good to me, & I feel well in health. I only hope I get through Macedonia all right.

When I return from Bursa I will write again. Good Bye old chap, good luck to you all.

Yours as ever

William Le Queux.

---

167. Ahmed Tewfik Pasha (1845–1936) was the last Ottoman Grand Vizier.
168. Sultan Abdülhamid II, Emperor of the Ottomans, Caliph of the Faithful (also known as Abdul Hamid II, and The Crimson Sultan), (1842–1918).
169. The Sweet Waters of Europe were the two streams that empty into the Golden Horn.

If You Can Walk With Kings

Apart from meeting Tewfik Pasha, the Minister for Foreign Affairs, he also met the Minister for War. According to his autobiography, Le Queux did succeed in having a meeting with Sultan Abdul Hamid, where they discussed politics.[170] The grey-bearded elderly Grand Vizier was said to be 'close to death', although remarkably clung to life for another twelve years. Le Queux left Constantinople on 4 December 1906, only first writing to another friend, the surgeon Cuthbert Hilton Golding-Bird, with whom he was more economical with the truth. Granted, Le Queux is unable to explain why he has been in the Balkans.

> Pera Palace & Summer Palace,
> Constantinople
> Dec 3 1906
>
> My Dear Golding-Bird
>
> I ought to have answered your kind letter long ago, but I have been on a four months' journey through the Balkans, & am just now on my way home by the Orient Express.
>
> I often wonder how you and Mrs Golding-Bird are.
>
> It was so good of you to write me such a nice letter about my book. The latter seems to have awakened the War Office a bit.
>
> Here, in the east, all is very interesting. I've had very hard travelling in Albania, Monténégro & Bulgaria, but it was very enjoyable.
>
> The weather here on the Bosphorous is quite spring-like. But to-morrow I shall take the Orient Express through to London, & will look in upon you. I'll 'phone first.
>
> So I won't write you a long yarn, but tell you all my news when we meet.
>
> Both kindest remembrances to Mrs Golding-Bird, & all good wishes to yourself.
>
> Yours very sincerely
>
> William Le Queux.

---

170. William Le Queux, *Things I Know about Kings*, p 106.

Mission to Albania 1906

A day later Le Queux tells George Beeforth where he really will be going and seems mightily concerned about his safety.

Pera Palace & Summer Palace,
Constantinople
Dec 4 1906

My Dear Old Chap

I am back from Bursa, & have had an audience of the Sultan. Very interesting!

To-night I leave for Macedonia direct. Don't worry about me. But if I'm missing on <u>Dec 21st</u> inquire of my whereabouts of –

Sir George Buchanan K. C. B.
British Minister
Sofia. Bulgaria

I hope you won't have to inquire. But I tell you this <u>in case of accidents</u>!

I am pretty weary, but am 'bucking up' for the last journey. The Bulgarian Government will be watching over me in Macedonia.

I shall be glad to be back in London. Of course I shall go straight to the Hotel Cecil, where I still have my room.

I have had no word from Beatrice, & cannot quite make out why. Her Paoletti affair is of course quite over, so that is all we need care about.

I hope she is not taking it to heart too much, poor girl. The only thing is for her to find another lover, & a decent chap. Here at the Embassy they are pressing me to stay another week in Constantinople, but I want to get on through Macedonia, before the snow comes. The weather here is just like June, & the Sea of Marmora [Marmara] is lovely.

I had a most interesting 3 days in Asia Minor, but it will take a long time to tell you all my experiences & quaint adventures.

If You Can Walk With Kings

As soon as ever I'm out of Macedonia, I will write you. I shall do all possible to be in London by Dec 20.

I think I told you that I shall have to be in Servia again in February.

You should come out with me – by the Orient Express from Calais to Belgrade – you would enjoy it. Thanks for the papers. I am first sending you a telegram wishing you good-bye.

Good luck old fellow, & daily remembrances of

Yours as ever

William Le Queux.

The promised telegram was sent a day earlier than the letter. As no letters were sent from within Macedonia we must assume that Le Queux was keeping, for him, a low profile. Despite extensive research I have been unable to track down exactly who Le Queux met or what they discussed during the next few days. His description of the country was stark: villages he went through had been recently massacred. A child decapitated. A mother and child burnt to death. Houses destroyed and men and women shot. 'That journey through Macedonia still haunts me like a nightmare.'[171]

Weighing charcoal in Scutari

William Le Queux

---

171. William Le Queux, *An Observer in the Near East*, p 296.

Unknown

William Le Queux – fully armed

If You Can Walk With Kings

Hotel Cecil,
Strand W.C.
Sunday night

My Dear old fellow

As I have just wired you, I am back again, after a pretty tough, but highly interesting journey. And thank God I'm safe.

Gabrielle wrote me to Constantinople but I have only just received the letter, & in it says you have a touch of gout! I am worried about it, & do hope it is not serious, & that you are not laid up. Do let me know <u>at once</u>.

I'm full up with diplomatic worries, but so far, all goes well. I am due again in Belgrade on Feb 1st.

I suppose I shall have to put in all day at the Foreign Office to-morrow, & probably Tuesday making my reports.

Macedonia was very interesting but somewhat unsafe.

Though, after all, Albania was far rougher & uncivilized.

I expect you are preparing for Christmas. I go to Kincardine Castle.[172] My friends the Reeds are in town to-morrow, they write, & remind me!

I have so many pleasant recollections of the jolly Christmas I spent last year with you, I hope we may meet again very soon to chink a glass!

I have a lot of amusing things to tell you, & I've often wished you had been with me.

Do let me know <u>at once</u> that you are all right.

Excuse a longer letter, but I'm very fagged & just going to bed.

With the best of good wishes to you, my dear old fellow from

Yours as ever

William Le Queux.[173]

---

172. Kincardine Castle, early-19th-century manor house near Auchterarder in Perthshire. The Reeds rented the castle on a number of occasions as a shooting lodge.
173. WmLQ letter to George Beeforth, 9 December 1906.

Having reported back to the Foreign Office, he would have been debriefed. It is not mentioned in any of his earlier letters whether he had actually spoken to then Foreign Secretary, Sir Edward Grey.[174]

Back at London's Hotel Cecil, where he maintained a room for fourteen years, he would have gone over the terms of the divorce proceedings that had continued whilst he was out of the country. It was reported in the national press that according to Luisa, it was in February 1904, four years after their marriage, that her husband returned to their home, the Villa Renata in Florence. After only four or five days Le Queux told Luisa that he had to go away again to work on his new book, which would have been *The Invasion of 1910*. Luisa sent him an affectionate letter asking him to return to her, to which Le Queux replied complaining of her extravagances and giving her the impression that he was not going to return. Remarkably this letter was printed in the national press for all to see, and it was only after this that Luisa pursued divorce proceedings:

> My Dear Willie
>
> Won't you put an end to this miserable state of affairs! We are, I feel, drifting further and further apart, and I can bear it no longer. Won't you come back to me or let me come back to you, either here or in Italy, whichever you prefer? Do let me hear from you at once.
>
> With salutations, your affectionate
>
> Piccina[175]

There is no indication of the date of this letter, except this must have been 17 May 1906, although from the letter sent to George Beeforth, and quoted earlier, Le Queux said he had had no word from Italy, which is at odds with Luisa's version. On 22 May 1906 Luisa filed for the restoration of her conjugal rights, which I take to mean that Luisa was

---

174. Edward Grey, 1st Viscount Grey of Fallodon (1862–1933). Liberal statesman, he served as Foreign Secretary from 1905 to 1916.
175. *Manchester Courier & Lancaster General Advertiser*, 25 July 1907.

applying for alimony whilst they were separated. In her petition Luisa stated that since their marriage in February 1902 they had lived as man and wife in cohabitation. She listed their various homes – Queen Anne Mansions, London; The Cedars, Castor near Peterborough; Villa Renata in Florence and the Villa Le Queux at Lastra a Signa. Currently the petitioner was residing at the Hotel Clifton in Welbeck Street, London. She also stated that there had been no issue from the marriage. Luisa confirmed that her husband had until recently been residing in Queen Anne's Mansions, but that his present address was unknown to her. Le Queux left the marital home, Villa Renata, on or about 5 February 1906 and had so far failed to render to her, her conjugal rights.[176]

Through his solicitor, Stanley Evans of Bedford Row, Le Queux offered a yearly allowance of £200, being paid monthly. In addition Le Queux would pay the rent and taxes on the Villa Renata during their separation, along with £34 to cover the cost of hotel bills and travel tickets for Luisa and her maid to allow them to return to Florence.[177]

Through Luisa's own solicitors, Messrs Markby Stewart, she claimed a further £43 13s 5d to cover her legal costs, and Le Queux also had to pay to the court £70 in assurances.[178] The following year the judge, Sir Henry Bargrave Deane, ordered Le Queux to return to his wife within fourteen days.[179] It can be believed that there will be problems in some marriages, especially where the partners will be separated for any length of time. That this would be Le Queux's second failed marriage does suggest, however, that he may not have been an easy man to live with. On the other hand a little more understanding from Luisa may have saved the day, but I guess not. Chris Patrick and Stephen Baister were able to quote from a letter written by a descendant of a Mrs William Chapman, who had once worked at The Cedars during this time, indicating that Luisa was unable to settle and wanted to return to Italy.[180] The comments

---

176. Court minutes, 22 May 1906.
177. Court minutes, 11 July 1906.
178. Court minutes, 24 July 1907.
179. Court minutes, 24 July 1907.
180. *Peterborough Evening News*, 17 February 1968.

about Luisa not being prepared to live in Northamptonshire on account of the climate might indicate that she was a little bit spoilt or it could be that she was suffering simply from homesickness.

For Le Queux life goes on:

> Hotel Cecil,
> Strand W.C.
> Dec 18. 6 p.m.
>
> My Dear old chap
>
> Since I wrote you this morning I have been thinking over the suggestion to come to York. It really is very <u>very</u> good of you, & you know how deeply I appreciate your kind thought. But for you to travel 80 miles to dine is too much on a winter's night, & I really cannot allow it.
>
> It would have been different if it were summer. Of course I'd have come & spent a night with you on my way north, if the girls had not objected. I however, can't see why they should be so [unreadable], for the whole affair is over and settled. Can you? But of course they know best.
>
> That Gabrielle is going to Dusseldorf is somewhat of a surprise! You <u>know to what I allude</u>!
>
> I've had a very heavy day at the Foreign Office, & have now to dine, go to the Gaiety & supper at the Savoy afterwards! How I long for a quiet few days, for I feel very shaky.
>
> You don't say how Miss Lizzie[181] is – well, I hope.
>
> With the best of good wishes my dear old fellow from
>
> Yours as ever
>
> William Le Queux.[182]

---

181. Elizabeth Lord Beeforth, George Beeforth's older sister who lived with him.
182. WmLQ letter to George Beeforth.

Le Queux spent Christmas with his friend Major A. J. Reed in Perthshire at his home in Kincardine Castle.

> Kincardine Castle,
> Auchterarder,
> N. B.
> Boxing Day

My Dear Beeforth

I thank you for your kind wire. I hope you all spent a merry Xmas.

The weather here is very Christmasy – snow & hard frost. And the Highlands looks lovely.

The reason of this brief note is to ask you <u>what day Gabrielle's birthday</u> is. I know it is immediately after Xmas, but do not know the day.

Will you please send me a line & let me know this? Now don't forget will you?

I know you must all be having a good time at the Belvedere.

Here, I don't get much rest, as the house-party is a very gay one. Still I am gradually getting over my journey.

With kindest regards, & looking forward to our next meeting.

Yours as ever

William Le Queux.

P. S. Remember me kindly to Mr & Mrs Normand

Le Queux remained as a guest of the Reeds until well into the New Year.

Mission to Albania 1906

Kincardine Castle,
Auchterarder,
N. B.
Dec 31. 06

My Dear old fellow

So many thanks for your card.

I wish you every good wish for the New Year, not forgetting good health. May you be less worried than you have been in 1906, & may God protect you & yours. Please give my best New Year wishes to Miss Lizzie.

I did not know that Gabrielle's birthday was so near. There is no time to get a little present for her, so I shall wait till I return to London.

I go back to London on Saturday next.

It is intensely cold here with much snow, but we have excellent curling everyday on the private curling pond in the park.

We had Haldane, the Minister of War,[183] to dinner the other night. He seems a merry fellow.

No more this time. Again, a Happy New Year, my dear old fellow is the heartfelt wish of

Yours as ever

William Le Queux[184]

Mr Haldane, who Le Queux refers to meeting in his book *German Spies in England*, assured the assembled guests that he knew Germany well and that there would never be a war.[185]

---

183. Richard Burdon Haldane, 1st Viscount Haldane (1856–1928), was a Liberal imperialist and later Labour politician, lawyer and philosopher. He was Secretary of State for War between 1905 and 1912.
184. WmLQ letter to George Beeforth.
185. William Le Queux, *German Spies in England*, p 15.

Lapland Expedition
1907

In his career and both his public and private lives, 1907 would be another momentous year for William Le Queux. For one, it saw the (anonymous) publication of his account of his mission to Albania as *An Observer in the Near East*. He was also expecting to be asked to return to Servia as early as February, as is mentioned in a letter to George Beeforth:

> Hotel Cecil,
> Strand W.C.
> Jan 13. 07

My Dear old chap

I was out when your wire came today.

So Many thanks of course, I'm longing to see you.

At present I am waiting, almost from hour to hour, to know whether I must return to Belgrade.

I hope not – at least not before I've seen you. Dispatches received at the F. O. yesterday give a better complexion to affairs, & my own idea is that the trouble will blow over before this present week is out.

If so, I could run up on Monday 21st. How about that? As soon as I hear definitely that matters are settled, & there is no risk of a revolution, I am free. At present I'm tied to London with my bags ready packed!

All this is very unsettling, but there is no doubt that big events are brewing in The Balkans in the near future, & I suppose I'll be in the thick of them.

I want to chat over things with you, & the earliest free moment brings me to you.

With all good wishes, & hoping you are no longer troubled with insomnia, dear old fellow

Yours as ever

William Le Queux.

A few days later, on the Thursday, Le Queux sent George Beeforth a telegram, and followed up with a letter, confirming that he is now able to get away from London for a few days.

Hotel Cecil,
Strand W.C.
Jan 17. 07

My Dear old chap

As I have just wired you. I shall be delighted to come down on Monday.

I would come down before, but I promised Sir Edward Grey not to leave London till Monday, & that if he wished I would go straight out to Belgrade on receipt of word from him.

I was at the Foreign Office today, & the tension seems lessened. Yesterday they had a despatch by wire from Whitehead,[186] our Minister, in Belgrade to say that things were nearly normal.

I have, however, arranged that I am to be in Belgrade on Feb 7th. How long I shall be there I don't know.

---

186. James Beethom Whitehead. Minister from 1906 to 1910.

Lapland Expedition 1907

I note what you say about Germany. We will chat it over.

I'm longing, old fellow, to have a nice long chat with you.

I'll be delighted to meet young Taylor. All news when we meet, & with the best of good luck from

Yours as ever

William Le Queux.[187]

Le Queux was able to meet George Beeforth as promised.

> Hotel Cecil,
> Strand W.C.
> Jan 25. 07

My Dear old chap

I ought to have written you before, but have been rushed to death all day.

I registered the girls baggage at York, & got the guard to look after them. I went as far as Doncaster with them, & I hope they had a good journey.

When I arrived last night I got a letter from Capt Howard at Parkeston, saying that he would see they had a good cabin.

So I hope they had a good journey.

As soon as ever I can I will run and have a gossip with you in ten days or so.

This time I had very little opportunity, as the girls were full of Paoletti & Dusseldorf!!

I only wish to come up and see you again, & have our old gossips as of yore!

All kindest regards to Miss Lizzie & yourself.

Yours as ever

William Le Queux.[188]

---

187. WmLQ letter to George Beeforth.
188. WmLQ letter to George Beeforth.

The day after this letter was written Le Queux attended a meeting at the Mansion House, in London, of the advisory committee of the Balkan Exhibition. Le Queux moved for a vote of thanks to the Lord Mayor, Sir William Treloar.[189]

Presumably Le Queux did go out to Belgrade as arranged, but there is no supporting evidence. The unrest in the Balkans finally flared up, as was thought possible when there was a Romanian Peasants' Revolt which took place in March, where it was estimated that thousands were killed. The Ottoman Empire was struggling on, but within twelve months it would start to break up after over six hundred years.

He was back over in Paris, possibly during the Easter period, before returning to stay with his old friend Sir William Cooper at Bournemouth. Le Queux was a regular visitor to Hume Towers, a large, imposing house dating from 1871, which had changed hands several times before being bought by Sir William Cooper in 1899. It remained his home until his death in 1924, when it became a nursing home. It was sold for redevelopment and finally demolished in 1966.

Hume Towers
Bournemouth,
Apr 16.07

My Dearest Old Chap

I only got your letter on my return from Paris on Monday morning, & then I came down here to stay with my old friend Cooper. I am so sorry indeed to hear you have a cold, but hope it is quite well by this time.

You are quite right in asking Fraulein for the truth concerning the desire of the girls to stay on in Dusseldorf, I hope there is nothing secret in the wind, yet I wonder they do not come home. The Academy is surely better than the art exhibition of a German provincial town!

---

189. Sir William Purdie Treloar, *A Lord Mayor's Diary 1906–7* (26 January 1907). London: John Murray, 1920.

Lapland Expedition 1907

There is a gay house-party here, & plenty of fun. My friends the Reeds, of Kincardine Castle are here, & a number of other pals. We are going to do the reel of cotton trick tonight.

I hope in about 8 days or so, to come up and see you. I know I am welcome. And we will have a quiet gossip together which I always enjoy with you.

With best wishes to your sister, & to you dear old chap,

Yours ever

William Le Queux.[190]

The rapidity with which Le Queux replies to friends' correspondence shows clearly a fondness that is as genuine as the concern.

Hume Towers
Bournemouth,
Apr 20

My Dearest Old Chappie

So many thanks for your letter, and your kind invite.

I will endeavour if possible, to run up and see you next <u>Saturday</u>, if at all possible. Only if I find I can't you will not be angry with me, will you?

I fear my brother will not be able to come, as the spring is his very busiest time.

I shall, however, see him on Monday, & give him your very kind invitation.

I look forward to a gossip with you old chap.

I am just off and the best of luck to your dear old self.

Yours always

William Le Queux.[191]

---

190. WmLQ letter to George Beeforth.
191. WmLQ letter to George Beeforth 20 April [1907].

Frederick Le Queux appears to have resembled his famous brother as a bit of a ladies' man. At this time, Fred was living in Acton and was occupied in advertising. Fred had already deserted his first wife, Julia, before she died suddenly in early 1905, and a son was born to his second 'wife', Hylda Sophia Weston, in December 1906. This actually mirrors what happened to his brother, William. As we have seen, his first wife died and in less than a year he had remarried. No marriage certificate for Frederick and Hylda has been found, which seems odd. What is even odder is that Fred appears to have deserted Hylda, in about 1918, leaving her with four children to bring up. Yet in Hylda's last will & testament[192] she appears not to have remarried but claims to have been a widow, suggesting she was still legally married to Fred! On 7 November 1918 Fred married his third wife, Lillian Mary Norris, a spinster, at St Luke's Parish Church in Wimbledon Park. The ceremony taking place just four days before the Armistice was called to end the Great War. Lilian had been born on 29 May 1887. In his previous marriage certificate, to Julia, Fred had put his father down as plain 'Deceased'. Intriguingly now his father is shown as 'Diplomatic Service (Deceased)'.

Fred Le Queux was said to have lived in a large detached house, Rosebank, off Wales Farm Road. One suggestion is that the house was later taken over by T. Walls for an ice cream factory.[193] Whether true or not, the whole area was transformed when the Western Avenue was constructed in the 1920s. Today large blocks of flats occupy the site.

It is rumoured that poor Fred Le Queux later suffered a financial disaster in a Stock Exchange scandal in the 1920s. Whether this had anything to do with the reason for leaving Hylda is perhaps for another day.

I have to say that I have no idea how William Le Queux kept up his prodigious output of books, short stories and articles. Apart from his entertaining, albeit at others' expense, and his travels, he hardly seems to have time to write. Plans were now being worked on for an expedition round the North Cape to the Kola Peninsula by reindeer sleds. The journey was to be to one of the least known, and seldom

---

192. Hylda died in Romsey on 17 June 1954.
193. Yvonne Vincent (nee Le Queux) letter to the author 19 March 1996.

explored, regions of the world: the Kola Peninsula, a bleak and treeless region of Lapland stretching out into the White Sea below the Arctic, and part of the Russian Empire.

Stafford,\
10 Holland Road,\
Hove,\
Brighton\
May 23. 07

My Dear Old Chap

If you want an interesting experience why don't you come up to Hammerfest with De Windt & I in early August? We shall be there about three weeks arranging for stores, reindeer, sleds and dogs, to prepare for our trip in November. Then we shall return to England direct.

The 'Land of the Midnight Sun' in August would be a new experience for you. We shall probably go up by the steam yacht of the P. O. the *Vectis*, which will drop us at Hammerfest, and return. So we shall come back down to Trondheim by a Norwegian boat, & then to Bergen & across to Hull.

I promise you will enjoy yourself & the sea is very calm in the fjords at that season. Indeed, *Vectis* follows the calm seas all the way.

Three weeks in the most northerly town in the world would certain [sic] to be of interest, even to you who have travelled such a lot. So why not come with us?

At present I'm here motoring with Jack Holdsworth, who wishes to be kindly remembered to you. Write me to the Cecil, as I don't know where I may be going!

Good wishes to you all from

Yours as ever

William Le Queux.[194]

---

194. WmLQ letter to George Beeforth.

If You Can Walk With Kings

There are those who in print have referred to Le Queux as a self-publicist, but they will now have to think again. He could certainly be flamboyant and liked to play a large part in society, but surely if he was so self-centred would he have thought twice about turning down a knighthood? Admittedly, the pending divorce court case was certainly his deciding factor.

> Hotel Cecil,
> Strand W.C.
> Jun 1. 07

My Dear old chappie

So many thanks for your letter from 'Spitzbergen'!

I quite <u>understand</u>. I think Beatrice's qualms are really too silly & childish. I'm at a loss to understand it all. But no doubt you will be able to settle matters.

You know well how I <u>Delight</u> to come and see you, & how I prefer to come to <u>you</u> in preference to my other friends.

I am due up in Scotland, but I have so many social engagements that all next week I must remain in town.

But I'm sick of London & long to wander again.

I will send you your copy of the Balkans book on Monday, which I hope you will accept.

I saw Newton Husbands here the other day.

And now I want to ask you your opinion, my dear old chappie.

On Tuesday last Sir Edward Grey called me to the Foreign Office, and after many kind words about my efforts (*The Invasion*) etc., and the years work I had done on the Continent in furtherance of our Diplomacy, he said he was about to recommend the King to give me the K. C. M. G.[195]

---

195. Knight Commander of St Michael and St George.

Lapland Expedition 1907

I thanked him and all that, but I told him that 'for private reasons' I did not 'at present' wish it. He was very surprised, and asked the reason. I asked him to excuse me for telling him.

He then said that the King had read, with very great interest *An Observer in The Near East*, and had told him that he wished to decorate me.

I asked him to allow me to decline – <u>at present</u>. And there it remains.

<u>Have I done right?</u>

I think Sir Edward Grey reads between the lines. Namely that I do not wish Mrs Le Queux, in the present circumstances, to become 'her ladyship' for he said 'Ah! I see, you have a family reason!'

I told him that His Majesty's opinion of myself was <u>quite sufficient</u> for me, the same loyal & patriotic subject. It was a difficult position, but I think you will agree that I have done quite right. After I have freed myself of my matrimonial encumbrance it will be different. Don't you think so?

When you have a moment, old fellow <u>Do write</u> & let me know what you think.

Yours as ever

William Le Queux.[196]

There are echoes of a knighthood similarly being offered to Le Queux's alter ego, Seton Darville, in the novel *Hidden Hands*. Here it seems that the honour was offered not once, but twice, and just as in real life it was refused on purely personal grounds:

> He spent most of his royalties earned by his books upon the great department the operations of which he directed, and few knew the truth beyond the members of the cabinet, his only reward being a gracious letter of thanks now and then

---

196. WmLQ letter to George Beeforth.

in the handwriting of the Prime Minister, and the offer of an honour at the hands of the Sovereign.

This he had twice declined. He had reasons, strong reasons, which he had never divulged to a living soul.[197]

Although Le Queux himself hardly mentioned his intended expedition to Lapland that coming winter in his autobiography, it was briefly referred to by Norman St Barbe Sladen. Le Queux and the adventurer Harry de Windt did do a preliminary reconnaissance in August 1908. His colleague was Captain Harry Willes Darell de Windt, born in Paris in 1856, who was aide-de-camp to his brother-in-law Charles Brooke, the Rajah of Sarawak.[198] He was best known as an explorer and travel writer featuring trips to Russia and Siberia, the near east and to China and India. Both men were members of the New Vagabonds Club along with *Who's Who* editor Douglas Sladen.

> Hotel Cecil,
> Strand W.C.
> Jun 3. 07

My Dear old chappie

So many thanks for your letter. I am glad you think I did right.

As regards the project in your letter, I think you do quite right to sketch out that your election as Mayor should be quite unanimous, & I certainly think that the Prince would be pleased to stay at the Belvedere – if it were suggested to him. This could not be done through his secretary. If I can assist in <u>anything</u>, only let me know in confidence and I'll work what I can.

---

197. William Le Queux, *Hidden Hands*, p 73.
198. Charles Anthoni Johnson (1829–1917). Brooke was his mother's maiden name.

Lapland Expedition 1907

I would like to see you as Mayor, and also I'd like to see [you] with an honour – even though you do not, like myself particularly care for one.

I am much interested, and so keep me au fait with what goes on.

This weather is fine for training for Lapland!

De Windt and I are very fussy about our stores and preliminaries. We find we have to take every ounce of food for the whole six of us, and also <u>all the fuel</u>!

I wonder when I shall see you again?

With all best wishes

Yours ever

William Le Queux.[199]

In a newspaper report given by Harry de Windt to the *Daily News*[200] he laid out their three objectives of the expedition. First, he and Le Queux would write a book of their adventure; second, they wanted to determine with the aid of a mineral expert the truth behind the rumours of mineral wealth; and third, they would photograph the scenes. We have what I believe was a possible 'press release', although unsigned, written by Le Queux.

The De Windt–Le Queux Expedition
Across Lapland in Winter

The expedition, comprising Mr Harry de Windt, the well-known explorer, Mr William Le Queux, also well known as a traveller, a mineralogist, a bioscope operator, two private members of the party, and a number of Lapps, will leave England about the middle of November 1907.

---

199. WmLQ letter to George Beeforth.
200. *Daily News*, 19 May 1907.

A preliminary journey will be made by Mr de Windt and Mr Le Queux to Hammerfest – the most northerly town in the world – and Alten Fjord for the purpose of making transport arrangements and fixing stores etc. for the winter journey.

Objects of the Expedition

First: To enquire whether the plan prepared by Russia of acquiring an open port on the Norwegian coast – at a certain point where only a narrow strip of Norwegian territory separates her from the sea – is practicable.

Secondly: To ascertain whether the reports of huge deposits of tin, said to exist from Lake Enare eastwards to Archangel, are correct.

Thirdly: To study the life and conditions of the remote Laplanders, who were last visited by Du Chaillu[201] more than twenty years ago – and therefore now practically unknown. A winter trip across Lapland from West to East has never yet been made by white men.

A Bioscope Expert will be taken to obtain 'living pictures' of the Lapps in their winter homes. Modern travellers have only seen them in summer-time, and these only a few belated specimens of the race – for in the open season the Lapps are scattered all over the country with their reindeer. Mr de Windt and Mr Le Queux will visit one of the remote Reindeer station where some thousands of these animals are herded in Winter.

The Route

The Route taken will approximately be as follows: From Alten Fjord (Norway) to Kansjok and south to Kantoke thence to Menesjarvi. From Menesjarvi to Ukkola and Sodankyla taking

---

201. Paul Belloni du Chaillu (1831 (disputed)–1903).

Lapland Expedition 1907

Enare (A large Reindeer station) on the way. From Sodankyla, the way is much more difficult, being very sparsely inhabited, but it is proposed to make a way to Kvolojarvi and thence to Kem on the shores of the White Sea. From Kem the way is clear to Archangel, but the journey from Kvolojarvi to Kem will be the hardest part of the trip on account of few natives, deep snows, and the furious blizzards which are met with in these regions in early spring.

The probable duration of the journey from Alten Fjord to Archangel will be three months.

As the first portion of the journey will be done in the partial darkness of the Arctic night, a very complete apparatus for photography under such conditions will be taken.

The journey throughout will be taken by means of Reindeer sleds.

From Archangel to Petersburg and thence to Paris and London.

As plans were still being made for their trip together, his other partnership was unravelling. In the divorce court on 24 July 1907 Luisa was granted a decree nisi for the restitution of conjugal rights against her husband. Whilst the couple had been cohabiting in Florence, Luisa claimed that Le Queux had told her that he needed to return to England to work on a new book. There was some correspondence between them but as we have already seen Le Queux had gone through periods of not receiving a letter from Luisa. On the other hand Le Queux did not appear to bother to travel over to Italy either. One of his letters apparently accused Luisa of extravagance and showed that he had no intention of returning to her. Le Queux did agree in principle to grant Luisa a substantial allowance.[202]

As planned, Harry de Windt and William Le Queux set off on their exploratory tour in early August 1907.

---

202. *Gloucester Citizen*, 24 July 1907.

If You Can Walk With Kings

> Hotel D'Angleterre
> Kjøbenhaven
> Tuesday Night.

My Dear old chappie

De Windt and I are here to-night to pick up the agent from St Petersburg who is going up to Lapland to assist us, & we go to Stockholm, via Malmö, in the morning.

We shall be in Stockholm till the 20th, for I believe we have audience of the King.[203] At any rate I'm going out into the country to visit my friend the Baroness de Barnebour, one of the ladies in waiting to the Queen of Sweden. So I expect we shall spend a few pleasant days in Sweden before we go north.

I have, as yet, nothing fresh to tell you.

Copenhagen has greatly improved. I have not been here for ten years, & see lots of changes. It is a very bright little place. This hotel is excellent, splendidly furnished, & of course correspondingly dear.

Please give the girls my best salutes, & tell them I will write to them in a day or two.

Meanwhile I am starting off Gabrielle's post-card for her new book 'Scandinavia'.

Lots of best wishes to you, dear old chappie.

I often think of you & wish you were with us.

I'll write again from

William Le Queux.[204]

On arrival in Stockholm Le Queux updated George Beeforth on his contact addresses.

---

203. Christian Frederik Vilhelm Carl (1843–1912) was King of Denmark from 1906 to 1912.
204. WmLQ letter to George Beeforth, circa 13 August 1907.

Lapland Expedition 1907

DE WINDT–LE QUEUX EXPEDITION, ACROSS ARCTIC LAPLAND, 1907.

> Address till Aug 17th
> Grand Hotel
> Stockholm
> Sweden

My Dear old chappie

Just a line to give you my address.
After Aug 17 it will be:- Poste Restante
Hammerfest
Norway

When we are back I will run up & tell you what the Arctic Regions look like!

We are travelling overland via Copenhagen, Malmö, Stockholm up to Narvik, & thence by steamer to Tromsö and another steamer to Hammerfest. The Russian agent sent from Petersburg is to meet us there, & we go into the interior for a day or two to buy our reindeer.

I will, however, let you know how we are getting on from time to time.

I expect you will go to the Lord's, won't you?

Let me have a line to Stockholm.

I hope you are all well. I was very disappointed not to be able to get back, but I've been very rushed with work.

With all good wishes dear old chap.

Yours as ever

William Le Queux.[205]

---

205. WmLQ letter to George Beeforth, circa 13 August 1907.

Unknown

Harry de Windt and William Le Queux in the palm court of the
Hotel D'Angleterre in Copenhagen

Lapland Expedition 1907

Le Queux and de Windt remained in Stockholm for a week. Amongst Le Queux's correspondence is a letter addressed to 'My dear Lambkin', who is presumably Beatrice Beeforth.

DE WINDT–LE QUEUX EXPEDITION, ACROSS ARCTIC LAPLAND, 1907.

Aug 15. 07

My dear Lambkin

Just as I left London the hankys arrived, I suppose. I got your kind letter forwarded to Copenhagen, but the hanky was in a separate packet, I presume, & has not been forwarded. However, I shall get it on my return.

Here in Stockholm, De Windt and I are having a very good time. His cousin Sir Audley Gosling[206] married the Swedish Prime Minister's daughter so we are in the swim here. Beyond that the Baroness de Barnebour, who is one of the leaders of society here is an old pal of mine, & often in London.

On Tuesday we say good bye to a decent hotel, & a decent bed, I suppose, for we go straight north to Narvik by train, & then nearly three days by steamer to Hammerfest.

We are advised to take tinned foods up there with us, as the so-called 'hotel' is only a kind of wood built shanty!!

So we are making the best of things here.

I'm glad Dad likes 'Roch'. I'm dying to see my new brother and to get him a collar.

You ought to come here. You & the Fraulein would like it – all except the sea passage across the Great Belt & the Sound, which are much like Dover–Calais only longer & rotten stinking boats.

---

206. Sir Audley Charles Gosling (1836–1913), formerly a soldier with the Royal Welsh Fusiliers before moving to the diplomatic service.

If You Can Walk With Kings

To my dear Lambkin. A bark to you from over the sea And lots of love your older Collie.

PS I am sending a secret snap – shotter on the beach in the early morning!![207]

Of these secret photographs we can only guess, but it may have been one of Le Queux posing in his beachwear. A few days later the expedition is about to get under way.

DE WINDT–LE QUEUX EXPEDITION, ACROSS ARCTIC LAPLAND, 1907.

Grand Hotel
Stockholm
Sunday night

My Dear old chappie

Many thanks for your kind salutations on the back of Beatrice's letter.

We have had a very jolly time here. The country about here is delightful. Yesterday we were at Saltsjöbaden, a little island out in the Baltic, where the Baroness Barnebour has her country house, & it was very beautiful. Stockholm is a kind of Venice – without the antiquity or architecture. I've sent Gabrielle some cards. I hope she has got them.

To-morrow night we leave direct for Narvik in Norway, & thence by Tromsö to Hammerfest – a six days journey. Our photographer to take the 'living pictures' left Hull last Thursday by the Wilson Line direct for Trondheim, & will join us up at Hammerfest.

The weather here is very chilly & autumnal. Everybody goes about in an overcoat & muffled up. The Swedish papers

---

207. WmLQ letter to Beatrice Beeforth, from Grand Hotel, Stockholm, 15 August 1907.

Lapland Expedition 1907

say that beyond the Polar circle there has already been heavy snow. So we are going into winter I suppose!

I hope I shall get a letter from you up at Hammerfest. Letters take about <u>10 days</u> from London. We intend to return via Trondheim to Hull.

I wonder how you are, & whether you are going to the Lords this summer. You really ought to have a change, old chap. Why don't you let me take you away somewhere or other when I come back?

Do let me hear all your news. I hope everybody, and especially Miss Lizzie, is well.

Likewise ye dogge!

And with every good wish to your dear old self from

Yours as ever

William Le Queux.[208]

Tromsö, which lies well within the Arctic Circle and is just over seven hundred miles north of Stockholm, was reached a week later, with a little help from their friends.

Tromsö – Aug 24. 07

My Dear old chappie

Just a hasty line to report progress.

A few days ago we were stranded in an out of the way hole on the Lofoden [Lofoten] Islands, waiting for a steamer north, when the Prince of Monaco[209] fortunately came in his yacht, the *Princess Alice*. He was awfully kind, & brought us up here, a two days steam. We had a magnificent time on board for the yacht is beautiful and the Prince was most merry & delightful. We came ashore yesterday & bought some of our furs. To-morrow we sail for Hammerfest. We, however, have

---

208. WmLQ letter to George Beeforth, circa 18 August 1907.
209. Albert I (1848–1922) was Prince of Monaco and Duke of Valentinois.

discovered that we cannot buy reindeer in Hammerfest, & that we must go on to Vadsø, in the Arctic Sea. We hope to be there next Wednesday.

The difficulties we find of crossing Lapland are much greater than we expected. The Lapps at our encampment about 10 miles from here we have visited to-day, & they say that the journey into the Kola Peninsula is impossible. But we don't believe them, & are going to Vadsø to see another tribe of Lapps.

Please tell Gabrielle that I have sent her about the last of the postcards, for we are going out of the civilized post card region.

Everything is very interesting here beyond the Arctic Circle. There is lots of snow everywhere, and the nights are bitterly cold. The Aurora Borealis is sometimes very fine. Winter seems to have already set. Thank heavens we are beyond mere tourists. Hotels have been very bad – and vermin frequent. What we shall get at Vadsø Heaven only knows. Still we keep merry, & life is full of change. With all good wishes, dear old fellow from

Yours as ever

William Le Queux.[210]

Le Queux mentions in his autobiography how he met the Prince of Monaco in Tromsö. It was thought Harry de Windt knew the Prince, who had been returning from a cruise to Spitzbergen on a deep-sea fishing trip. The whole incident is played down by Le Queux in print, suggesting they only spent a few hours on board. Perhaps he did not want to show that the two intrepid explorers were given a lift by a mere Prince in his luxury yacht. Exactly how much further Le Queux and de Windt got is not certain, but it appears they did reach as far as Vadsø before having to turn back.[211]

---

210. WmLQ letter to George Beeforth.
211. *Manchester Courier & Lancashire General Advertiser*, 17 September 1907.

Lapland Expedition 1907

DE WINDT–LE QUEUX EXPEDITION, ACROSS ARCTIC LAPLAND, 1907.

Monday

My Dear old chappie

I've just got back and received your kind letter sent to my brother. It was so very good indeed of you to invite me.

I've also found a letter from Beatrice which says that the Newtons were due with you on Saturday, so I will postpone my visit till they have gone.

I feel rather shaky after the rough journey, and the change of temperature has upset me a bit. Still thank God! I'm fit enough. De Windt turned very green in Hamburg, & I got a doctor for him. The latter got him normal all right, & he travelled home fairly well. It is a shock to the system to come from the Arctic direct south.

We have done all we set out to do, but we find that the winter journey will be beset with many more difficulties than we imagined. The Lapps we've got seem a pretty tough crowd, very dirty oily and forbidding looking. I have taken some of their photos & hope to bring them.

I forgot to send you these gloves before. They have been laying here all the time I've been away! I hope the girls are all right. I hear you're been very gay of late.

I'm longing for a chat with you, for I have many quaint things to tell you.

With very best wishes, dear old fellow & trusting you are quite well

Yours as ever

William Le Queux.[212]

---

212. WmLQ letter to George Beeforth, [Hotel Cecil, London] September 1907.

The winter expedition was never attempted, so perhaps the Lapps were right in saying that it was impossible to attempt such a journey. In a newspaper interview given by Harry de Windt upon their return, he divulged that they had been told of petroleum springs which were yielding a limitless supply of oil and that he was making arrangements with the Russian Government for concessions, provided the oil was found. It appears that the mission was being bankrolled by a Paris-based syndicate and, had things gone to plan, the mission proper would have begun on New Year's Day and taken up to five months to complete.[213] Starting from Vadsø the mission would cover about three thousand miles by reindeer during which time they could discover a new race of people.

William Le Queux did write an article presumably based on his experiences in Lapland, entitled 'Lonely Lapland'. I feel it must have been published, but have no knowledge of where.

The explorer Harry de Windt

---

213. *Manchester Courier & Lancashire General Advertiser*, 17 September 1907.

Lapland Expedition 1907

DE WINDT–LE QUEUX EXPEDITION, ACROSS ARCTIC LAPLAND, 1907.

Sep 19. 07

My Dear old chappie

Your very welcome letter to hand.

Of course I shall be most delighted to come. I don't know, however, if my brother can get away as he seems so very busy just now.

I'm feeling 'fit' again and go motoring with Col Holdsworth & his son till Monday.

I'm looking forward to seeing you all again. It seems an age since we met.

My very kindest regards

Yours as ever

William Le Queux.[214]

No sooner was Le Queux back in London than he found himself running into trouble in high places. In a dingy registry office in Henrietta Street, Covent Garden, Le Queux attended the marriage of the Countess of Montignoso and the brilliant Italian pianist Enrico Toselli, when he was a witness to the ceremony on 25 September 1907. The Countess was born Archduchess Louise of Austria and as the great-great-granddaughter of Charles X of France, she held the title of Archduchess until she married Frederick Augustus, Crown Prince of Saxony. They divorced in 1903 after she had fled from her husband. As the Emperor Franz Joseph did not acknowledge the divorce it created a scandal in central Europe. Her new husband was some thirteen years her junior.

---

214. WmLQ letter to George Beeforth, Hotel Cecil, London, on expedition notepaper.

If You Can Walk With Kings

Le Queux was acting as one of three witnesses, along with Mr and Mrs Witt. After the ceremony the couple adjourned to the Hotel Cecil, but were recognised by a waiter. They soon left the Hotel Cecil and moved across to the Hotel Norfolk before leaving England shortly afterwards.

William Le Queux, Countess Montignoso and Enrico Toselli

Lapland Expedition 1907

In a letter to George Beeforth Le Queux explains the fuss his actions had unwittingly caused.

> Hotel Cecil,
> Sep 26. 07

My Dear old chappie

As you have seen in the papers, I'm having a most exciting time. The King of Saxony is furious about the marriage & has sent a messenger to me with certain proposals. I fear I shall have to go to Paris tonight. But, as I have just warned you, I will be with you for certain on Monday. This I have told Col Holdsworth in his letter.

His address is-
Col J. J. Holdsworth[215]
5 Lansdowne Place
Brighton

The Princess & her husband have gone off. And I'm left to bear the brunt of things! What will happen I don't know. Between ourselves the King threatens to upset the marriage in Italy.

I alone know where the child is, but a dozen German detectives are searching for it!

Excuse haste, for I am living on the edge of a volcano.

I will tell you all about it when we meet – a perfect romance it has been. Love to the girls & to yourself.

Yours as ever

William Le Queux.[216]

---

215. Lieutenant Colonel John Joseph Holdsworth, born France *c.*1844, died Sussex 1920. Commander-in-Chief of the Gorakhpur Light Horse.
216. WmLQ letter to George Beeforth.

The child mentioned was her daughter by Frederick, who was born only after she had deserted him. There was an exciting mission carried out by Le Queux on behalf of the Princess involving diamonds:

> A jewel adventure in which William Le Queux was actively concerned happened when the ex-Crown Princess of Saxony asked him to deposit her famous pearl necklace in French, Lemon & Co.'s Bank at Florence. The necklace consisted of three hundred and seventy large, perfectly matched pearls, which had originally formed part of the Dresden Court jewels, and had been secretly brought to London by Louisa. She now decided to remove them from the care of Mr Massey, of the London and Westminster Bank at Temple Bar, and send them to Florence, as she contemplated remaining in Italy for a considerable time.
>
> William Le Queux agreed to convey the precious necklace to Florence, and it was securely stowed away in a belt which he wore under his clothes. He was very friendly with Mr Haines, of the Dover Customs, who met him on his arrival and crossed over to Calais with him. Just before they reached Calais, Mr Haines asked William Le Queux whether he was acquainted with a tall, well-dressed man who had been looking at them on the boat with some degree of interest. Le Queux answered in the negative, and the journey to Paris passed off without any untoward incident.
>
> At Paris Le Queux dined, drove to the Gare de Lyons, and afterwards left for Florence by the 10.45 p.m. Rome Express. But he was most disagreeably surprised to discover that the other berth in his sleeping-compartment was occupied by the man to whom Haines had directed his attention on the boat! His suspicions were instantly aroused, and, under the pretext of having his ticket examined, he went into the corridor and spoke to the conductor of the *wagons-lits*, with

whom, as a constant traveller to and from Florence, he was well acquainted. William Le Queux remained with the conductor until the train reached Aix. The strange individual who shared his compartment then got out, and was presently joined by two other men who had evidently travelled in a different part of the train. There was not the slightest doubt that Le Queux's mission was known, and that he had been watched from London; and, doubtless, his presence of mind had alone prevented the theft of Louisa's necklace, which had been arranged to take place in the express.

When the train arrived at Bardonnechia, William Le Queux told the whole story to the Commissario of Police, and, to his intense relief (as the three hundred and seventy pearls by this time represented three hundred and seventy millstones round his middle), a special detective was ordered to accompany him to Florence, where he eventually deposited the necklace safely in French, Lemon & Co.'s Bank.[217]

Back in the divorce courts Le Queux was served with a decree of restitution of conjugal rights by his wife at his solicitor's office on 8 October 1907, with which he had failed to comply.[218] Thereby he was found guilty of desertion without reasonable cause. Luisa further claimed that her husband had been domiciled in the Hotel Cecil, but his whereabouts were unknown. This seems to be a falsehood or had he just gone to ground for few days? Although his letters of this period are addressed from the Hotel Cecil, they are not on hotel headed notepaper.

---

217. Maude M. C. Ffoulkes, *My Own Past*. London: Cassell's, 1915.
218. Court minutes, 25 August 1908.

If You Can Walk With Kings

Hotel Cecil,
Oct 10. 07

My Dear old chappie

I have heard from Holdsworth who I'm sorry to say cannot come up this week. I expect he has written to you. He says he has had a nice letter from you with information re the genealogy.

Now as regards my own movements. I have promised to speak at a lecture by De Windt at the Armstrong College Newcastle-on-Tyne on Saturday night.

I would like to come & spend Sunday night with you, but I see that to do so I will have to be travelling all night – save 3 or 4 hours at – York – arriving Scarboro at eleven in the morning. This I think I will do, if I may, as I should like to have a day with you all, dear old fellow.

I will, however, let you know by wire on Saturday.

This week I have been very upset over the death of a little child to whom I was devoted, and at this moment I am just going to its funeral. It was the little daughter of an honest working man & his wife, & for years I had taken a great interest in it. She died suddenly of heart disease, & the last words of the child was a message to me!

I hope you are quite well, & to see you on Sunday.

Yours as ever

William Le Queux.[219]

Speculation on who this child was does open up several possibilities. I do not believe that Le Queux was the real father of this child, but another child was born around this time that may have been his. This will be discussed at a later stage.

---

219. WmLQ letter to George Beeforth.

Lapland Expedition 1907

Hotel Cecil,
Strand. W. C.
Oct 11. 07

My Dear old chappie

You have sent me too much for the gloves were only fcs 16.

I'll give you the balance when we meet – which I hope may be Sunday, but it is still uncertain. To add to my troubles, I've got a bit of a chill.

Your Sunday train service York–Scarboro is <u>rotten</u>!

I hope you are all quite well, and I look forward to seeing you, my dear old fellow.

Yours as ever

William Le Queux.[220]

For Bonfire Night Le Queux was invited to dinner by another old friend, Golding-Bird, at his house in Cavendish Square.

Hotel Cecil,
Strand. W. C.
Oct 29. 07

My Dear Golding-Bird

I would be most delighted to dine on Nov 5th – the Day of Guy Faux!

I want so much to meet your brother again, & also to see your dear old self!

Kindly thank Mrs Golding-Bird & say that I'm looking forward to our meeting. Best wishes.

Yours

William Le Queux.

---

220. WmLQ letter to George Beeforth.

If You Can Walk With Kings

The following month Le Queux finally decided to call off the proposed winter expedition to Lapland.

> Hotel Cecil,
> Strand. W. C.
> Nov 12. 07

My Dear old chappie

So many thanks for your kind and cheery letter.

I feel quite with you that I ought not risk the lives of those with me by leading the Expedition myself, for if anybody died I would never forgive myself. Of course the equipment is all perfect, but one never knows what might happen.

I have a lot of worries about the affair, & I should be down to see you. However, I hope to come in a few days.

De Windt is up at Edinburgh lecturing, but he returns to London to-morrow.

London is in uproar over His Nibs of Germany.[221] Streets decorated, and all sorts of rot. The public do not recall the Kruger telegram.[222] What short memories people have!

The instant I can leave London I shall run up to see you. I'm sick of London & now I'm not going to Lapland, shall probably spend the winter in the East.

Already two men have volunteered to go with me through Lapland both experienced travellers. But I have not sufficient confidence.

With the best of good luck, & longing to see you again.

Yours as ever

William Le Queux.[223]

---

221. The visit of the Emperor and Empress of Germany and the King and Queen of Prussia.
222. Telegram sent by Kaiser Wilhelm II to Paul Kruger, president of the Transvaal Republic, on 3 January 1896, congratulating his repelling the Jamieson Raid.
223. WmLQ letter to George Beeforth.

Lapland Expedition 1907

With the expedition to Lapland out of the way, Le Queux had to tackle another tricky situation, which ultimately would bring him down.

Divorce
1908–1909

Now back in England Le Queux had to face what he probably wanted to get away from – and somewhere in the Arctic Circle, you are well out of the way of lawyers. This was never going to be a 'quickie' divorce. In his subsequent letter to George Beeforth, Le Queux's optimism is short lived and it would be almost another year before the judicial separation was finalised.

Devonshire Club,
St James's, S. W.
Nov 19 [1907]

My Dear old chappie

I have just got your very kind letter. Oh! What trouble servants are. I'm glad you have not had a tragedy in the house.

I'd be most delighted to come & see you, only I have to go to Dusseldorf on business & shall not be back till the end of next week.

So I will come & see you very soon. I hope the girls & Fraulein are quite well. I caught a bad chill motoring the other day, but I'm better after a day's rest in bed.

If You Can Walk With Kings

I suppose you know that at last Mrs Le Queux's case is settled & she has signed a deed of separation. So that is one worry the less.

I'm glad you are quite well. My friend Sir Wm Cooper wants me to spend this winter with him at his villa at Beaulieu near Nice, & at present I'm undecided. He is rather erratic like myself!

With all good wishes my dear old chappie, & hoping you are quite well.

Yours sincerely

William Le Queux.[224]

Sir William Earnshaw Cooper had been born in 1843 and attended Wellington College. He was knighted in 1903 and had been an Honorary Colonel in the Indian Cawnpore Volunteer Rifles. He died at Castle Cary on the island of Guernsey in 1924 and is buried close by. In 1911 Le Queux wrote an introduction to Sir William's book *Spiritual Science: Here and Hereafter,* in which Le Queux himself says he had looked into the subject only a year or so earlier. Cooper is described by his friend as both a deep thinker and level headed.

Whether Le Queux spent the winter along the Mediterranean is by no means certain. If he had done so I am sure he would have written to his friend. In fact I have no correspondence between Le Queux and George Beeforth for the next seventeen months. During this time Le Queux managed to publish a handful of new books and a few short stories. With rising divorce costs something had to pay the bills.

One of those books was *The Spies of the Kaiser* published by Hurst & Blackett in May 1909. It had first been serialised in the *Weekly News* in March of the same year. Once again Le Queux continues his theme of underlining the proposed threat to Britain from foreign spies. It opens with the statement that the plans for a naval station to be built at Rosyth had already been stolen and were in German hands. Yet again you can

---

224. WmLQ letter to George Beeforth.

Divorce 1908–1909

feel that Le Queux is being fed this information from government sources. He was in effect a spokesman for the British Government without the word 'official'.

Although Luisa had signed her deed of separation, her husband had not, it seems, been paying any alimony, for her lawyers were back in court on 25 August 1908 when they filed for a judicial separation. Luisa gave her address as 89 Vis Babuino, Rome.[225] Le Queux's solicitors made a counterclaim on 14 October 1908 stating that he denied failing to comply on the grounds that Luisa had left the country and was residing in Italy, and as she had not returned, he was therefore unable to comply.[226] Luisa had by now signed an affidavit witnessed at the British Consular Office in Rome. Le Queux finally lost his case on 9 November 1908, and a month later, on 9 December 1908, he was given seven days in which to pay Luisa costs amounting to £33 6s 8d plus several sureties of £30 each, totalling £120.[227] This Le Queux also failed to comply with and on 26 January 1909 an order for non-payment was lodged.[228] Following further delays in payment a settlement was finally reached on 17 December 1909 for an undisclosed amount of maintenance, except that Le Queux was then given seven days to pay £89 10s 10d to Luisa's solicitors, Messrs Mills & Morley of Lincoln's Inn Fields, for their costs.[229]

According to his autobiography, Le Queux spent some time in the Sudan in north Africa in 1909. It was not the first time he had visited this part of the world, as just over a decade earlier he had been in Algeria and the Sahara. Unlike the previous occasion, it does not seem to have provided the inspiration for any literary effort. This may be because he spent more time in Egypt than Sudan.

---

225. Court minutes, 25 August 1908.
226. Court minutes, 14 October 1908.
227. Court minutes, 17 December 1909. This could represent up to £12,000 in today's money.
228. Court minutes, 14 February 1909.
229. Court minutes, 8 July 1910.

Devonshire Club,
St James's, S. W.
April 14. 09

My Dearest old chappie

I got back from the south three days ago, & I got your kind note to-day.

Your letter from Wiesbaden is evidently following me somewhere or other! I am so sorry you have not been well, & I do hope you will take care of yourself & get quite well.

You have planned a pleasant summer holiday & I hope you will all enjoy yourselves. I too, shall probably be abroad a good deal this summer. If I can possibly come up and see you before you go I will be delighted to do so. To-morrow, however, I'm due at Bournemouth, & am going for a round of visits. Still, I shall try to see you before you go away again. The girls have not written me <u>at all</u>. But I hope they are all right, & enjoying themselves. I wrote to Beatrice my regards, but she did not answer.

Paris is very gay just now. It looks its best, and the Riviera is crowded.

So you will be back in August, old chappie. Do take care of yourself in travelling. I was in Cracow about 8 years ago, but I believe it has much improved since then. Lots of Jews there – also in Lemberg![230] But Galecia is full of Hebrews.

Let me know how you are, won't you, as I shall be anxious about you. If you write either to the club or the Cecil my letters are forwarded.

Wishing you good health again dear old chappie – and quickly

Yours as ever

William Le Queux.[231]

---

230. Now Lviv in Ukraine.
231. WmLQ letter to George Beeforth.

Divorce 1908–1909

From the tone of this letter you sense his embarrassment that the Beeforth girls do not wish to have anything to do with him and that he seems to be avoiding staying in one place for too long. He still had his loyal friend in George Beeforth.

Hotel Cecil,
W. C.
May 5. 09

[On headed notepaper Ashley, King's Somborne, Hants]

My Dear old chappie

Your very welcome letter and kind invite to hand. I would be <u>delighted</u> to come to see you – and <u>much want</u> to see you – but I am away just now with friends motoring – and I have to be back in London all next week – or greater part of it, so I will have to defer my visit until you are all back again.

What day shall you <u>be in London</u>? If I knew, I would try & be there also, so as to get an hour or so with you. So let me know to the Cecil. I suppose you will be at the Midland Grand, as usual?

Towards the end of May I go motoring again on the continent – I think to Bordeaux, Biarritz, and along the Pyrenees. But I am not yet certain. I have a lot of travelling before me this summer amongst other things, I am due to pay a visit to my little Republic – San Marino! You should go there with me.

If you go to <u>Belgrade</u> or to <u>Bucharest,</u> let me know, & I will give you letters of introduction which I daresay may be of service to you. I quite understand what you say about Beatrice. She is happily out of it, I think.

I hope you are quite well, dear

Old chappie. A hearty hand-grip to you from

Yours as ever

William Le Queux.[232]

---

232. WmLQ letter to George Beeforth.

If You Can Walk With Kings

What is the meaning behind the reference to Beatrice? Does this suggest that Beatrice could have been implicated as 'the other woman' in his divorce case? Unlikely but far from impossible.

The Hampshire village of King's Somborne features in Le Queux's *Lying Lips*.

> I left Waterloo for Andover Junction, where I changed upon the branch line, which took me through sleepy old Stockbridge on to Horsebridge Station. There Fred met me in his big red 'Mercedes' and drove me over the hills, through the village of King's Somborne, with its squat little church, a place once the residence of John o' Gaunt, and out upon the broad open highway, where, a mile further on, we turned sharp to the right up a steep hill. Into a lovely wooded country, picturesque in all the fresh green of spring, we went, and through a tiny hamlet of homely thatched cottages called Ashley, beyond which we suddenly swung past a lodge and up the long drive that led to Charlwood Manor,[233] a big, long, spacious, seventeenth-century house partly covered with ivy, with pretty, well-kept gardens, and splendid woods beyond.[234]

* * *

Devonshire Club,
St James's, S. W.
May 15. 09

My Dearest old chappie

I was away in the country, but only received your welcome letter of the 9th, and also the newspaper. I feel sure the Corporation will jump at your very generous offer. It will be a great benefit to the town to have those lovely gardens. But

---

233. Charlwood Copse is nearby.
234. William Le Queux, *Lying Lips*. London: Stanley Paul, 1910, p194.

Divorce 1908–1909

I do so want to come up and spend a couple of days with you before you go away. I have been on a round of visits in the country, & this week I have a lot of engagements in town now that the season has started.

But I <u>will</u> come down in the course of ten days or so.

Let me know when you decide to leave. If you remain another fortnight I will be down before you go, for I feel I must have a chat with you.

I suppose you saw that Mrs Le Q has been at me again in the Courts for judicial separation & payment of her costs. I have to shell out for her costs this week £122.

I'm so sorry to hear you are so seedy. But this bright weather will soon set you right again, dear old chap.

My brother sends his kindest regards to you.

With the best of good wishes, & hoping to see you in a few days.

Yours as ever

William Le Queux.[235]

The gardens which now form part of the South Cliff Gardens were originally purchased by George Beeforth in 1883 and finally sold to Scarborough Borough Council in 1912.

> Devonshire Club,
> St James's, S. W.
> June 2. 09

My Dearest old chappie

I find that Carmichael of Leghorn arrives in Paris on Saturday & I am going over to spend a day or two with him there, so I fear I shall not be in London on Tuesday when you come. I am very disappointed, as I would so much like to go

---

235. WmLQ letter to George Beeforth.

to the Academy with you. I, however, promised him I would spend a week or ten days in Paris with him & then for a day or two at Étretat. So I cannot very well get out of it.

I shall give him your kind regards. I [will] tell him you are away or you would have asked him to Scarboro.

I hope you are quite well & fit for your journey. May God protect you, dear old chappie, & may you come back hearty & well. Write and let me know your movements from time to time, won't you. I shall often think of you.

I am longing to go travelling again, either to the Arctic or to the Antarctic – to me it matters not which!

Till we meet a letter always finds me either at the Cecil or here.

Yours as ever

William Le Queux.[236]

That last part was not strictly true, for after four years, Le Queux finally gave up his room at the Hotel Cecil. It has to be because of his crippling and ongoing financial obligations to Luisa. His financial difficulties really must have been that bad as the next letter is sent from his brother Fred's, home in Maida Vale.

89, Elgin Avenue,
Maida Vale, W
July 6 [1909]

My Dearest old chappie

Got your two letters. I've left the Cecil for a bit, after 4½ years. Grown tired of it. At this moment I'm motoring with some friends in Hampshire. But I shall strain every effort to be back in town on Thursday. If I can. I shall wire to you at the Midland before 5 o'clock. If you don't get a wire you will know I cannot be back in time.

---

236. WmLQ letter to George Beeforth.

Divorce 1908–1909

If I don't chance to see you & say good bye. I wish you bon voyage, & a very pleasant time. I shall be spending part of the summer in Russia I think. I have many friends there, & lots of visits to pay.

But we shall meet again in the autumn, I trust.

Do you see my new novel about 'Socialism' in 'Black & White'.[237]

I shall do my utmost to see you, & bring Carmichael along.

Yours as ever

William Le Queux.[238]

Le Queux's new novel was *The Unknown Tomorrow*. It was originally subtitled *How the World Will be Divided after the War, Aspirations of the Allies*. Later this was changed to *How the Rich Fare at the Hands of the Poor*. Aimed at his more affluent readership perhaps?

> Devonshire Club,
> St James's, S. W.
> July 9. 09

My Dearest old chappie

Just a line to hope you arrived safely. I rushed down to Charing Cross this morning, but your train – the 9. am, had just left. I was too late!

Carmichael and myself had a most pleasant evening last night. It was so jolly for all three of us to meet again.

I hope you will have a pleasant time & return in better health.

Let me have news of you from time to time. I shall get your letters if sent to the club.

With all good wishes to the young people & to Fraulein.

---

237. William Le Queux, *The Unknown Tomorrow*. London: F. V. White, 1910.
238. WmLQ letter to George Beeforth.

And lots of luck to your dear old self.

From

Yours as ever

William Le Queux.[239]

Although Le Queux was expecting to spend the summer of 1909 away in Russia he appears to have gone to Germany instead, on another secret mission.

> Metropole Hotel,
> Folkestone.
> Aug 16. 09
>
> My Dearest old chappie
>
> I was surprised to get yours an hour ago! I am so sorry that the circumstances make you cut off your holiday like that! But I do hope Miss Lizzie is better by this time. Since you have been away I have also been across the water on a confidential mission – a rather interesting one! I will tell you all about it when we meet.
>
> I note what you say about the German preparations, but I have reason to believe that we are now waking up. I have – and am still, engaged upon more secret work for the Intelligence Department of the War Office, & what I have already seen means that we have really awakened to a sense of our peril.
>
> Give my kindest regards to the girls, & tell them to let me know how they are. I hope Fraulein is also well. I was in Berlin a fortnight ago!
>
> I hope you will soon be all right again dear old chappie, & that we shall quickly meet.
>
> Yours as ever
>
> William Le Queux.[240]

---

239. WmLQ letter to George Beeforth.
240. WmLQ letter to George Beeforth.

Divorce 1908–1909

As the summer days passed into September, Le Queux continued to be on the move, avoiding London as if the plague was back.

Royal Oak Hotel,
Betws-y-Coed.
Wednesday

My Dearest old chappie

I am motoring with Sir William Cooper through Wales, the Lakes, & then up to Perthshire. I expected we should go the East Coast road. In which case we should have come to Malton to see you. But Cooper wanted to go to Wales, so here we are. We have already done about 500 miles – from Bournemouth, & have had a lovely run.

I wonder how you are & the girls. Are they on their tour? I wrote to Beatrice, but she has not replied. Will you please tell her to write to Scotland when she visits. This part of Wales is very picturesque. I expect you know it. The hotels are very full of holiday folk just now.

Let me know how Miss Lizzie is & how you are.

Address me –

at Kincardine Castle

Auchterarder N. B.

We go from here to Bangor, Chester, Liverpool, Lancaster, Windermere, Carlisle, Gretna, Moffat, Lanark, Glasgow & Perth.

Give my regards to Fraulein & my love to the girls.

And with all good wishes to you, dearest old chappie from

Yours as ever

William Le Queux.[241]

---

241. WmLQ letter to George Beeforth, [1 September] 1909.

We know how Le Queux enjoyed travel of any kind and he seems to have taken to motoring from a very early date. According to his autobiography he was a passenger in one of the first automobiles purchased in the country. The first mention of regular motoring comes from 1906, the same year that he published *The Mystery of a Motor Car*.[242] It must have been shortly afterwards that he obtained his own car. In his books a Mercedes has been mentioned, as has a six-cylinder forty-horse-power Napier,[243] the latter being his more likely motor of choice. After he wrote *The Count's Chauffeur* in 1907 and *The Lady in the Car* in 1908, the novelty of motoring seems to have waned and it no longer features in any of his book titles.

Kincardine Castle,
Auchterarder,
N. B.
Sep 7 [1909]

My Dear Beeforth

We arrived here to-day, & I got your letter.

The weather in North Wales last week was horribly wet & dull.

We stayed at Llangollen, Betwys-y-Coed, & Bangor.

The girls would like the Royal Oak Hotel, at Betwys-y-Coed. Not too dear & very comfortable. A good centre for walking excursions.

We are a pretty gay party up here for the shooting. Let me know when you decide to go to Wales. I am so glad Miss Lizzie is better. Please give her my kindest regards. Also to the girls. And with best wishes to yourself from

Yours always sincerely

William Le Queux

---

242. William Le Queux, *The Mystery of a Motor Car*. London: Hodder & Stoughton, 1906.

243. In a later edition (London: Greenhill Books, 1986) of *The Count's Chauffeur*, the Napier is replaced by a six-litre Bentley. Are we seeing an early form of 'product placement'?

Divorce 1908–1909

Deene Park, Northamptonshire

Le Queux's next house party during the shooting season was in Northamptonshire at the castellated Tudor mansion, Deene Park, home of the Countess of Cardigan.[244] She was the widow of the Earl of Cardigan, who led the infamous Charge of the Light Brigade at Balaklava. Le Queux would describe the Countess as having a squeaky voice and wearing a yellow wig and a dress of pale carnation satin. She was extremely eccentric, even more so in her old age. In one of the few references to his father he claimed that the old Earl had once been a friend of his father.[245] When in London the Countess lived in Deanery Street, off Park Lane.

From Deene Park we find Le Queux writing both to Trottie[246] and her grandfather, George Beeforth.

---

244. Adeline Louisa Maria, Countess of Cardigan and Lancastre (1824–1915).
245. William Le Queux, *Things I Know about Kings*, p 131.
246. Beatrice May Crawford Beeforth.

If You Can Walk With Kings

Deene Park,
Wansford,
Northans.
Oct 10. 09

My Dear Trottie

Many thanks for your letter. It was real good to see your <u>neat</u> handwriting again. I thought you had forgotten 'poor little Willie!'

So you are back at Scarboro again. By Jove! You have been wandering about, haven't you?

Your dad wrote that you were going to Wales, & I suggested that he should take you to Betws-y-Coed – where I had just been with 'God'. Then I hear from you that you've re-entered residence at Scarboro.

How is the Kidkin? I've written to her twice, but she hasn't answered my letters. I hope she is alive & well.

As you see, I'm here shooting, but I go in two or three days. There is the usual gay party here, smart people & lots of fun.

Have you read *My Recollections* by Lady Cardigan. I suggested that she should write them. Some of them are very <u>naughty</u>! You can get it at the library, but there's a tremendous rush for it, & over 1,000 people are waiting for it at Mudies.[247] The publishers are just reprinting it for the 6th time!

I was flung out of a motor-car the other day & hurt my leg badly. For some days I hobbled with a stick. Much better now.

I wonder if Fraulein ever means to write to me again. She owes me a letter. I wrote to Wiesbaden, & never got a reply. Will you give her my regards, & tell her so.

To you, my dearest darling Trotlet, much love from

Yours ever sincerely

William Le Queux

---

247. Mudie's Circulating Libraries, eventually killed off by the Public Library movement.

Divorce 1908–1909

Deene Park,
Wansford,
Northans.
Oct 10. 09

My Dearest old chappie

Just a line to ask how you are? I have not heard from you lately, though I heard from Beatrice that you had returned to Scarboro.

I expected that you had gone to Wales.

I hope you are all right, & are feeling the benefit of the change you have had.

I have been wondering if you have come to any conclusion with the Corporation regarding your gardens.

Let me have any news of you when you have a moment to spare.

I am shooting here for a day or two more, with a very smart party, & with much amusement.

I trust Miss Lizzie is much better, & that you are in your usual health.

With every good wish dear old chappie.

from

Yours very sincerely

William Le Queux

Wansford is mentioned in a number of novels, but Le Queux does not seemed to have used Deene Park as the setting for any of his plots.

The main reason Le Queux would have to leave Deene Park 'in a day or two' was that he was heavily involved in England's first aviation meeting due to be held at Doncaster. The show would run over a week from 15 to 23 October 1909 and take place on Doncaster Racecourse. Amongst the early flying pioneers attending would be Samuel Cody, Leon Delagrange and Hubert Le Blon. Both the two latter flyers were to be killed within a year and Cody died in 1913 and is buried in the military cemetery in Aldershot.

One of the judges was Le Queux himself, perched high up in a wooden tower situated in the middle of the racecourse where he was supposed to be timing the circuits, that is if he remembered! Among his fellow judges was his old travelling companion, Harry de Windt.

Cody was the big draw as he had the honour of being the first man to fly a heavier-than-air machine in Britain. However his craft came to grief whilst taxiing and never did fly. On several days the weather for these early pioneers was simply too windy and no flying was possible. Despite several records being set, the meeting was a financial disaster and cost the local Doncaster Corporation a great deal of money.

Dec 14. 09
Devonshire Club,
[On headed notepaper Metropole Hotel, Folkestone]

My Dearest old chappie

I have just got yours forwarded from London. I intended accepting your very kind invite, but I had a lot to do about my aunt's affairs & I had to 'cross the Channel' as well, and am just back yesterday! I fear therefore I shall not be able to come up to see you before Xmas, but as soon as your Xmas party is over I will run up for a day or two. Of late I have been travelling incessantly.

I am interested to hear that you intend going to Constantinople. Take my advice & do the journey from Constantinople to Salonica <u>by sea</u>. The train is a dreadful one – the slowest in the world I should say. The hotel in Salonica is only <u>fair</u>. If I were you I would go by steamer – the same steamer which comes from Constantinople to Alexandria, & take the girls to see Cairo. You can then get from Alexandria straight to Corfu, & on to Trieste.

Divorce 1908–1909

There is really nothing to see in the extreme south of Turkey. It is not interesting like Albania or Macedonia.

You will find the Constantinople–Alexandria steamer though small – excellent. You would get good weather too. It is never very rough there.

But we will have a chat over it when we meet.

I hope you are all well, & though I am not near you you are <u>very often</u> in my thoughts my dear old chappie.

All good luck to you from

Yours as ever

William Le Queux.[248]

Yet despite his own mounting problems Le Queux was, as always, willing to lend a helping hand when it was required. On 8 September 1905 there was a strong earthquake which struck central Calabria. This appears to have left around six hundred dead and as many as three thousand injured. Much of the property was also destroyed. In a letter to *The Times*, Le Queux writes that he accompanied Victor Emmanuel, the King of Italy, to the disaster area. There followed an appeal from the Lord Mayor asking for donations for the Mansion House Fund. In all nearly £9,000 was raised by the public. The King of Italy had just in the previous year awarded Le Queux the Order of the Crown of Italy, and now the King wrote a warm letter to Le Queux thanking him for his efforts on behalf of the victims.[249] At some point Le Queux was summoned to the Quirinale Palace in Rome to meet the King. Apparently it was at the suggestion of the Duke of Abruzzi, for whom Le Queux had translated and published his *The Stella Polare* in 1903, and at their private audience King Victor Emmanuel III presented Le Queux with Italy's National Order awarded to civilians. Then at the very end of the December 1908, there was another terrible earthquake which again hit Sicily and Calabria, this time being centred on Messina.

---

248. WmLQ letter to George Beeforth.
249. *The Star*, 10 March 1906.

If You Can Walk With Kings

It was estimated that this time as many as 120,000 people may have lost their lives in the disaster. Once again we find Le Queux writing to *The Times*. However, Le Queux's 'Letter to the Editor' is concerned more with the scandal surrounding the distribution of aid. He stated that from the previous request for aid less than a fifth of the money subscribed reached the poor and destitute.[250] In a follow-up letter, Le Queux tries to reassure the public that the British Ambassador, Sir Rennell Rodd,[251] would oversee the distribution of funds in future.[252]

At the end of the year Le Queux wrote to Douglas Sladen and in a rare moment mentioned that he was due to visit Serbia again and that from 18 January 1910, he would be in St Petersburg.[253] In his autobiography Le Queux recalled a meeting with the Tzar of all the Russias. He was staying at the Hotel de l'Europe in Petrograd[254] when an officer of the Imperial Guard called and presented him with an envelope containing a command from the Tzar. Le Queux duly took the train to Tzaeskoye Selo, known as 'the Village of the Tzar', where the royal residences of the Russian Emperors were located. He recalls feeling ill-at-ease in such grand surroundings. Fortunately, Le Queux was accompanied by Count de Redetski who reassured him that as this was to be a private audience the Tzar would in all probability not be wearing his dress uniform. Passing through countless corridors Le Queux finally meets Tzar Nicholas II, whom he describes as a short bearded man wearing a rough shooting jacket. The Tzar was aware of Le Queux's previous trip to Siberia and his more recent excursion accompanied by Harry de Windt. Of their meeting all that Le Queux revealed is that the Tzar was in agreement with his belief that the mobilisation of Germany is in preparation for an invasion. This new year would see Le Queux spending a large part of the summer in Russia possibly on intelligence work, as he was about to go under cover.

---

250. *The Times*, 7 January 1909.
251. James Rennell Rodd, 1st Baron Rennell (1858–1941).
252. *The Times*, 1 February 1909.
253. WmLQ letter to Douglas Sladen, from Devonshire Club, London, 31 December 1909.
254. At the time of writing (1923) St Petersburg had been renamed Petrograd and in 1924 changed again to Leningrad.

William Kelly
1909–1912

There appeared in an early edition of the magazine of the William Le Queux Society an obituary which had been printed in the *Daily Herald*.[255] It was spotted by Dag Hedman, who was struck at once by an odd comment in the news report. The newspaper repeated what almost all the other obituaries had mentioned about Le Queux being born in London, son of a French count and studying in Paris etc. However, the writer may have known more than he wanted to say, but it is the last line, almost a throwaway comment, that is of the greatest interest:

'His real name was Kelly'.[256]

So was William Le Queux working under cover as a real spy with an alias?

If you read any early John le Carré novel you get an idea of the activities of his character George Smiley, working for MI6 and the organisation of the 'London Circus'. This is counter-espionage. Today, we think of the foreign spies such as Gordon Lonsdale, the Portland Spymaster; and Peter and Helen Kroger, who masqueraded as antiquarian booksellers; the Cambridge spies, Kim Philby, Donald Maclean and Guy Burgess and the fourth man or the fifth man, the list

---

255. *Le Queux Magazine*, issue 14, Autumn 1999.
256. *Daily Herald*, 14 October 1927.

could go on. They all acted under cover and infiltrated as part of their plan in order to gather information.

This is very much the opposite to the activities of William Le Queux and the German and Russian spies of which he writes. For in the days before the Great War, spies were well educated and on the face of it seemingly acceptable to society. Their aim was to gain access to embassy functions, to be seen around town, where they hoped to pick up gossip and to generally mix with diplomats where a careless or unguarded word would be reported back to their paymasters. This is the very role that Le Queux played, using travel to gather local colour for his novel writing as his cover. His acquaintances were titled nobility, foreign embassy staff and even minor royalty. His work is littered with references to the top European hotels where he was instantly recognised and welcomed.

It seems he was very much a spy and his activities appear to have commenced around 1905. We do not need to guess at this as he himself admits it:

> At Rosyth, I lived in an obscure hotel in Queensferry under the name of William Kelly, enduring three weeks of wearisome idleness, boating up and down the Firth of Forth, and watching, with interest, the movements of two Germans. They had arrived in Edinburgh from a tourist-ship which had touched at Leith. The first suspicion of them had been conveyed to me by my friend Mr D. Thomson, proprietor of the *Dundee Courier*, and I sped north to investigate.[257]

D. C. Thomson[258] had begun to publish Le Queux's series *Spies of the Kaiser*, in the *Weekly News* in March 1909. According to Roger Stearn it was a fortnight before the appearance of the first instalment that the *Weekly News*, for 27 February 1909, inserted an advertisement offering

---

257. William Le Queux, *German Spies in England*, p 53.
258. David Coupar Thomson took over the business in 1905 and today is best known for the children's comics *The Dandy* and *The Beano*.

readers £10 for information on spies.[259] It is clear from this that Thomson's 'Spy Editor' had passed on to Le Queux any likely sightings that were sent in by readers. The *Weekly News* was particularly strong in Scotland and northern England which explains why Le Queux was skulking around Queensferry.

The *Weekly News* series was subsequently expanded into a book version published by Hurst & Blackett. It opened with the revelation that the plans of the new Rosyth Naval Base, which opened in 1909, had already fallen into the hands of the Germans. I have not seen whether this was an actual fact, but we know that in October 1914 a German national, George Dunnet, claiming to be a Frenchman, was arrested at Rosyth, where he was in charge of the telephone switchboard. As Le Queux always maintained, spies would be, or claim to be, other nationalities such as French, Swiss or Belgian.

It was in March 1909 that Colonel James Edmonds,[260] later Brigadier General who in 1907 was promoted to head up Britain's fledgling Secret Service, MO5, was called to address a meeting of the Defence Committee.

> On Tuesday 30th March 1909, a sub-committee of the Committee of Imperial Defence met in secret session at 2 Whitehall Gardens, Westminster, to consider the question of foreign espionage in Britain. The first witness was Colonel James Edmonds, head of MO5, military operations counter-intelligence, whose job was to uncover foreign spies in Britain. He had a staff of two and a budget of £200 a year. Edmonds painted a picture of hordes of German spies in Britain preparing to take by stealth what Germany could not gain in open combat. Lord Esher, who apparently thought Edmonds had spies on the brain, asked him, 'Colonel, do you feel any apprehension regarding the large numbers of German waiters in this country?'

---

259. Roger T. Stearn, 'The Mysterious Mr Le Queux', p 17.
260. Brigadier General James Edward Edmonds (1861–1956), a Royal Engineer who served in the Boer War.

But the sarcasm was lost on Edmonds, who had quickly realised that in order to persuade the sub-committee to act, he would have to present a list of cases packed with convincing detail. Fortunately, help was at hand in the unlikely figure of William Le Queux, Queen Alexandra's favourite novelist. Le Queux provided Edmonds with a list of fictional cases he had prepared for his bestseller *Spies of the Kaiser*.

When Edmonds presented his new 'evidence', the atmosphere in the sub-committee changed.[261]

It should be borne in mind that in March 1909 Le Queux's book *Spies of the Kaiser* had not yet been published, appearing two months later in May. Therefore any list did indeed come first hand direct from the author. However I very much doubt that any list of names would be the same as the fictional ones that appeared later in his book. Still, this is a clear indicator that Edmonds of MO5 and Le Queux were in close contact from an earlier date.

Le Queux's mission to Scotland reads like a scene from Alfred Hitchcock's adaptation of *The Thirty-Nine Steps*, with Le Queux resembling the character of Richard Hannay. The book *German Spies in England: An Exposure* is signed and dated 'Hawson Court, Buckfastleigh, Devon, February 1915', although this was not his address at the time of publication. Hawson Court lies off the road from Buckfastleigh to Scorriton, a road described in a later book:

> On the steep stony road which winds up from Buckfastleigh through Holne village, that remote little place where Charles Kingsley lived and wrote.[262]

Hawson Court had once been owned by the notorious Richard Capel. He was the Lord of the Manor at Buckfastleigh in the 17th century and

---

261. Philip Knightley, *The Independent*, 27 May 1993.
262. William Le Queux, 'The Duck's Egg', *Sovereign Magazine*, August 1922. Charles Kingsley (1819–1875) was born in Holne Vicarage.

kept a pack of hounds. This became the basis behind Conan Doyle's Sherlock Holmes story *The Hound of the Baskervilles*. Until the turn of the 20th century it had been the home of Mr Fearnley Tanner JP. Le Queux moved into Hawson Court some time around September 1910 according to a letter sent to George Beeforth:

> Hawson Court
> Buckfastleigh,
> S. Devon
> Sep 30. 10
>
> My Dearest Old Chappie
>
> I am just back in England again, having been wandering once more on the other side of the channel.
>
> I found your letter awaiting me, & was so glad to hear that you are all quite well, and as usual.
>
> I would dearly love to meet up & see you all again, but only just coming back I cannot yet make up my plans. Still if I may leave it open I will meet up and see you as soon as I can manage.
>
> I have been absent from England most part of the summer and partly in Russia and partly staying with some people in Normandy.
>
> I want to see you & to hear of all your adventures during your late trips. Next time you should do Roumania & southern Russia. It would greatly interest you all. I am sure.
>
> I expect you wondered why you did not get a reply to yours, but my letters were not forwarded, as I am constantly on the move.
>
> Please give the girls my best wishes. I hope they are quite well, and that the pack of hounds still flourishes.
>
> All my kindest regards to you my dear old chappie, & longing to have a chat with you soon.
>
> Yours as ever
>
> William Le Queux

If You Can Walk With Kings

Is Le Queux referring to the Baskerville Hounds?

However, we know that Le Queux was away from home once again a few weeks later as he was then writing to George Beeforth from the home of Sir William Earnshaw Cooper in Bournemouth.

Hume Towers
Bournemouth,
Oct 22. 10

My Dearest Old Chappie

I only got your two kind letters when I arrived here yesterday, as they had been following me about.

I would have loved to have come up and joined your merry party, but I have to return to Paris on Monday night, as I have some important business there. I have been telegraphing today, trying to put it off, & to come up to you over Sunday – but alas, to no avail.

I am so sorry that it is impossible for me to come up to you this time, but I shall be back <u>in about a fortnight</u>, and I will move up & see you all, if I may.

Of late I have been travelling incessantly, & long for a few days quite with you & a gossip.

I would have loved to have come & joined in the fun with Newton Husbands, but I have just received a wire from Paris in reply to mine, in which I find it impossible to postpone crossing.

With all good luck my Dear Old Chappie, & the best of good wishes to you all.

Yours as ever

William Le Queux

Unfortunately, matters dictated that Le Queux was unable to spare the time to visit Scarborough, and within the month he was sailing with HMS *Antrim*. HMS *Antrim* was a Devonshire Class Armoured Cruiser built at John Brown's yard, launched in 1903 and fitted out eighteen months later. At the time that Le Queux was on board she formed part of the Home Fleet.[263] What he officially did between 1910 and 1911 seems to be shrouded in mystery!

HMS *ANTRIM*
Home Fleet,
Nov 23. 10

My Dearest Old Chappie

I must apologise for not answering your kind letter of invitation before but I have be[en] abroad, & mostly at sea ever since. We are on our way home from Madeira, & been into Lisbon & are due in Torbay tomorrow when I shall post this.

Weather has been pretty bad in the Bay of Biscay, but it does not make much difference to a big cruiser.

I expect you are at Mr Lords, if so, please give them both my kindest regards. I hope you are all quite well. I was so sorry I could not get up to you when Newton Husbands was there, but I had to go to Paris, & then on to Brest to join this ship.

I shall by <u>most delighted</u> to come up and see you all when you are home again. I feel that it is ages since I had a yarn with you.

Please give my best regards to Beatrice and Gabrielle I expect they are enjoying themselves with Mrs Lord.

<u>When writing, please write to the Club.</u>

All good wishes your dear old self & hoping you are well.

Yours very sincerely

William Le Queux[264]

---

263. This vessel is mentioned in the opening chapter of his book *The White Lie*. London: Ward Lock & Co., 1914.
264. WmLQ letter to George Beeforth.

H.M.S *Antrim*

H.M.S. ANTRIM.

Home Fleet
Nov 23. 10.

My dearest old chappie

I must apologize for not answering your kind letter of invitation before but I have been abroad, & mostly at sea ever since. We are on our way home from Madeira, & been into Lisbon, & are due in Torbay tomorrow when I shall post this.

Stephan Baister makes a point that during the years 1910, 1911 and 1912 Le Queux's earnings took a dip due to ill health.[265] From Le Queux's letters there is no indication of any illnesses. On the contrary, he appears to be heavily engaged working with or for the British Government on fairly secret work, although as we learn later, he does suffer from occasional bouts of malarial fever.

At no time is there any mention of his home life, even when he returns to Devonshire for Christmas:

> Hawson Court
> Buckfastleigh,
> S. Devon
> Dec 12. 10
>
> My Dearest Old Chappie
>
> I got your kind wire only to-day, forwarded from the Club.
>
> I find I have so much to do & have several business appointments that I cannot get north till about 22nd. Of course then you will have your Xmas party arranged, so had I not better come up later on, in the New Year?
>
> I am busy writing here until the 20th, & then go to London. After the 22nd I am free.
>
> I did not think you expected me this week-end just past, & it was a surprise to get your wire this evening.
>
> I am hoping to have a good yarn with you, as of old. I hope you & the girls are all quite well. I had a very kind letter from Beatrice a few days ago.
>
> With my very kindest regards Dear Old Chappie, from
>
> Yours ever sincerely
>
> William Le Queux[266]

---

265. Stephen Baister, 'Le Queux and the World of Insolvency', *Le Queux Magazine*, issue 19, Winter 2000, p 31.
266. WmLQ letter to George Beeforth.

If You Can Walk With Kings

Having spent Christmas in Scandinavia, in February Le Queux was once again abroad on official business, staying with an old friend, the British Consul, Monty Carmichael:

> C/O British Consulate
> Leghorn
> (Italy)
> Feb 11 [1911]

Dearest Old Chappie

I only got your kind letter the other day, as it has been following me about for weeks. I have been abroad ever since just after Xmas in Copenhagen, Malmö, & Danzig – in a spot you know well. Mr & Mrs Carmichael, with whom I dined last night, were anxious in their inquires [sic] after you, & send you their kindest regards.

I am sorry I've not yet been able to get to Scarboro to see you, but I am such a traveller more-a-days, & nearly always on the continent. Still I hope to be home again in about a month & then I shall see you. At the end of March I go to sea again until the naval manoeuvres. I am very fond of it, & have such a good time with the fleet. My friend William with the '*Antrim*' is stationed at Harwich now, & is always cruising up and down the North Sea. So I shall induce him one day to anchor off Scarboro & we shall 'bombard' no 66. He has promised to do this when we have an opportunity. You and the girls will then be able to come on board.

My immediate movements are uncertain. I go from here to Milan & then to have a look at the winter sports in Switzerland.

I hope the girls are quite well, & also your sister & Fraulein. Please remember me very warmly to them all.

And with the best of good wishes to you, my Dear Old Chappie, I remain

Yours as always

William Le Queux

PS The Palace Hotel here where we stayed was burnt down yesterday![267]

The 1911 Census in William Le Queux's own handwriting

William Kelly (as Le Queux was then calling himself) was back in Devonshire for the National Census taken on Sunday night 2 April 1911. The occupants of Hawson Court in Buckfastleigh were William Kelly, head of the household, a 42-year-old married man who described himself as engaged in 'novel writing'. This would indicate he was born in Kensington in about 1869, losing some five years off his real age. His 'wife' is shown as 30-year-old Emily Elizabeth Kelly, and having been born in Hammersmith. They, or rather she, had one child, Gertrude Miriam Kelly, aged 11 years old, having been born in Greenwich. The way the form has been completed, in Le Queux's own handwriting, gives a strong impression that he is not the father of the child. The

---

267. WmLQ letter to George Beeforth.

remaining members of the household are the governess, Edith Priscilla Rowe, a 20-year-old girl from Camborne in Cornwall, and two servants, Florence Ada Macey, 22 years old from Paddington who was the laundry maid, and Sarah Ann Wheaton, a year younger, a general servant from Broadwood Kelly in Devon.

Despite his close relationship with George Beeforth it appears that Beeforth was ignorant of Le Queux's relationship with 'Emily'. This was apparently no brief or even casual affair.

Hawson Court
Buckfastleigh,
S. Devon
June 17. 11

My Dearest Old Chappie

I was so glad to get your letter & to know you are well. Of late I have been on the continent a great deal. Indeed I have been three times to Italy & once to Greece this year, & in October I am going up to Khartoum for the winter.

Meanwhile the above address always finds me, for I have the house and their shooting and fishing – a very pleasant place high up on the edge of Dartmoor. I find I can write here well, and as you know I love a country life.

So you will be at the Isle of Wight. Shall you be there at the Review. I shall be on board the *Antrim* to see it. I wonder if there is any chance of seeing you while I am there? Perhaps we might meet on the Sunday following the review.

Please give my very kindest regards to the girls & Fraulein. I hear nothing of them now-a-days, but probably I am the culprit for not writing.

I shall be most delighted to come up to Scarboro to see you when you get back – if the girls want me. I fear they don't!

Though I have not written to you lately, Dearest old chappie you are <u>very often</u> in my thoughts. But we will meet very soon,

& have a gossip. By return of post send me your address in the Isle of Wight, & how long you will be there. I shall leave here for the *Antrim* on Friday next.

I had a card from Newton Husbands, who is in Brussels. He seems as merry as ever.

Well, my Dear old Chappie the best of poor health to you, & we will give each other all the news when we meet.

Write to me at once & tell me where you are.

Yours as ever

William Le Queux[268]

With Buckfastleigh not being far from Devonport Royal Naval Dockyard, there is a thought that this was perhaps the main reason for taking Hawson Court.

So what role was Le Queux fulfilling? We know HMS *Antrim* did dock at Rosyth, so was he officially being used to track spies? In one letter he mentions that his future plans are uncertain, which indicates that he was not in control and could be sent to wherever he was needed next. The captain or senior officer on board ship is mysteriously referred to as 'William'. The captain of HMS *Antrim* at this time was Captain Henry Douglas Wilkin, who must have been carrying instructions allowing him to ferry his passenger and take him wherever he liked.

Hawson Court
Buckfastleigh,
S. Devon
June 20. 11

My Dearest Old Chappie

Have just got your very kind letter. So pleased you are going up the Nile. I start with some people named Whittens – he is an Australian millionaire, by the way – & we leave London the first week in November. But of this more anon.

---

268. WmLQ letter to George Beeforth.

I hope to see you while you are at the Isle of Wight. I arrive on the *Antrim* on Friday night. I believe there is a very gay party to be on board. How far Totland's Bay is, I don't know. But I expect you will steam past us on Saturday, & I shall be on the 'look-out' for you!

The *Antrim* will be anchored near the Stokes Bay end of the line. She has <u>four</u> funnels.

Give my best wishes to the girls, & tell them that I hope to see them.

All kind wishes to you all. Looking forward to seeing you.

Yours as ever

William Le Queux

(Turn over)

PS I found that Totland Bay is a long way from our anchorage. So perhaps I will not be able to get over to you. Anyway I will wire.[269]

From a letter sent on the following Tuesday it is clear that the friends did not meet as planned.

Hawson Court
Buckfastleigh,
S. Devon
June 27. 11

My Dearest Old Chappie

I am just back home. I got yours just before leaving the *Antrim* & I was so sorry not to have seen you. <u>I am often in London. So very soon I shall look you up</u>.

I was so sorry not to let the girls have an opportunity of seeing over the ship, but as I shall be with them on manoeuvres in the North Sea this summer, I shall try to get William to put into Scarboro. Then they will be able to see it.

---

269. WmLQ letter to George Beeforth.

We had a pleasant time during the review. Luncheons, Dinners, Dances, Concerts, & all sorts of festivities both afloat & on land.

I hope you will have a good time in London. You and I will have a quiet dinner at the Club. I hope to be up next week.

<u>Meanwhile, address me here</u>. It is lovely on Dartmoor just now.

All good luck Dear old chappie from

Yours ever sincerely

William Le Queux[270]

For urgent communication Le Queux would use the Post Office Telegraph. He sent a telegram from his former residence, the Hotel Cecil in The Strand, handed in on 21 July 1911:

> To Beeforth 66 Esplanade
> Scarborough

Only today returned to London and got your card so very sorry you have gone expected you would be here this week Kindest regards to all Le Queux

* * *

> Hawson Court
> Buckfastleigh,
> S. Devon
> July 25. 11

My Dearest Old Chappie

I got your letter. Only just back here this morning. I am awfully sorry to hear of the girls' loss. This is most unfortunate.

---

270. WmLQ letter to George Beeforth.

If You Can Walk With Kings

The worst of it is that all hotels exhibit in their reception office a notice that they are not responsible for valuables.

A county solicitor is no good against the Midland Railway. You want a smart London man who can 'fluff' them. Why don't you get my man Stanley Evans, 20 Theobalds Road,[271] to go for them straight away? If you like I'll see him for you & start on the matter. Let me know. He is just the man for the job.

I do hope that your sister[272] will get round again all right. Give her my very best wishes for a speedy recovery. I am not very well myself. This hot weather has brought on my old enemy malaria fever & I can hardly hold my pen.

I hope that the girls are quite well. Tell them how sorry I am about their loss. I should suspect the servants – probably male servants.

My best love to you Dear old chappie. How worried you must be! I hope to see you soon always.

Your sincere friend

William Le Queux[273]

With regards to publishing, 1911 was a quiet time for Le Queux. Only two novels appeared and three collections of short stories which had been collected from various magazines. It is strange that we should think of this as a small output when compared to modern-day authors who would be lucky to produce one novel every couple of years. The author himself was still involved in what is looking like surveillance work.

---

271. Stanley Evans & Co., 20–22 Theobalds Road, Bedford Row, London.
272. Elizabeth Lord Beeforth.
273. WmLQ letter to George Beeforth.

William Kelly 1909–1912

Hawson Court
Buckfastleigh,
S. Devon
Aug 3. 11

My Dearest Old Chappie

I am anxious to know how your sister is. Please send me word. I feel that what with one thing and another you must be pretty worried, dear old chap.

How about the theft? Can I help you.

I was on the *Antrim* in the North Sea for five days last week, but we were out at sea 100 miles so could not touch Scarboro'. On the 17th I sail again for three weeks in the Atlantic making Berehaven[274] our headquarters & then to Cromarty.

Unfortunately I'm not very well. Have a touch of malaria. I've visitors here, & it makes it rather wretched.

When you are back from the Newtons I shall come & see you.

Give my love to the girls, both of whom I hope are well, & also kind regard to Fraulein.

Let me know how Miss Beeforth is. Kindest regards

Yours as ever

William Le Queux[275]

People's reminiscences of Le Queux do say how he would genuinely want to help a friend in need. One such recollection comes from Maude Ffoulkes from her own autobiography:

> When I first made his acquaintance, I was disposed to believe that he was rather superficial and slightly insincere, but I soon discovered my mistake. William Le Queux is good-hearted in the best sense of the word, and he is, as well, an indefatigable

---

274. Castletown Berehaven is on the west coast of Ireland at the entry to Bantry Bay. This was a Royal Naval station until the 1930s.
275. WmLQ letter to George Beeforth.

helper of lame dogs; when once he counts you as his friend, nothing is too much trouble if he thinks he can be of any service to you, and in prosperity and adversity he remains unchanged.[276]

* * *

Hawson Court
Buckfastleigh,
S. Devon
Aug 9 11

My Dearest Old Chappie

I think I <u>certainly</u> would take a good solicitor. You will never get anything out of a railway company by private arrangement. The pistol must be held at their heads.

The enclosed cases are interesting & I return them. The manager of the Midland Hotel would certainly not admit liability. I quite agree with you to go for them in the County Court. Any way in which I can help you, I will.

I am so glad to hear of your sister's improvement & I hope to come & see you again.

Please remember me kindly to Miss Beeforth, the girls & Fraulein, and to you. Dear old chappie the best of good health.

Yours as ever

William Le Queux[277]

From late November and over Christmas and New Year Le Queux visited Egypt and the Nile valley. An inscription dated the end of November was placed in one of his books whilst he was staying in Wadi Halfa, just south of Abu Simbel, on the Soudanese side of the River Nile.

---

276. Maude M. C. Ffoulkes, *My Own Past*.
277. WmLQ letter to George Beeforth.

As ever Le Queux would describe his travels in one of his forthcoming books, in this case *Her Royal Highness*, where he recalls arriving in a little white steamer as it pulled up, in the evening light, alongside the stone quay at Wadi Halfa. It would be a trip he would hardly forget in a hurry. For on a boat excursion down the Nile his craft overturned and Le Queux and his six Soudanese boatmen desperately fought for their lives in the swift-running waters in the rapids above the Second Cataract. Fortunately they managed to scramble onto some rocks in the middle of the river, from where they were rescued by some locals.[278]

Hawson Court
Buckfastleigh,
S. Devon
Feb 27. 12

My Dearest Old Chappie

So very much thanks for your cheery letter, which is so welcome.

I do so much want to come & see you, & to gossip as of yore. At the moment I'm fitting in time at home, writing a novel about Egypt.[279] And I shall stay over the first week in March to start the salmon fishing. After that I will do all I can to come and pay you a flying visit.

You know, Dear old chappie, what a wandering spirit I am now-a-days. I have been away from home all the time since the first of November.

I am so sorry to hear of your sister's illness. Please give her my very kindest regards & good wishes. I am sorry, too, about Fraulein's sister.

My publisher wants me to write my reminiscences of 'Half a Life'. I'm not yet decided to do so. It would be a fine opportunity to have a sly dig at my enemies!

---

278. *Western Times*, 9 January 1912.
279. William Le Queux, *The Hand of Allah*. London: Cassell & Co., 1914.

If You Can Walk With Kings

> In a week or two I hope to grasp your hand once again, Dear old chappie. I often & often think of you & wonder how you are.
>
> My love to the girls, whom I hope are as merry as ever.
>
> And with best wishes to your dear old self
>
> Yours as ever
>
> William Le Queux[280]

For reasons which will become clear this would be the last letter to George Beeforth for well over two years.

In May 1912, 'William Kelly's' cover was well and truly blown in the most unfortunate of circumstances that were way beyond Le Queux's control. One of the domestic servants at Hawson Court, 23-year-old Ann Ellen Bunstow, underwent an operation at the local hospital only to die whilst under the anaesthetic. At the following inquest held in Ashburton, conducted by Mr S. Hacker, the county coroner, William Le Queux was called under his own name as a pertinent witness.[281] Whether it was the unwelcome publicity on top of severe financial loss is uncertain, but Le Queux soon left Devonshire for good. Just when that was is not clear.

According to his autobiography Le Queux had been summoned by telegram from his Devonshire home to London when war broke out in the Balkans. The First Balkan War had been brewing for some months until it was declared in October 1912. After just two hours in London Le Queux had been dispatched to Serbia, taking the Orient Express, and within three days he was at the Serbian front line. With him were eight boxes of first-aid appliances for the wounded, supplied by the Serbian Minister in London. Le Queux would remain in the Balkans for seven months. He took part in the triumphal return of King Peter to Belgrade, before returning home.[282]

---

280. WmLQ letter to George Beeforth.
281. *Western Times*, 10 May 1912.
282. William Le Queux, *Things I Know about Kings*, p 82.

In a magazine article written some years later, Le Queux explains that he was staying in Constantinople, probably as part of his mission to the Balkans, where he met a self-styled count who turned out to be a German spy.

> At the time the Germans were very anxious to arm Turkey, in view of the coming Great War. But I was equally anxious to know what was in progress in the German arsenals. I saw in my friendship with the count an opportunity, more especially because I was on friendly terms with Tewfik Pasha, then Grand Vizier of Turkey, the official who could give a contract for arms and ammunition. I let my friend the count into the secret of my influence in high quarters, whereupon he urged me to join forces with him. He was the representative of the great Erhardt Gun Factory, in Dusseldorf; therefore, after a show of reluctance, I consented to go to Dusseldorf with him, see the directions, and make necessary arrangements by which I was to share in the plunder to be obtained from a contract with the Turkish government.
>
> This I did, and not only was I shown every courtesy as a friend of the Grand Vizier's but I was conducted over the Erhardt factory and also the great Vulcan works as well! I actually saw one of the Big Berthas in the making, and in consequence the British War Office were in possession of certain German secrets of which they had never hitherto dreamed.[283]

Le Queux's information gleaned may have been insignificant as regards the technical details, but he would not have failed to notice the organisation behind the armaments construction. Perhaps the Germans were only too pleased to show off their big guns knowing the information would get back to the British Government.

---

283. Quoted from *T.P.'s and Cassell's Weekly*, in *Gloucester Citizen*, 15 January 1925.

The Mummy's Curse
1912–1913

Any mention of Egypt and Egyptology immediately recalls the work done by Lord Carnarvon and Howard Carter with the discovery of the Tomb of Tutankhamun, the boy king, in the Valley of the Kings. It was Carter who broke through the sealed doorway for the first sight of the royal sarcophagus for over three thousand years.

Carter had first travelled to Egypt in 1891 and later worked under Flinders Petrie. In the early years of the 20th century he was transferred to Thebes. Here Carter met Gaston Maspero who introduced him to Lord Carnarvon. From 1914 until 1923 Carter persevered in searching the area for antiquities. In 1922 the steps leading to the tomb were uncovered. And the rest is history.

The famous curse is dismissed by most critics. It began mainly because of the sudden death just four months later of Lord Carnarvon, who was present when the tomb was opened. Carnarvon's half-brother also died in the same year, and there followed a few other deaths of those who were closely associated with the dig. Howard Carter, however, lived on for another decade, casting doubts on the curse affecting all those who disturb the tomb. The curse did not just apply to Tutankhamun but to any royal tomb.

Some years prior to this Le Queux had met the French Egyptologist Gaston Maspero at Thebes, who in turn introduced him to an old Arab. The Arab was apparently acting as an agent for the British Museum, amongst others, in acquiring antique objects not required by the Cairo Museum. During this current visit Le Queux bought a number of fine items including a string of beads, a human eye of lapis-lazuli taken from a sarcophagus, several amulets and Ushabito figures along with an alabaster jar. The prize object was a gilded mask of a priestess of Isis, dating from 1600 BC and found near Aswan. These were all packed and sent back to Hawson Court to be added to his earlier collection.

On his return he had the gilded mask displayed in a glass case. The next day upon entering the room he found the mask had fallen from its stand and smashed to pieces. He had it repaired and within a week following this calamity he suffered from financial problems and one of his servants died from a disease, and a second, Ann Bunstow, died in hospital. A relation died the following week, as did his collie dog. The next week Le Queux suffered further financial problems which resulted in him having to vacate Hawson Court. The implications are that this was connected with the disturbance of the priestess' tomb.

Le Queux said that as a result he packed off the Egyptian artefacts to the Peterborough Museum, where he thought they had been on exhibition ever since. Up until 1912 the museum was known as the Victoria Museum, but then the collections were transferred to the Carnegie Public Library. Today's museum was opened in 1931, so, with the various moves, records could have been mislaid. However, it does look as if this part of Le Queux's life may be more fiction than fact.

There was a good reason why Le Queux chose Peterborough Museum for his collection. Whilst living at Castor back in 1904 he undertook some excavations and uncovered one wing of a Roman house in his grounds. The person who accompanied him on the dig was the first curator of the Peterborough Museum. The Peterborough Museum was contacted in recent years to enquire about the collection, but they insisted they had no record of any such treasure![284]

The Ethnographic and Foreign Archaeological collections forming this museum had been divided many years earlier between Cambridge University Museum of Archaeology and Anthropology and the

---

284. Peterborough Museum Services in a letter to Geoffrey Fitzsimmons, 12 May 1994.

The Mummy's Curse 1912–1913

Horniman Museum in London. Cambridge were unable to trace any such donation. The Horniman Museum in Forest Hill likewise were unable to throw any light on the matter.

In his autobiography Le Queux says:

> I am by no means a superstitious man except in one direction, and it has been forcibly brought back to me by the recent death of my friend Lord Carnarvon ...[285]

The conclusion was that Le Queux may well have been frightened by the thought of the curse and quietly sold the items, as many did around this time.

There is a possibility that he sold off his collection to settle his payments to Luisa and the courts. Certainly his literary output had dropped, which was not helped by his involvement in serving the Government, paid or unpaid. In 1911 he published only two new books and three collections of short stories gathered together from a variety of magazines. None of these commissions probably paid very handsomely. The following year he published three new novels and reissued *An Observer in the Near East* under a slightly different title by adding *The Balkan Trouble* to the beginning.

Le Queux also 'wrote' *The Death Doctor*, being the remarkable confessions of Archibald More d'Escombe, MD of Kensington, London, selected by Lawrence Lanner-Brown. It was published by Hurst & Blackett in 1912. The story opens with a note written by Lawrence Lanner-Brown in which he explains how he came by a sealed manuscript by Dr d'Escombe, with whom he had been friends in the Devonshire town of Okehampton, and later in Kensington. He goes on to say that, having been left the manuscript, it was up to his discretion what he should do with it. So he proposed to enlist the help of his friend, Mr William Le Queux, to publish a few episodes.

Here Le Queux is blurring the gap between fiction and reality. It was some years ago that I became a founder-member of the William

---

285. William Le Queux, *Things I Know about Kings*, p 147.

Le Queux Society set up by Yvonne Vincent, nee Le Queux. Sadly I have heard that Yvonne died a couple of years ago, and although we corresponded, we only met once. On that occasion Yvonne passed me a note about a claim that *The Death Doctor* was actually ghost written by a Dr Richard Leonard Bealy Smith. The information itself had come from the daughter-in-law of his son, Leonard, via his granddaughter. So we are dealing with information from a third hand. It was suggested that it may have been written when money was tight. This, I very much doubt, as Dr Bealy Smith had been the medical officer of Eastleigh & Bishopstoke in the years prior to moving to Honor Oak.[286] On the 1911 census his occupation is that of Physician and Surgeon. Dr Bealy Smith had been born in Bridgewater in 1868 and died 25 May 1921. For his efforts, for which he got no recognition, he was paid a sum said to be £30.

This does open up the question of just how many other books could have been ghost written. In 1914 Le Queux published eight books, in 1915 it was ten, in 1916 nine and in 1917 an incredible fifteen books or collections of short stories. In this last year certainly a number could have fallen into the same category as *The Death Doctor*.

The pressing reason that may lie behind the decision for Le Queux to take on one or more ghost writers is that his financial position was becoming intolerable. For, on 30 July 1913, Le Queux was declared bankrupt in the Bankruptcy Court in London for an outstanding amount due to Luisa Le Queux of £276, dating back to 1909.[287] This, in today's terms, is approaching £90,000. Le Queux, in writing to the court, claimed that he was stuck in Brussels as he was without sufficient funds to be able to travel to London. The meeting was adjourned for a week.

Le Queux was still careful to avoid being in London where he was a well-known figure. At some point in 1913 he rented a fully furnished house in Cromer on the Norfolk coast.[288]

---

286. 1911 Census.
287. *London Gazette*, 30 July 1913.
288. William Le Queux, *Things I Know about Kings*, p 121.

The Mummy's Curse 1912–1913

On 20 August 1913 his affairs were further investigated at the London Bankruptcy Court.[289] Le Queux had surrendered to the court that day and now a preliminary investigation was being made. Mr Sidney Steadman, appearing for Le Queux, requested an adjournment as he believed that a number of his client's creditors had not yet proved their debts. Steadman was also at pains to stress that Le Queux's present predicament was in no way as a result of the falling off of any demand for his works. One of the reasons put forward for Le Queux not being able to produce more publications was his work in the Balkans for the Government. This prevented him from fulfilling some of his contracts. One of the creditors made the point that Le Queux had the ability to earn considerable sums from his writing and was confident that they would all be settled in full. Whether that included Luisa is another matter. Le Queux had always maintained that Luisa had been overextravagant. In one newspaper it was reported that Mrs Le Queux's villa in Florence had been sequestrated in settlement of a debt of her husband for £120.[290]

As the bankruptcy hearing went on the general public were told of Le Queux's various financial schemes, which included him trying to acquire a casino in Corfu, although the licence was later withdrawn. He also acquired a concession to supply Serbia with £80,000 worth of military equipment and stores, which again was cancelled, and he is said to have personally lost £1,200,[291] or close on £120,000 in today's terms.

Le Queux's bitter experience of married life was expressed in a comment gathered from one of his latter books when all the bills had been paid and the adventure over. Yet it still rankled with him.

> Marriages are said to be made in Heaven, but judging by the result of many such unions, it would seem better if Heaven interfered less. For statistics show that only one marriage out of five can be described as 'satisfactory'. That does not mean

---

289. *Dundee Courier*, 21 August 1913.
290. *Auckland Star*, 4 October 1913.
291. *The Times*, 3 November 1913.

that four out of five end in divorce or separation. It means that in one marriage out of every five do the 'contracting parties' remain faithful; in other words, love endures from marriage to death only one out of five times.[292]

On 31 October 1913 his liabilities were said to amount to £8,851, or getting on close to nine hundred thousand pounds in today's value. Of this amount, £672 was due to Luisa in respect of arrears in alimony and associated costs. With his assets at only £2,683, he was still confident of being able to pay up his debts in full. The Official Receiver did consider Le Queux's personal expenses were in part responsible for his precarious position, amounting as they did to £9,000 spent over the past three years.[293]

One of the ways out of his financial mess was to turn to the fledgling film industry. Once the initial novelty of seeing moving pictures had begun to wear off, film directors were looking to recruit accomplished writers to produce better scripts and stronger story lines. The earliest of his film connections dates from 1914 when his novel *The Invasion of 1910* was turned into a film, *If England Were Invaded*. Le Queux was credited as being the writer, but I doubt very much if he produced the screenplay, and no copy of the film is known to exist. It was produced by the Gaumont British Picture Corporation and directed by Fred Durrant, his first picture. It was released in October 1914 and starred Leo Lilley as Lt Dick Pontifex and Diana Shaw as Elsie Ashcroft, neither character appearing in the original novel. There seems to be some confusion over the actual title of the film as the IMDb has it listed as *The Raid of 1915*. According to Chris Patrick and Stephen Baister, this was the intended film title that the film company were going to use in order to perpetuate the dramatic effect of a forthcoming war, just as the original novel had done. The film was apparently finished by the end of 1913, but its release was held up by the British Board of Film Censors.[294]

---

292. William Le Queux, *Cipher Six*. London: Hodder & Stoughton, 1919, p 270.
293. *Evening Telegraph*, 31 October 1913.
294. Chris Patrick & Stephen Baister, *William Le Queux*, p124.

The Mummy's Curse 1912–1913

The hold-up of *If England Were Invaded* allowed another film based on a Le Queux novel, *The White Lie*, to be released in May 1914. It was a French production which, in the silent era, did not matter. It starred Anne Regina Badet, although credited as Madame Bartet, playing Maude Ansel, whereas in the book the character is Jean Ansel. Her co-star was Charles Decker, playing her husband, Ralph Ansel. Regina Badet was a French ballerina, born in Bordeaux in 1876, who was later to appear in another Le Queux plot.

The third film for which Le Queux is credited with providing the scenario was director George Loane Tucker's *The Sons of Satan*, taken from the novel of the same name. Produced by the London Film Productions Company, it was released in June 1915 and starred the one-time matinee idol Gerald Ames as Henry Normand. Tall, with an athletic build and with dark eyes and moustache, he went on to star in nearly seventy films, until the start of the 'talkies' when, as with so many silent stars, his career was over.

The last of the silent movies with a connection to William Le Queux was *No Greater Love*, produced by the Selig Polyscope Company and released in October 1915. Once again it starred Regina Badet, as the dancer Sadounah, alongside co-star Max Barbier. Along with Louis Mercanton, Le Queux is also officially credited as being a co-director! The 'book of the film' was published in 1917 by Ward Lock.

It is perhaps not surprising that that there is no correspondence between Le Queux and his close confidant, George Beeforth. Embarrassment over his financial affairs may have been one thing, but I hope it was because Le Queux did not want to be seen as perhaps asking for financial hand-outs. It has to be said that for Le Queux, struggling under the threat of bankruptcy, the advent of the Great War could not have come at a more convenient time. Going into overdrive, Le Queux was responsible for producing over fifty novels and collections of short stories at the rate of ten per annum, over the course of the war.

No war has ever started on the day it was declared. Resentment, animosity and fear would have been building up over time, sometimes years. Perhaps it was the launching of HMS *Dreadnought* back in 1906 that set the course for the Great War. It was certainly the same year that Le Queux published his *The Invasion of 1910*. In the immediate years that followed Le Queux continued to bang the Hun drum. Many years ago I was told that Le Queux's name was on the German Kaiser's death list. I have no written evidence to support this, but it is highly likely, given his high profile. It may also be the reason that in the later editions of *Who's Who* Le Queux described one of his recreations as revolver practice, possibly giving the impression that he carried a gun for his own personal safety.

The Great War
1914–1919

After leaving Devonshire in 1912 Le Queux appears to have used his London club, The Devonshire, as his home base. This was the address that is mentioned in the Bankruptcy Court. At some point, probably in the summer of 1914, Le Queux moved out of London and took up a year's lease on Sunbury Cottage in Halliford Road, Upper Halliford, on the Thames. This may well have been the cottage described in one of Le Queux's later books:

> By road to Beech Cottage, Lower Halliford, a little village in the Thames Valley … a pretty little cottage overhung with climbing roses, facing the river.[295]

When war broke out on the continent on 28 July 1914 Le Queux was abroad in Belgium, where the citizens had been butchered by the German invaders and a whole swathe of the country laid waste. Whether he was there on 'active service' or personal business we do not know. On his return to England, which may have been before Britain declared war on Germany on 4 August, he settled down by the Thames, or rather tried to. In the National Archives at Kew there is a Metropolitan Police file regarding Le Queux's concerns over his personal safety and the

---

295. William Le Queux, *Stolen Statesman*. London: Skeffington & Son, 1918, p 137.

If You Can Walk With Kings

safety of his family.[296] The file begins with a written overview and covers a period from 17 August 1914 until 1 March 1915.

The overview begins by stating that Le Queux was a well-known novelist who had only recently published his latest book entitled *German Spies in England*,[297] the implication being that he was a fiction writer who specialised in sensational thrillers and was therefore just being over dramatic. Shortly after the book's publication Le Queux had written a letter to the Commissioner of the Metropolitan Police at New Scotland Yard from Upper Halliford in which he mentions his interest in spies and spying. This, he claimed, may single himself and 'his family' out for possible harm.[298] Sensibly he asked if the Metropolitan Police would instruct the local constabulary at Sunbury to keep an eye on his home, in view of his high profile. The reply from New Scotland Yard advised Le Queux that Sunbury Police had been asked to do so.

Apparently a beat officer was deployed to patrol the area, but after about a week this seemed to have stopped. Was this sudden withdrawal ordered by 'someone' in higher authority in the hope that Le Queux may be silenced? After complaining to the local station the patrol was restarted, until it again suddenly ceased. In his subsequent letter[299] to the local 'Super' Le Queux mentioned having sent his servant out on the previous four days to search for a constable without success. Le Queux reiterated that he was promised police protection by the Commissioner, which is not what the letter from New Scotland Yard had actually said. Not having receiving any satisfaction Le Queux gave up with the divisional superintendent and wrote again to the Commissioner. He informed him that his house was two miles from the nearest police station and that he had no telephone and that Upper Halliford

---

296. National Archives, Kew, MEPO 3/243.
297. William Le Queux, *German Spies in England*.
298. WmLQ letter to Commissioner of Metropolitan Police from Sunbury Cottage, Upper Halliford, 17 August 1914.
299. WmLQ letter to Superintendent 'T' Division, Hammersmith from Sunbury Cottage, Upper Halliford, 15 September 1914.

was only patrolled infrequently.[300] Unbeknown to Le Queux the police had been in contact with the War Office, who appeared to have said that Le Queux had brought it upon himself by communicating with the press. Which is precisely why Le Queux was requesting police protection now!

In a letter dated 17 November 1914 Le Queux claimed that a stranger was found on his premises at two in the morning, but fortunately driven off by his dogs.[301] It was noted in the overview that no action was taken. A simple enquiry to the neighbours would have proved whether they had been awoken by dogs barking in the early hours. However, later that same day Le Queux followed up in another letter stating that a second prowler had been spotted with 'evil intent', or was it because of his private wireless station?! I don't think Le Queux endeared himself when, in the same letter, he mentions a couple of articles which would be appearing the following week in *Lloyds Newspaper* and the *Daily Mail* intending to expose the police failures.[302] This would seem a rather silly threat as it would tell anyone who really did want to do him harm that his house was left unprotected. In all he sent three letters, including one to the Commissioner at New Scotland Yard, all on the same day. So either he was genuinely scared or was being over melodramatic.

At some stage Le Queux had begun dabbling with the new-fangled radio waves which had been discovered since the turn of the century. We know he had set up his own private wireless receiving station at Sunbury Cottage. And in a newspaper report which appeared in August 1914 it mentioned that Le Queux had suggested to the Postmaster General that the other 2,000 or so holders of experimental licences in wireless telegraphy should be enrolled in a volunteer corps for the duration of the war.[303]

---

300. WmLQ letter to Commissioner of Metropolitan Police from Sunbury Cottage, Upper Halliford, 17 September 1914.
301. WmLQ letter to Station Sergeant, Sunbury-on-Thames from Sunbury Cottage, Upper Halliford, 17 September 1914.
302. WmLQ letter to Superintendent 'T' Division, Hammersmith from Sunbury Cottage, Upper Halliford, 17 September 1914.
303. *Evening Telegraph*, 5 August 1914

If You Can Walk With Kings

There is now a gap in the tirade directed to the police until February 1915.

In between this correspondence with the police we find Le Queux writing to George Beeforth, and from the tone of the letter they appeared not to have been in contact for some time.

> Sunbury Cottage,
> Upper Halliford,
> Shepperton-on-Thames
> Sep 20. 14

My Dearest Old Chappie

I was so glad to hear from you, & to know that you are all right. You must have had a wretched time!

I, too, was in Belgium at the outbreak of the war – at Dinant & Givet. I then came home to start my history. Last-week I was over in Amiens to have a look round. Next week I shall cross again for a day or two.

Our Government are now afraid that [omitted as even I feel this is still too sensitive]. One thing is certain & that is that the German bubble is finished, once & for all.

They would not believe my warnings, nor Lord Roberts' either. But the public now acknowledge we were quite right. Now that Russia has put 4½ million men into the field – or they will be there within a fortnight, I think we can laugh at the sad spectacle of the madman invested with a crown.

My history is very popular, 80,000 copies are sold each week. It is written in a more popular style than *The Times*, or *Daily Mail*, hence its popularity.[304] I am glad you are better again. I'm very overworked, & do a lot of travelling as usual. I was in Albania again in the early spring, & then over to Cairo.

---

304. William Le Queux, *The War of the Nations*. Volume 1. London: George Newnes, 1914 (part-work).

I have a little house here – an old farmhouse 300 years old modernised – but I'm only here for a year, so as to be near London & to have a pied-a-terre.

Is Fraulein with you now? What does she think of things.

The Department I joined at the War Office[305] has been very successful in searching out German spies. Two have been shot at Aldershot – though it is naturally denied. One had cholera bascilli [sic] in his possession!

Please remember me very kindly to the girls, I often see Dr Hakin, & we talk over old times, and how good you were to us all.

Write me again when you do have time, as I always like to hear from you.

And with the best of good wishes to you all.

I remain

Yours as ever

William Le Queux[306]

If you look up the number and names of foreign spies shot in this country during the Great War you will find listed about a dozen, but none at Aldershot. However another web site claims that of the thirty-one German spies arrested, nineteen were sentenced to death and ten imprisoned. In a book recently published by the Oxford University Press, according to the diary of one Annie Brunton, she recalls having heard from a friend that two spies were caught 'poisoning the water' and shot at Farnborough in Hampshire on 23 August 1914.[307] Another German, possibly a spy, was named by Le Queux as Schmitt and his address was given as the Blue Boar Inn, Aldstone, up in Cumberland. This information was communicated to the War Office at their

---

305. M.O.5 Intelligence Department at the War Office.
306. WmLQ letter to George Beeforth.
307. Catriona Pennell, *A Kingdom United: Popular Responses to the Outbreak of the First World War in Britain and Ireland*. OUP Online, 2012. NLI: Diary of Annie Brunton: Ms 13,620/2, 23 August 1914.

request[308] – more proof, if any more proof were needed, that Le Queux was much more closely connected to the security services than is generally believed.

The history book that Le Queux was writing was *The War of the Nations: A History of the Great European Conflict,* published weekly by George Newnes for 4½d. In issue number 4 is a report of the naval Battle of Heligoland which was regarded as a great victory for the British. Le Queux only wrote the first volume before Edgar Wallace took over and saw it through to the end. It was a part-work that would run for nine volumes.

Sunbury Cottage,
Upper Halliford,
Shepperton-on-Thames
Dec 26. 14

My Dearest Old Chappie

A line to send you & the girls seasonal greetings.

I was in Rouen, at the base hospital when the raid on Scarboro took place.[309] I saw in the paper that a shell fell onto your house, & I referred to the fact in my article in last weeks *Lloyds*. Curious that I predicted the raid in my book *The Invasion*, but nobody believed it then – except Lord Roberts.

I have just finished a book of exposure of German spies. It will be out in about a week.[310]

How are you? Are you still at Scarboro?

Write & let me have news of you. Your last letter was very welcome. Where have you spent Xmas, I wonder? The bombardment must have upset you. The girls do not think so highly of Germany <u>now</u>, I expect!

---

308. WmLQ letter to Director of Military Operations, MO5, War Office, London, from Sunbury Cottage, Upper Halliford, 16 September 1914, National Archives. Kew KV 6/47.
309. 16 December 1914.
310. William Le Queux, *German Spies in England*.

The Great War 1914–1919

It is a good job you took out your insurance policies.

I have spent Xmas here, but I shall be off to the Continent again soon. It is very interesting, but very fearful there.

The Times want me to go as a war correspondent with the Russians at Warsaw, but I don't relish a winter campaign. I had enough of it in Macedonia with the Servians in the Balkan war. Still it would be interesting, & I am half inclined to go.

Please give the girls the compliments of the season from me, & to you the best of good health & good fortune in the coming year.

Yours as ever

William Le Queux[311]

These last two letters show just how much Le Queux had been put under pressure. He even mentions being overworked. He had been focusing on closely following the progress of the war in order to continue writing the weekly *The War of the Nations*. Yet with sales running at 80,000 copies a week he was surprisingly replaced by Edgar Wallace. Surely this was not a decision taken by George Newnes alone. I feel he was being pushed by the War Cabinet to produce more and more books which outrightly attacked the German war effort. From the titles of his next five books there can be no ambiguity of their intentions – *German Atrocities*; *The German Spy*; *The German Spy System from Within*; *German Spies in England* and *Britain's Deadly Peril*. As he said in his last letter, this last book had been completed and within a week was expected to be out, and so it would have been on the railway book stalls by New Year, and this was all over the Christmas holiday period.

With the New Year Le Queux returned to badgering New Scotland Yard over his personal protection, at whose premises he arranged to meet a Mr Edwards. In their interview Le Queux mentioned that he had received upwards of thirty threatening letters. It was not stated whether these letters were sent to Le Queux's home address or anonymously to

---

311. WmLQ letter to George Beeforth.

If You Can Walk With Kings

a national or local newspaper or publisher. Mr Edwards' thought is that Le Queux must have imagined it. The day following the meeting Le Queux put his version of it in writing to Sir Richard Henry,[312] Commissioner of the Metropolitan Police, the essence being that the police had now agreed to take full responsibility for his and his family's protection.[313]

Mr G. H. Edwards filed a memo of his own version of what took place at their meeting and he intimated that he had not gone as far as Mr Le Queux believed. Apparently a reply confirming that this was the situation was sent, but it all reads like a fudge.

A clearly frustrated Le Queux next spoke to, and was in correspondence with, Superintendent Patrick Quinn, of the Special Branch of the CID.[314] In a remarkable letter Le Queux is seen asking Quinn if he would be willing to take over from the Home Office the responsibility for counter-espionage and, if so, Le Queux would do his utmost to enlist a number of members of the House of Lords to achieve this aim.[315] Quinn felt that if he was to proceed along these lines it would amount to disloyalty and he told Le Queux that he would be placing his letter in the hands of Sir Basil Thomson,[316] head of the Criminal Investigation Department. Nothing is heard of from Sir Basil Thomson.

In Le Queux's eyes his presence did demand police protection from possible danger from the German spy organisation. The police on the other hand felt he was over dramatising the situation and clearly felt that there was nothing that needed to be done. In a letter to Mr Lambton,[317] to whom Le Queux was well known, he mentions that only the day before he had spent nearly twenty-four hours with the Royal

---

312. Sir Edward Richard Henry (1850–1931).
313. WmLQ letter to Sir R. Henry, Commissioner of Metropolitan Police, from Sunbury Cottage, Upper Halliford, 20 February 1915.
314. Later Sir Patrick Quinn, knighted in 1919. He died in 1936.
315. WmLQ letter to Superintendent Patrick Quinn, Special Branch, from Sunbury Cottage, Upper Halliford, 21 February 1915.
316. Sir Basil Home Thomson (1861–1939).
317. Arthur Lambton, former member of Scotland Yard's Special Branch and son of General Arthur Lambton. Died 1935.

The Great War 1914–1919

Naval Air Service. He was taken in an armoured car into the Surrey hills where they witnessed signals being flashed from the Kent coast to London. Having obtained the identity of one of the signallers, whose name had previously been reported to the police, who appeared to have done nothing about it,[318] Le Queux asked Lambton to show Quinn a copy of his letter and if necessary he would produce a record of the night's events along with a half a dozen witnesses.

Le Queux finally gave up his quest for police protection with a veiled threat to publish all their correspondence which was not marked 'confidential'.[319] In this last letter Le Queux was true to his word. In an article printed in the *People*, the sub-heading is 'How the Home Office turned a blind eye to Treason-mongers and Traitors'.[320] He also laments the utter incapability of the Commissioner of the Metropolitan Police and his hopeless department in not only failing to deal with spies but not even replying to his correspondence.[321]

If the police thought they had heard the last from Mr Le Queux they clearly underestimated him.

Sunbury Cottage,
Upper Halliford,
Shepperton-on-Thames
March 18. 15

My Dearest Old Chappie

Can you find out for me the name of the Chief Constable of the East Riding, & where he lives?

I have some <u>very important</u> information to send to him regarding the spies near Hull.

---

318. WmLQ letter to Mr Lambton, from Sunbury Cottage, Upper Halliford, 24 February 1915.
319. WmLQ letter to Mr Lambton, from Sunbury Cottage, Upper Halliford, 1 March 1915.
320. William Le Queux, 'Hotbeds of Alien Enemies and Spies in the Heart of the Metropolis', *The People*, London, 28 February 1915.
321. William Le Queux, *German Spies in England*, p 55.

We have nabbed one & he was shot at The Tower of London last Thursday. Another whom I discovered, is to be <u>shot to-morrow</u> at the same place!!

You will see by the enclosed that I am still hard at work.

If Miss Kloss wants any relaxation of the order I will try & get it for her. But I expect she don't. Please give her my kindest regards & good wishes.

The same to the girls. I shall come & see you soon.

To you dear old chappie, a hearty hand shake from.

Yours old friend [sic]

William Le Queux[322]

In February 1915, the *New York Times* printed an article on a speech made by the Kaiser at Potsdam way back in June 1908 in which he announced that Germany was ready for war. It was only being mentioned now as this was referred to in Le Queux's new book *German Spies in England: An Exposure*.[323] Le Queux in his book mentioned having indeed received a copy of this secret speech. He went on to say that he drafted a manuscript based on this report and gave a copy to his friend, the publisher Eveleigh Nash, who placed it in a locked drawer in his private office. A couple of days later Nash discovered that the manuscript was missing; it had been stolen. Le Queux mentions this incident as a footnote and I am sure that if this was not true Mr Nash would have denied it. The *New York Times* said that Le Queux had handed a report to the British Government and it must still be in the archives of the confidential department.[324]

Following shortly on after this, the *New York Times* also reported that the War Office in London had forced the censor to place a ban on Le Queux's new book, *Britain's Deadly Peril: Are we told the Truth?*, which purported to expose German spies working in Britain.[325] This was a

---

322. WmLQ letter to George Beeforth.
323. William Le Queux, *German Spies in England*, p 24.
324. *New York Times*, 17 February 1915.
325. *New York Times*, 29 April 1915.

follow-up to his *German Spies in England: An Exposure*. This ban came into being on 14 April 1915 and this action was taken under the 'Defence of the Realm Act'. A few days later the *New York Times* published a two-page article enlarging on the British Government's action, although most of their article was a straight copy taken from Le Queux's book. Of Le Queux himself, the *New York Times* had accepted that he had been formerly a member of the British Secret Service.[326] It was not so much that the censors believed that Le Queux was giving the enemy information but that he was critical of the Government's handling of the outbreak of war, in total opposition to Lord Kitchener. True, Le Queux was critical of the way that Britain had relied on the use of volunteers rather than conscription, with the result that far too many men signed up who were not able to be assigned and trained and had to be turned away. Also, the pay in the services was far lower than many able men were receiving in employment, which gave no incentive to join up. This in turn led to resentment amongst those who had. This, coupled with the withheld information on just how bad the situation had become at the front, made Le Queux certain that if the true state of affairs were known to the British public they would have responded more readily.

> We have been at war for eight months and we have not yet got the men we require. Recruits have come forward in large numbers, it is true, and are still coming forward. But there is a very distinct lack of that splendid and enduring enthusiasm which a true realisation of the facts would inevitably evoke. Priceless opportunities for stimulating that enthusiasm have been, all along, lost by the persistent refusal to allow the full story of British heroism and devotion to be told.[327]

Thousands of copies of *Britain's Deadly Peril* had already been distributed and the publishers, Stanley Paul, had been prevented from

---

326. *New York Times*, 2nd May 1915.
327. William Le Queux, *Britain's Deadly Peril: Are We Told the Truth?* London: Stanley Paul, 1915, p 78.

printing further copies.[328] At the time it would seem that the official line was that the authorities were concerned that this book might inflame the Germans and result in retaliation against British subjects already interned in Germany. When finally the truth of Britain's perilous position was becoming known the ban was relaxed as the book did appear in March 1915, by which time editions of *German Spies in England: An Exposure* were then in the sixty-thousands.

The last letter I have seen which was sent from Upper Halliford was written on 1 May 1915 saying he was going to be staying with his old friend Colonel Jack Holdsworth in Hove, as he was lecturing there.[329]

An undated letter, but presumably summer 1915, was written to Douglas Sladen advising him that 'we are up here for the summer'; it was addressed from Hambleden near Henley-on-Thames.[330] With the lease at Upper Halliford now up, Le Queux was about to move permanently to the Guildford area, from where we find him writing to Douglas Sladen in July 1915. He firstly moved to The Hermitage at Guildown on the slopes leading to the Hog's Back, where he took a year's lease. The house with its three gables is still perched high above Beech Lane, a few minutes' walk from the centre of Guildford, along the River Wey.

At the suggestion of Lord Northcliffe, Le Queux now set out on a new venture which was to be a series of lectures given up and down the country on the subject of 'German Spies and Spying', partly we must say, to promote two of his most recent books, *German Spies in England* and its sequel, *Britain's Deadly Peril*. We know he had been speaking in Hove on 3 May 1915 where he graphically explained how the spies of Germany and Austria were stretched out across southern England. He said that those operating east of a line from Eastbourne to Gravesend were Saxons, one of whom was known to be an adviser to the Crown Prince of Saxony. Those operating in the Brighton to Croydon corridor were with the Hanover Army Reserve, and those east of a line from Littlehampton

---

328. *New York Times*, 29 April 1915.
329. WmLQ letter to Mr Cock, from Sunbury Cottage, Upper Halliford, 1 May 1915.
330. WmLQ letter to Douglas Sladen, from The Thatch Cottage, Hembleden, Henley-on-Thames [1915].

The Great War 1914–1919

to Uxbridge originated from Frankfort, the original English spelling of Frankfurt. On 7 May 1915 Le Queux appeared at the Music Hall, George Street, Edinburgh, with the Marquis of Linlithgow being the chairman. Two weeks later, Le Queux was speaking at Hanley, in the Potteries. Amongst the warnings given was the threat that the Germans had the intention of dropping glass bombs on London containing bacteria as part of their germ warfare campaign.[331] Running into the beginning of (4th) June Le Queux was speaking at the Pavilion in Torquay with Lord Leith of Fyvie presiding. If the meetings were anywhere near as well attended as compared to the sales of *German Spies in England*, they would be sell-outs, as copies were running at 6,000 a day. On part of a lecture circuit he wrote to George Beeforth to tell him he would be close to Scarborough, at Buxton, in a few days' time.

> The Hermitage,
> Guildown,
> Guildford
> Aug 01. 15

My Dear Old Chappie

I was so glad to get your letter yesterday.

I lead a life of which I am lecturing at <u>Buxton</u> – the Opera House – <u>at 3 o/clock on Wednesday</u> next. Staying at the Crescent Hotel. Do you know Buxton? Can you come over? I am lecturing on what I know, & what I have done through all these years regarding 'German Spies'.

I am speaking night after night throughout August, & in September I go back to the front. I am lecturing before the British Colony in Paris at the end of the month.

I do wish you could come to Buxton. <u>Do</u>.

I arrive at the Crescent Hotel at 6 on Tuesday afternoon, & lecture next afternoon.

---

331. *Manchester Evening News*, 26 May 1915.

Tell Gabrielle that I have joined the Suffragettes, she will laugh.

Also give my kindest regards to Beatrice.

I do want so much to come & see you, my dear old chappie, but my hours are taken up. I am doing my best to wake up the country & I live in railway trains.

If you can come over to Buxton wire me to the Crescent Hotel Buxton. But in any case I mean to come and [unreadable] a plate with you soon.

I have just written a new book called *The Devil's Spawn*,[332] not out yet. To you dear old chap, & to all my best love.

William Le Queux

The speech that Le Queux made in Buxton was reported in *The Times*. The reporter found some of the writings about the war and its spies 'very entertaining'. They also highlighted that a report of the speech had been previously sent to an unnamed journal, to which Le Queux had referred. The censor subsequently wrote to the editor of that journal telling him not to publish the report![333]

Whether or not George Beeforth ever saw Le Queux speaking at the Buxton Opera House we shall never know as sadly this was the last letter sent to his old friend. George was by now well into his nineties so he may even no longer have been fit enough to undertake a long journey to the Peak District. The war would have devastating effects on many friendships during the years of conflict.

Domestic problems continued to mount up when Le Queux was summoned to Feltham Magistrates Court by the Brentford Gas Company for non-payment of gas supplied to Sunbury Cottage, in September. The amount was for £4 9s 8d, but had since been paid and the case was dismissed.[334] This may simply have been a case of it being overlooked

---

332. William Le Queux, *The Devil's Spawn: how Italy will defeat them*. London: Stanley Paul, 1915.
333. *The Times*, 23 September 1915.
334. *The Times*, 28 September 1915.

as Le Queux was still heavily involved with his series of lectures. On 3 October 1915 he was due to speak at the Winter Gardens, New Brighton, followed by a talk at the Knightstone Pavilion in Weston-super-Mare.

D I Chapman

The Hermitage, Guildford

The late Lord Salisbury said:—"*No living Englishman knows more of the under-currents of Europe than Mr. William Le Queux.*"

OPERA HOUSE, BUXTON.

Wednesday Afternoon, August 11th, at 3 o'clock.

A Non-Political LECTURE:

"The German Spy Peril"

BY

WILLIAM LE QUEUX

the well-known writer, who for years, has made a careful study of the German Secret Service. His recent Books, "German Spies in England" and "Britain's Deadly Peril," have created a profound sensation, and certain of his suggestions have been adopted.

The Lecture is a Startling Exposure of Astonishing Facts and Outspoken Revelations.

Photo by Russell & Sons, Baker Street, W

Stalls, 3s.; Dress Circle, 2s. 6d.; Pit Stalls, 1s. 6d.; Pit and Upper Circle, 1s.

Plan and Tickets now ready at the Box Office.   Telephone 114.

A copy of the flyer of the series of lectures undertaken in
1915 sent to George Beeforth

The Great War 1914–1919

Le Queux was certainly staying at The Hermitage in the early part of 1916, as in a letter from there to a Douglas Smith he advised him that he would be staying at the Midland Hotel in Bradford, from where he would get a taxi over to the Saltaire Institute to give a further lecture.[335] In all, Le Queux claimed to have given 228 lectures from as far as Aberdeen in the north to Hove in the south.[336]

Apart from his new book *The Devil's Spawn*, Le Queux also wrote the preface to another spy book, *The German Spy System from Within* by an Ex-Intelligence Officer.[337] He continued with his series of spy and war books during 1916 including *The Spy Hunter, Number 70 Berlin* and *Annette of the Argonne*.

The Zeppelin raids on Britain began in 1915 when at first London was excluded. The following year Le Queux was quick to react to the circumstances, bringing out *The Zeppelin Destroyer*. In this a device is invented, based on an original German invention by Heinrich Hertz, from which it is hoped that by creating a spark this would strike a Zeppelin and cause it to explode. If that did not frighten off the Jerrys, then they had to contend with *Beryl of the Biplane*. Le Queux would later make an unsubstantiated claim, in the *Daily News*, that in 1913 he had persuaded Count Zeppelin's chief engineer to come to London with secret plans for a new airship. After a week's interrogation he was paid off and dismissed.[338]

His lecture circuit of *The German Spy Peril* continued well into the new year. In March he was at the Borough Halls in Guildford in aid of prisoners of war from The Queen's Royal West Surrey Regiment, on Saturday 4 March 1916 with Viscount Midleton presiding.

---

335. WmLQ letter to Douglas Smith, from The Hermitage, Guildford, 25 March 1915.
336. William Le Queux, *Things I Know about Kings*, p 264.
337. An Ex-Intelligence Officer, *The German Spy System from Within*. London: Hodder & Stoughton, 1915. It has been suggested by some that the identity of the 'Ex-Intelligence Officer' is Lional James. This is not a position taken by the British Library. James did write under the by-line of 'The Intelligence Offlicer', which may have led to some confusion. The true identity is not known with any certainty. Possibilities are Colonel J. E. Edmonds of the Royal Engineers or the Rev Tinsley Such, a Baptist minister from Leicestershire.
338. *Evening Telegraph*, 8 November 1921.

Le Queux began producing a series of articles written exclusively for the *Post Sunday Special*, published by D. C. Thomson's in Glasgow; an early one was entitled 'The Unknown To-Morrow'.[339] In it Le Queux literally maps out his vision of just how the German territory would be divided up by the allies after the war. At this point there would still be two years of fighting to go, although he earnestly believed it would be all over by the autumn of 1917.

Le Queux did not pass up the opportunity to remind his readers that he had actually predicted the war with Germany in his book back in 1906. In backing up his claims he mentions once again how he foretold the shelling of Scarborough and the Battle of Jutland. He's not going to let the British public forget.

His belief now was that once the cat's paw Austria fell, then Germany would have to sue for peace. One of the conditions would be to then see a much-reduced Germany compelled with the confiscation of her ports to prevent her from ever again being a major sea-power.

Le Queux went on to describe how the Allied powers sat down at the London Peace Conference and how the spoils of war would be parcelled up. To Belgium, her lands would be restored along with the Rhinelands, to be shared with France. France herself would be ceded Westphalia. Russia would be the big winners, taking most of Prussia and the Baltic ports. Italy would absorb Austria, which itself would have had its eyes on Venice, had things gone their way. Also Italy would occupy the Dalmatian coast to Sebenico. From here the remaining stretch of the Dalmatian coast along with Bosnia and Herzegovina would all become Serbia, whilst also embracing northern Albania.

The Roumanian and Bulgarian question would need extensive negotiations, whilst also taking in parts of Albania, with Montenegro retaining a foothold along the coast.

Britain, for her part, would secure the Dardanelles, as she had a greater claim over this area than the Russians. British control would safeguard the Muslim interest in Constantinople. Le Queux was

---

339. 'The Unknown To-Morrow', *The Post Sunday Special*, 24 September 1916, p 12. Not to be confused with a book of the same name published in 1910.

adamant that Britain should claim the Kiel Canal and thereby reinforce its position as the greatest sea-power in the world.

Le Queux pursued his long series of articles for the *Post Sunday Special* which began to be published from late October 1916. He states some names, some of whom can be vouched for as genuine from various sources. One of the earliest is the spy Frederick Gould, a publican from Rochester in Kent,[340] a loyal British subject with a hatred of the Germans, or so he said. When finally arrested for spying at Chatham he was found to have been born in Berlin under the name Frederick Schroder. He was sentenced to six years' imprisonment. He was the typical German spy for which Le Queux kept reminding the British public and the authorities they should be on the look-out.

Then there was the case of Karl Burgdorff. Le Queux had been contacted by a major in the British Army who needed a confidential manuscript to be typed. He had seen an advertisement for a typing agency, McLays Commercial School & Academy of Languages, in Glasgow's Buchanan Street. The college's advertisement purported to provide typists for Admiralty work, which the major believed sounded secure. On entering the college the major was surprised to find that the managing director, instead of being a Scotsman, was a German who spoke in broken English. Feeling unsatisfied, after their meeting he left and informed the police. The major also contacted Le Queux, who himself felt the matter needed personal investigation. Le Queux records interviewing Burgdorff in his top flat in Buchanan Street. After their meeting Le Queux placed on record the German's declaration that he had been interned in September 1914 and released in February of the following year following efforts made by his wife, something he had initially overlooked. Burgdorff also let slip that he had left Germany just eight days before the declaration of war. Le Queux had taken with him an unnamed witness who countersigned his findings at the time. Le Queux wanted to know why, if in 1914 Burgdorff was considered a threat to Britain, he was no longer under suspicion.[341]

---

340. 'Enemy Aliens in Scotland', *The Post Sunday Special*, 5 November 1916, p 6.
341. 'William Le Queux's Discoveries in Glasgow', *The Post Sunday Special*, 12 November 1916, p 6.

The following week Le Queux printed further revelations regarding Burgdorff. Le Queux had obviously been tipped off by one Andrew Hunter that in 1911 Burgdorff had specially led a group of Scottish freemasons to meet a German lodge in Hamburg. From Hamburg they went on to Berlin where Burgdorff seemed to be, as Le Queux states, persona grata.[342]

Four weeks after the appearance of Le Queux's newspaper articles the matter was raised in Parliament by Sir John David Rees, only to be told by the Secretary of State for Scotland, Robert Monro, that Burgdorff had been re-interned.[343] It should be pointed out that Burgdorff did reappear as principal of the college throughout the 1920s and '30s. So perhaps in this particular case Le Queux was wrong.

Le Queux now turned his attention to Herr Walter Heinricht. Heinricht was working as a musical instrument maker and owned a number of shops in Glasgow and Govan selling gramophone records. In about 1908 Heinricht married a local girl, Molly, and by then had changed his name to Walter Hendrie. Soon after the outbreak of war Heinricht or Hendrie had been interned. However, just two days before the start of the war Heinricht's elder brother and sister-in-law were both arrested in Portsmouth. It was whilst in prison that the elder brother died of what was said to be the shock of his arrest. Back in Glasgow, Walter Hendrie's wife campaigned to have him released into the care of a responsible person. This objective was ultimately achieved.

After fully investigating Hendrie's past Le Queux decided that it was time to call upon Hendrie's Gramophone Stores. Le Queux put to him a few statements that he, Le Queux, knew to be incorrect, yet Hendrie was able to correct him. Le Queux stated that this was the form of questioning perfected by the French Sûreté Nationale. Hendrie told Le Queux he had been expecting him and reasoned that it was due to the publicity aroused by his brother. On Le Queux's departure he

---

342. 'Herr Burgdorff's Masonic Trip from Glasgow to Berlin', *The Post Sunday Special*, 19 November 1916, p 6.
343. Hansard, vol. 88, 19 December 1916.

judged Hendrie not to be dangerous but wondered why a German should be treated differently to other foreign nationals.[344]

The affair of Walter Heinricht's brother, Max Power Heinart or Heinricht, has been included in an important history of MI5 by Nigel West. Heinart, along with his wife, Lina Mary Heine, was living in Portsmouth. It was discovered that Heine had been sending messages to various hotels in Germany. In May 1914 Heine made a trip to Ostend where she was followed. Evidence was found relating to Portsmouth Dockyard and in August she was arrested, along with her husband. They were held in Portsmouth awaiting deportation when suddenly she confessed, but claiming that her husband was innocent. This did not save him as he died a few months later. Although the autorities wished to release Heine she was detained on the order of the secret service until the end of the war. It was whilst she was incarcerated that Heine was in correspondence with her brother-in-law, which is how he became ultimately embroiled in the suspicion of spying. Apart from Le Queux's version of events surrounding Hendrie's involvement it seems nothing was publicly known until West's history was published in 2014.[345] However, in April 1917 Hendrie's businesses were closed down by the authorities under the Trading with Enemy Amendment Act, 1916.[346]

Le Queux, in his series of *Sunday Post* articles, questions why if 30,000 Germans had been interned, were a further 20,000 allowed to roam freely. Many of the examples he cited were men who have been seen on numerous occasions in sensitive areas along the River Clyde and in the vicinity of Rosyth, men who were, for example, employed as humble barber's assistants yet who were able to visit their home country once or twice a year.

There are cases which do not, on the face of it, threaten our national security, but of Huns who were well treated, to the detriment of natural Scots. It seemed to him that Britons living in Germany would never

---

344. 'Prussian Sells Gramophone Records in Glasgow', *The Post Sunday Special*, 10 December 1916, p 6.
345. Nigel West, *MI5 in the Great War*. London: Biteback Publishing, 2014.
346. 'Prussian Who Sold "Blighty' Records", *The Post Sunday Special*, 8 April 1917, p 3.

If You Can Walk With Kings

be treated as fairly as German nationals or naturalised subjects were in Scotland.

The Scottish public still came forth with further examples of Germans, Swiss or Dutchmen, men who since the declaration of war had been seen acting suspiciously or spotted in the same place at various times of the day or night. Le Queux was urging the security services to keep tabs on these individuals as it was more than likely that some of these men were up to no good. Whilst they remained free they presented a direct threat to our national well being.

In July 1917 there was another case, which Le Queux had briefly mentioned earlier, concerning a Glasgow boarding-house. The propriator, Heinrich Meina, had married a woman named as Annie Burley, and since 1913 they had carried on running the place together. Despite Meina's claims to have applied and paid for British citizenship, it was never granted, which made Le Queux suspicious. As a result of the publicity the Scottish Command notified all troops that the boarding-house was 'out of bounds'.[347]

Back in July 1913, Le Queux had been invited to a dinner party held in London's Mayfair by a society hostess. There Le Queux was introduced to a Dr von Kuhlmann,[348] then a councillor at the German embassy, and who later would become the German Secretary of State for Foreign Affairs. It was not long afterwards that a certain Otto Hirschberg arrived in London, who was a close friend of von Kuhlmann. Hirschberg took up rooms in Ryder Street, St James', from which he could enter daily the German embassy by a side door which led off the steps from the Duke of York's Monument and almost directly into the private rooms of von Kuhlmann.

Hirschberg was one of many aliases of Franz von Rintelen.[349] In 1915 Hirschberg had entered the United States on a false Swiss passport where his instructions were to control a vast group of spies and to sabotage

---

347. 'German's Hotel in Glasgow', *The Post Sunday Special*, 22 July 1917, p 5.
348. Richard von Kuhlmann (1873–1948). German diplomat and industrialist born in Constantinople.
349. Franz Dagobert Johannes von Rintelen (1878–1949). German naval intelligence officer.

The Great War 1914–1919

American shipping carrying supplies to Britain. Le Queux claims that amongst his many dastardly acts Hirschberg was directly responsible for the sinking of the RMS *Lusitania* on 7 May 1915.[350] Hirschberg, or von Rintelen, was arrested at Southampton on 13 August 1915 and interned at Donnington Hall[351] before being extradited back to the USA two years later. Almost unbelievably von Rintelen returned to Britain to live out the rest of his days until his death in London in 1949.

Over the course of about twelve months Le Queux had contributed a about a dozen articles for the *Post Sunday Special*, all aimed at the Scottish audience. In addition they had also printed his *Life Story of the Ex-Crown Princess of Saxony*. Many more persons were mentioned as being involved in some form of espionage; some were named and others just hinted at. Those named included Karl Ernst,[352] a hairdresser in the Kingsland Road, London, who acted as the Kaiser's 'post office'; Karl Graves, arrested in Glasgow for spying in Rosyth and along the Clyde; Herr Kirchner, whose activities in the Firth of Forth were noted, was questioned as to why he had so often watched the construction of the naval base at Rosyth; and Anton Baumberg, alias Count de Borch, who had seduced the wife of Lieutenant Douglas Malcolm. Count de Borch was shot and killed by Malcolm when he was home from serving on the Western Front. At the trial held at the Old Bailey it was claimed that Count de Borch was a dubious character and womaniser and a German spy. The jury seemed to agree as Malcolm was acquitted. Le Queux's exposé of Count de Borch came just two days after the end of the trial.[353]

Le Queux seems to have spent most of this period, up until that moment when the guns finally fell silent in France, beavering away at his desk. However, there is a letter written to Douglas Sladen from the Colwyn Bay Hotel on personalised headed notepaper in early May of that year so it is clear that at some point he must have moved from the Guildford area to north Wales. We do get some idea of his movements

---

350. 'Von Kuhlmann: German Man of Mystery', *The Post Sunday Special*, 23 September 1917, p 7.
351. Castle Donington, Leicestershire.
352. Not the Karl Ernst who was implicated in the 'night of the long knives'.
353. 'Secret Life of Count de Borch', *The Post Sunday Special*, 16 September 1917, p 7.

from this letter to Sladen[354] as he explained that he intended to remain there until August 1918, when he would then travel north to Scotland for a month, staying at Ivercauld House near Braemar, with a Canadian jute millionaire, and probably for the 'shooting'. Despite the ravages of war, for the social classes some things never changed and the 'Glorious Twelfth', with its gay house parties and days out on the hills, seems to have gone on uninterrupted. Le Queux mentioned that he would be returning from north Wales to London in middle to late October[355] then back to Colwyn Bay for the remainder of the year.

He also bemoaned the fact that he was unable to travel to the continent and certainly not able to reach Italy, and that London did not hold any attraction. Apart from being unable to travel, the war seems to have caused little in the way of disruption to him. Le Queux was in north Wales when the armistice was signed in November 1918. Yet long before the end of hostilities Le Queux had realised that the defeat of the Germans would not be the end of the matter. Like the United States General, Jack Pershing, he called for their total unconditional surrender, or the job would need doing again. In time they were both proved completely correct:

> Here lies one of the gravest perils by which our country is to-day faced, and it is a peril immensely exaggerated by the foolish peace-talk in which a section of malevolent busybodies are already indulging. It is certain as the rising of the tomorrow's sun that, when this war is over, Germany would, if the power were left within her, embark at once on a new campaign of revenge.[356]

---

354. WmLQ letter to Douglas Sladen, from Colwyn Bay Hotel, Colwyn Bay, 4 May 1918.
355. WmLQ letter to Mr Robert H. Edleston, from Colwyn Bay Hotel, Colwyn Bay, 4 September 1918.
356. William Le Queux *Britain's Deadly Peril*, p 25.

The Great War 1914–1919

Those words were written not in the last months of 1918, but in early 1915.

His own contribution to the war effort seems to be totally propaganda. In 1917, his fifteen printed books included five collections of short stories and a series of five books which claimed to be the confessions from top-ranking German officers. The first three were *The Secrets of Potsdam, More Secrets of Potsdam,* and *Further Secrets of Potsdam,* all revealed by Count Ernst von Heltzendorff, commander of the Black Eagle and late Personal Adjutant to the German Crown Prince. All these were chronicled by William Le Queux, thereby leaving the door open for these to have been ghost written and lightly edited. They were cheaply printed by the *London Mail* in hardback for a shilling each. These were followed by further confessions, *Hushed Up at German Headquarters,* this time from Colonel Lieutenant Otto von Heynitz, Principle Aide-de-Camp to His Imperial Highness the German Crown Prince in the field. It would seem that the Crown Prince's closest officers were leaving the sinking ship in their droves. Close on its heels was *Behind the German Lines,* the second series of confessions.

The final story in *Hushed Up at German Headquarters* dealt with the murder of the Russian Mad Monk, Rasputin. And late in 1917 Le Queux did indeed publish the story of *Rasputin the Rascal Monk,* recorded for the first time from official documents. Le Queux followed this up in 1918 with *The Minister of Evil,* taken from a bulky manuscript sent to him after the earlier publication.

Now into 1918, we are fed more of the same, starting with the *Love Intrigues of the Kaiser's Sons.* Then more exposé, this time of Alexandra Feodorovna by her Maid-of-Honour and confidante, the Baroness Zeneide Tzankoff, printed in *The Secret Life of the Ex-Tsaritza,* from another manuscript that had fallen into his hands. According to the book, the Baroness sent a letter to him on 16 November 1917 from France, accompanied by the manuscript. Alexandra Feodorovna was the last Empress of Russia[357] being the consort of Tzar Nicholas II. Their entire family, the last of the Romanoffs, were all executed in Tobolsk,

---

357. Alix of Hesse (1872–1918).

a mean and sordid place somewhere in Siberia. Finally, Colonel Vassili Grigorieff, the Personal Attaché of the late Tsar, reveals to Le Queux the truth, which he translated into *The Secrets of the White Tsar*.

There were two other spy stories published in 1918 in the same cheap bindings, which are amongst the most difficult of Le Queux's books to find these days. By far and away the most difficult to track down is *Bolo, the Super Spy*, published by Odhams of London. It contains the amazing confessions of Bolo the traitor as told by Armand Mejan, Ex-Inspector of the Paris Sûreté, and once again Le Queux is on hand to edit. Le Queux described Bolo as being the 'Black Force of Paris' and in many ways resembling the Russian monk, Rasputin. The other hard to find book is *Sant of the Secret Service*, being the memoirs of Gerry Sant. An even harder to find book and therefore little known is *The Life Story of the Ex-Crown Princess of Saxony* as told by herself and related by Le Queux. The reason for the scarcity of all these titles must have been because they were printed on very flimsy wartime paper.

Apart from the very real possibility of many of these books having been ghost written we know that Le Queux now took on a secretary, Mabelle Lodge.[358] Miss Lodge's duties were, apart from the business side, typing, and whether Le Queux dictated drafts of his new books directly to her or they were typed up from a manuscript is far from certain. Without her it would be almost physically impossible for one man to have kept up this tremendous output since 1914.

In his autobiography, Le Queux makes one mention of his:

> ... valued secretary, Miss Mabelle Lodge, who had typed my books for some years, and who is an outspoken critic, ...[359]

Having left north Wales, Le Queux settled back in Guildford, this time at Lavender Cottage, situated in Mount Street. This was once the old coach road leading up to the Hog's Back, the ridge of hills stretching out towards Farnham. In the garden there once stood a garden feature:

---

358. Mabelle Lodge (1888–1971).
359. William Le Queux, *Things I Know about Kings*, p 119.

The Great War 1914–1919

... grey old sundial! He recollected the quaint inscription upon it: 'I mark ye Time; saye Gossip dost thou so.' Yes, the weather-beaten old dial was there beside a lily pond with a pretty rock garden beyond.[360]

Although this quote applies to a house in Welwyn, Le Queux has transferred the sundial from his home on The Mount.

In his personal life there was at least some encouraging news. It was reported that Le Queux successfully applied for discharge from bankruptcy which had been in force since August 1913. Counsel settled for a payment of £1,247, or getting on for nearly £200,000 in today's terms, to cover his liabilities.[361]

We know that Le Queux was living with the mysterious 'Emily Elizabeth' at the time of the previous National Census taken at Buckfastleigh. However, there is no positive indication of whether they were still living together. In one of his letters to the police from Sunbury, Le Queux once again mentions 'his family', again without being in any way specific. The most significant comment direct from Le Queux comes in his autobiography when he mentions: 'my two stepdaughters'.[362]

In the same sentence Le Queux refers to the Crown Prince of Johore, in the Malay States,[363] who had two sons, Ismail and Ahmed, and that they have often been his house guests at Guildford. Both sons were Oxford educated and spent much of their time in England. Le Queux, in writing to Douglas Sladen, said that he would be unable to visit as he had the young Crown Prince staying with him for a day or so.[364] Once again, how and when, or even where, Le Queux initially became friends with the Crown Prince of Johore eludes us.

---

360. William Le Queux, *The Voice from the Void*. London: Cassell & Co., 1922, p 118.
361. *Aberdeen Journal*, 1 November 1919.
362. William Le Queux, *Things I Know about Kings*, p 119.
363. Sultan Ibrahim Iskandar Al-Masyhur ibni Abu Bakar or Sultan Ibrahim II (1873–1959). He took over as Sultan in 1960, shortly before his own death a year later.
364. WmLQ letter to Douglas Sladen, from Lavender Cottage, Guildford, 24 July 1919.

Moving from Devon may have caused Le Queux's relationship with the mysterious Emily Elizabeth to cease. However, I am fairly sure that she was the same person as one Ada Chatfield.

Ada's husband was Alfred Chatfield, who had been born in Lambeth on 7 March 1864 and was the middle child of five children. He married Ada Searle at Clapham Holy Trinity Church on 12 October 1891. She was four years his junior, having been born in Epping in 1868. Together they went on to have three children, Frances, Alfred and William. The eldest child, Frances Elizabeth, always known as 'Dolly', was baptised at St Mary's Church in Balham on 2 May 1894. Sadly her father died in June 1906. Not too sadly perhaps for Ada, as she gave birth to a second daughter, Mabel Elizabeth, on 1 September 1907. Mabel's birth certificate, however, shows no father's name. The natural conclusion is to believe that Mabel's father is William Le Queux, and the dates do tie in with his having returned from the Balkans in early December 1906. The question we cannot answer is how and when Le Queux and Ada Chatfield met in the first place.

Referring back to the 1911 census for William and Emily Kelly, we may assume that the mysterious Emily is the same person as Ada Chatfield. For Ada Chatfield does not appear anywhere in the 1911 census, nor does her youngest daughter, Mabel. It is of little consequence that none of their ages tie up on the 1911 census form as Ada was forty-three whereas 'Emily Elizabeth' is shown as thirty years of age, but then Le Queux had knocked off five years from his own age. Only one child is shown, 'Gertrude Miriam' – Frances would have been seventeen and her half-sister, Mabel, only four. However, Frances does crop up elsewhere on the 1911 census staying with her uncle, Benjamin Chatfield, his wife, Alice, and her cousins, Benjamin and Elizabeth, living at 26 Ellora Road, Streatham.[365] Her occupation was shown as a domestic servant. This leaves Mabel as a possible figure for 'Gertrude Miriam', despite her apparent increase in age.

Thus his new family now consisted of the two girls, both the natural daughters of Ada Chatfield. It has been suggested that Le Queux

---

365. 1911 Census.

adopted both girls, but with the use of the term 'stepdaughter' it is strongly suggestive that a form of marriage had taken place, not that any marriage has been traced between Ada Chatfield (or Searle) and anyone resembling Le Queux. However they would become Le Queux's stepdaughters at some point in time, whether official or unofficial. Le Queux's remaining family included his minature Pomeranians, Toby and Tweedles,[366] who were his constant companions when working at his desk.

In 2000 Yvonne Le Queux was able to make contact with Beverly Johnson, the eldest daughter of Frances Chatfield, who was living in Canada. In her letter Beverly states that her mother and her two brothers were left orphaned in about 1906.[367] However, evidence proves that only their father had died, leaving them to be brought up by their widowed mother. Some years later Frances Chatfield was said to have been 'adopted' by Le Queux as a companion for his own daughter, though tantalisingly, Beverly could not remember the child's name, but there is little doubt that this child was Mabel Elizabeth.

---

366. William Le Queux, *Things I Know about Kings*, p 120.
367. Beverly A. Johnston letter to Yvonne Le Queux, April 2000, reprinted in *Le Q Magazine*, issue 18, Autumn 2000.

Radio Days
1920–1921

If anyone had felt that, once the war was over, they would not hear from William Le Queux again, they were to be mightly disappointed. With any cessation of conflict there is bound to be a period of euphoria with the boys coming home and the country getting back to some sort of normality. Except this did not last as the Great War affected the common man, and more importantly the common woman, as no war had done before. As we have learnt, Le Queux was a supporter of Women's Suffrage and he shows in many of his books that the woman plays a leading rather than a supportative role.

Yet for Le Queux the real 'unrest' lay with the damaged but not unbroken 'Hun'. In an article published in the *Royal Magazine* in 1919, Le Queux highlighted the secret world where money held in German banks was being used to undermine Britain.

> Those behind the scenes know well that before the war every preparation was made in Berlin in case of defeat. The Wilhemstrasse long ago warned Junkerdom that the unexpected usually happened in war.
>
> It did happen, whereupon, at the moment of the Armistice, all the secret machinery of a certain unsuspected bureau in a dingy house in the Krausen-Strasse, a few doors from Donkohh-Platz in Berlin, was set in motion, and millions of marks were released from German–Swiss and German–American banks

If You Can Walk With Kings

for the financing of the Cult of the Extreme ... to create a propaganda against law and order in hated Britain.[368]

Le Queux further accused Germany of being the paymasters behind Rasputin, the spy Protopopoff and the Prime Minister, Sturmer, allowing them to betray their country and set in motion the Bolshevik revolution in Russia. He also accused Germany of its secret hand behind the unrest in Ireland, as proved at the trial of Roger Casement.

He now called upon the workers of Britain and her colonies to face an even greater problem than war itself. Only by working together, he said, can we save the Empire from the insidious Hun. In his last battle call Le Queux writes:

> Let us drop the idea of a working class, and let us be a broad-minded working nation. The sunshine of Peace is upon us. Let us at last open our eyes to the vile wickedness of the Hun plots and the sly underground workings of the Hun propaganda. The German has proved times out of number, to be the enemy of civilisation. Therefore, why should we dance to his diabolical tune any longer?
>
> Let us pay our own piper. We have done so since 1914 with all heart and patriotism. Let us continue.
>
> If Britannia is still to rule the waves ... then our working nation should hound out her traitors who are receiving Hun doles – and alas! They are in the least suspected walks of life – give them their due punishment, and keep before it that motto, which, by the way, I invented myself nearly twenty years ago, 'Britain for the Briton'.[369]

For some years now Le Queux had been experimenting with radio waves and had set up his own station in Upper Halliford. But earlier, in about 1911, he had set up a 'spark set' on Cromer cliffs close to

---

368. William Le Queux, 'Who stirs the Mud?' *Royal Magazine*, October 1919, p 463.
369. Ibid., p 464.

Runton, with the permission of the Post Office, from which he regularly transmitted news to the Cross Sands Lightship anchored in the North Sea. His masts were some ninety feet high with a double aerial some 320 feet long. Both masts and aerial were eventually destroyed in a gale.[370] Le Queux does mention allowing certain interested visitors to inspect it. Of these he thought about eight had slight accents and were spies, all of whom were interned.[371] It was only after the war, early in 1919, that he did set up another experiment, this time in Guildford. Did he select a house on The Mount just because it was an ideal place to erect an aerial? It was also within easy distance of Britain's top-secret spy headquarters at Wanborough Manor, the First World War equivalent to Bletchley Park.

Why a novelist should get caught up with wireless telephony has always intrigued me. He was not a boffin and could have had little time as he must have been constantly scribbling all day and every day just to keep up with demand. He must surely have had outside help with the setting-up and operation. So was this help forthcoming from the Intelligence Department? What Le Queux did say was that for six months, presumably in early 1920, he gave up writing to concentrate on his wireless. Then how could he have still published ten books in 1920 and another seven in 1921?

One highly likely reason Le Queux was able to keep up with supply and demand is certainly suggested by a film that was produced in Italy. Released as *I Borgia* and directed by Luigi Caramba it first appeared in October 1920. Subsequently the following year a book of the film appeared under Le Queux's name. However, Chris Patrick and Stephen Baister described 'Le Queux's' *The Power of the Borgias; The Story of the Great Film* as one of his worst books. There has to be a thought that this could just have been a hasty translation of the original storyline from Italian into English, and with Le Queux still looking for the easy buck, he agreed to have his name associated with it. As Chris and Stephen have said, the best thing about the book is the illustrations taken from

---

370. William Le Queux, 'Early Adventures in Wireless', *Radio Times*, 21 December 1923.
371. William Le Queux, *German Spies in England*, pp 85–6.

the stills of the film. Strange how the dustwrapper should have a dirty big '?' on the front cover. Perhaps even the book was asking why.

According to his autobiography Le Queux first became interested in wireless communication during his time spent in Leghorn. He records watching Guglielmo Marconi at work on one of his earlier experiments, and that he was present with the British Consul when Marconi signed an agreement. According to an article Le Queux wrote for the *Radio Times* in 1923, he actually took over the flat vacated by Marconi's mother. He claims his interest stems from those early days and we know he had a wireless installed in Upper Halliford in 1914, but it is in Guildford that Le Queux developed his skill early in 1919.

> It may be of interest to know that I was the first person to broadcast speech and music to amateurs and experimenters. This I did for one hour each evening during the first seven months of 1920 – the early days of radio-telephony.[372]

Le Queux did mention that in setting up his transmitter he received help from Captain Duncan Sinclair, later attached to the Wireless Section of the Air Ministry, and Messrs Ernest Brown and F. A. Love, both well known in the wireless world. Work on his transmitter was beset for months with problems, including the failure of his generator, after which he was on the point of giving up. The condensers were pierced and the microphone ruined. He tried replacing expensive burnt-out valves, but to no avail, except that there were reports of mumblings from his muffled call sign. Then he began to receive a message that his call sign of '2AZ' was being picked up as far away as Manchester. With further persistence the signal even reached beyond the Scottish border, finally as far away as Aberdeen.[373] Encouraged by his successful transmissions Le Queux began a series of nightly gramophone concerts from 8.30–9 and talked to those who could pick up his signal. What

---

372. William Le Queux, *Things I Know about Kings*, p 157.
373. William Le Queux, Member of the Institute of Radio Engineers, 'Early Adventures in Wireless'.

could not have helped was his worn-out gramaophone and use of scratched records!

Le Queux was a member of the Institute of Radio Engineers and was re-elected as president of the Wireless and Experiments Association and vice-president of the Radio Association. Later when he was a resident of Hastings he was honoured to be made president of the newly founded Hastings, St Leonards & District Radio Society.[374]

It is said that some time in 1925 Le Queux broadcast *Children's Hour* from a radio station somewhere on the south coast, under the name of 'Uncle William'.[375]

Sir Hugh Carleton Greene, at one time the Director General of the BBC, in writing a small biography for his *The Rivals of Sherlock Holmes*, a collection of early detective stories, mentions under the entry for William Le Queux a small collection of letters written by Le Queux to another early wireless pioneer, Mr Wallace. These letters today are kept by the Emory University Library in Atlanta, Georgia. Apart from being of interest to those knowledgeable on the subject, they cast little light on Le Queux's personal life or career. I should imagine he could be quite boring on the subject.

While Le Queux may have said he had put aside his novel writing for six months this was certainly not the case. On 7 April 1920 Le Queux agreed a contract with The Macauley Company of New York City to supply two books a year for the next five years, the contract being witnessed by his secretary, Mabelle Lodge.[376] Interestingly, seven of the books are named, probably recorded some years later after the actual titles were printed.

The seven titles were: *The Intriguers, Mademoiselle of Monte Carlo, The Stretton Street Affair, The Golden Face, The Voice from the Void, The Dangerous Game*[377] and *The Tattoo Mystery*.[378]

---

374. *Hastings & St Leonards Observer*, 12 April 1924.
375. Stories for all Moods. *John O'London's Weekly*, 20 May 1938.
376. Contract in the author's possession.
377. Also published in Britain as *Hidden Hands*.
378. Also published in Britain as *The Letter 'E'*.

If You Can Walk With Kings

One of Le Queux's stories not given to Macauley for publication in the United States was *The Elusive Four*[379] which came out in 1921. It is quite an elusive book to find in first edition, even the British Library does not have a copy, and neither was it published in the USA. Fortunately the cheap 1930 edition is plentiful albeit in a somewhat flimsy construction.

Le Queux, whilst he has always described himself as a wanderer, was about to make his penultimate move. Just when he moved is uncertain and the reason is that the Guildford electoral register for spring 1922 shows no entry for Lavender Cottage. It would appear that Lavender Cottage was renamed as West Mount, in 1921 or early 1922.[380] I have a short note from Le Queux to an autograph hunter, George Smith, on headed notpaper from Lavender Cottage, dated June 1920.[381] The last entry for Le Queux showing him living in Guildford was for the spring of 1921, for by the following year, he had again moved on. West Mount no longer exists, having been replaced by a block of flats which can be clearly seen from the top of Guildford's historic cobbled High Street.

William Le Queux pictured at the end of the Great War

---

379. William Le Queux, *The Elusive Four*. Cassell & Co., London, 1921.
380. West Mount, *Lasham's Directory*, 1922.
381. WmLQ letter to George Smith, from Lavender Cottage, Guildford, 9 June 1920.

Journey's End
1922–1927

Nineteen twenty-two proved to be the final year that Le Queux brought out a really large number of new books, his total for the year being seven, including three collections of short stories. Apart from further novels, he had by now begun working on his autobiography *Things I Know About Kings, Celebrities, and Crooks*, published in October 1923.

Some time in 1921 Le Queux had left the Surrey hills to return to London, possibly leaving his stepdaughters to remain in Guildford. Although Le Queux must have been still in London in early December 1921, a few days later he had moved to the south coast. His new home for him and his family was in St Leonards-on-Sea, at 93 Marina, occupying a flat in a narrow house with four floors and a sub-basement, facing directly onto the sea. In a newspaper interview, given late in 1924, he remarked that about three years earlier he was looking for a pied-a-terre in England. He settled on Hastings because of the sunshine.[382] There was a reference to what was certainly his new home:

> We found ourselves in an old-fashioned but very comfortable hotel on the Marina at St Leonards, our rooms overlooking the long, well-lit promenade, the pier and the sea.[383]

---

382. *Hastings & St Leonards Observer*, 25 October 1924.
383. William Le Queux, *The Peril of Helen Marklove and Other Stories*. London: Jarrolds, 1928, p 87.

Here we certainly know he shared the accommodation with both Mabel and Frances. We can date approximately his arrival on the south coast from a letter to William Robertson Nicholl[384] as 15 December 1922.[385] This was a rather odd letter in which Le Queux thanked the older man and remarked that they had never met. Why he should have been moved to write is unclear.

We find Le Queux writing from his club, the Devonshire, a letter to the editor of the *Daily Graphic*, dated 11 December 1922. It was on the subject of the origin of the fountain pen, regarded by Le Queux as a blessing to men. According to the *Encylopedia Britannica* such pens had been around since the beginning of the 18th century, which Le Queux was able to substantiate from references in several books, but he would still like to have known the name of the actual inventor.

Amongst Le Queux's novels appearing in 1923 were *Where the Desert Ends*, which I feel may have been originally written some years earlier. Also one of his more difficult titles to find is a collection of short stories about *Bleke the Butler*. Most of these stories had already appeared in the *Royal Magazine* for the second half of 1922.

Finally in 1923 Le Queux produced his own autobiography, *Things I Know About Kings, Celebrities and Crooks*. It had been a decade since the idea of an autobiography had been mooted by a publisher back in 1912. That it contained little in the way of personal details and instead concentrated on anecdotes of celebrities and socalites should not have come as a surprise as it was never promised to be anything else. However, that has never prevented it from being criticised. It was dedicated to Sir William and Lady Earnshaw Cooper, in whose own book Le Queux had provided an introduction a decade earlier. It is littered with stories, some third hand, of various people Le Queux had known over the past forty years. It would be very difficult to tie down any story to any particular date. Then in early November 1923 Le Queux broadcast on the BBC a short fifteen-minute radio programme entitled *Other Things I*

---

384. Sir William Robertson Nicoll (1851–1923).
385. WmLQ letter to William Robertson Nicholl from 93 Marina, St Leonards-on-Sea, 15 December 1922.

know.[386] Unfortunately, no script has survived and the BBC archives have no further details.

It was whilst living at St Leonards that Le Queux sought out the inventor of the television transmitter/receiver, the Scotsman John Logie Baird.[387] An early photograph shows a more than interested Le Queux peering eagerly at Baird's apparatus set up in his workshop in Queen's Arcade in nearby Hastings. Baird's move to Hastings must have only been made a short time after Le Queux took up residence in St Leonards. There was a comment made at the time that Le Queux was one of only three men who showed any interest in Baird's work. This meeting occurred less than two years before Baird was successfully able to demonstrate the capabilities of television.

Norman Sladen is mistaken in his biography when he states that in December 1923 Le Queux called upon a well-known tourist agency in London,[388] probably Thomas Cook & Son, and that this was Le Queux's first winter sports holiday. I suspect this was, in fact, a year earlier than recorded by Sladen. For in his autobiography, which was published in 1923, Le Queux mentions skiing in Mürren with Noel Mobbs the previous year.[389]

In the later edition of *Who's Who* Le Queux mentions that amongst his recreations are winter sports, listing several clubs of which he was a member – Mürren Ski Club, Swiss Alpine Club and the British Ski Association. How accomplished a skier he was is difficult to tell for, according to a newspaper report from January 1923, he suffered a mishap. He was skiing in the Bernese Oberland when he fell into a deep drift from which he was unable to free his legs. With darkness approaching and in falling snow, the situation was becoming dangerous when fortunately his shouts were heard by a guide, who came to his rescue.[390]

---

386. BBC, 3 November 1923, 7.15 pm.
387. John Logie Baird, born Helensburg 13 August 1888, died Bexhill-on-Sea 14 June 1946.
388. Norman St Barbe Sladen, *The Real Le Queux*, p 221.
389. William Le Queux, *Things I Know about Kings*, p305.
390. *Evening Telegraph*, 4 January 1923.

If You Can Walk With Kings

Back home there were more legal problems waiting for him. A committal order was made against Le Queux by the county court in Kingston-upon-Thames for an unpaid grocery bill of £7. The plantiff remarked that the novelist had recently published a new book and appeared to have enough money to allow him to go skiing.[391] I can find no follow-up to this, so assume it was paid and the matter settled.

One of the sides to Le Queux's character is his willingness to help charity when he was able. So when he was approached by the committee of the St Leonards Children's Convalescent Home, Le Queux readily agreed to give a public lecture on their behalf. It took place in the St Leonards Pier Pavilion on 22 October 1924, in the form of episodes from his recently published autobiography.[392]

One book that has never appeared was *Dr Carclew*, written under the pseudonym of 'Tufnel Traill'. It was intended to be the first of three titles agreed to be published in the United States. It is highly likely that Le Queux failed to honour his contract and this is the reason for the titles failing to appear. The three-book contract with Macaulay was signed on 31 January 1924 and witnessed by M. B. Chatfield.[393] From this can we conclude that at this time Mabel had not yet taken the name of her stepfather?

There is still much mystery surrounding the two stepdaughters of Le Queux, not helped by what was to follow. In late 1924 Frances Elizabeth Chatfield, the natural daughter of Alfred and Ada, married a Canadian, Franklin Stanley Willsie, who had been born in Ontario, Canada on 8 October 1893. On the wedding certificate Frances is married under the surname of Le Queux, but clarified as 'properly Chatfield', the ceremony taking place at the Hastings Register Office on 5 December 1924. The single address of all the parties involved is shown as 93 Marina, St Leonards-on-Sea and the marriage was witnessed by both Le Queux and Mabel Chatfield Le Queux. Franklin's occupation is shown as that of a mine owner, although he had been a house-painter,

---

391. *The Advocate*, Tasmania, 21 January 1924.
392. *Hastings & St Leonards Observer*, 11 October 1924.
393. Contract in the author's possession.

prior to joining up for the war. Franklin had only arrived in London on 21 November 1924, so the couple must have met when Franklin was serving with the Canadian Military during the Great War. Franklin had enlisted as a private in the Canadian Infantry and joined the Royal Air Force some time late 1914 or 1915, where he rose to the rank of lieutenant, having, it is said, secured a commission with the RAF with the help of Le Queux.[394] What is most mystifying is just how and when Le Queux and the young Canadian met.

Ada Chatfield had died on 15 December 1914 in the Union Infirmary in St John's Hill, Wandsworth, this being close to her home address at 66 Noyna Road, Tooting. Ada died of Phthisis Pulmonalis, a form of TB and a common cause of death. The death was witnessed by her sister-in-law, Alice, who was present at the time, and Ada Chatfield was described on the death certificate as being the widow of Alfred Chatfield. Neither Le Queux not any of her children were mentioned. Accepting his responsibilties, Le Queux must have arranged to 'adopt' Frances as well as becoming the guardian for possibly his own daughter, Mabel, around this time.

At some point Le Queux, now responsible for a grown woman and a child, must have come into contact with Franklin Willsie. Franklin in turn must have met Frances and fallen in love. He was still stationed in Britain at the end of the war as he was elected to the Royal Aero Club of the United Kingdom in 1918, having risen to the rank of lieutenant.[395] Franklin returned to Canada and by 1920 he was resident in Michigan. Frances waited for her Canadian airman to make his way in the world, when at last he was able to return for her.

Franklin and Frances, accompanied by her younger half-sister, Mabel Le Queux, all left Southampton Water on the Cunard liner *Ausonia* on 8 May 1925 bound for Montreal in Ontario, arriving on 17 May. Mabel's passage was paid for by her 'guardian', William Le Queux. Their last addresses were all shown as c/o William Le Queux, Devonshire Club,

---

394. Beverly A. Johnston, letter to Yvonne Le Queux, April 2000, reprinted in *Le Q Magazine*, issue 18, Autumn 2000.
395. *Flight*, 18 April 1918, p 422.

London. After arriving in Ontario, Franklin and Frances moved to northern Manitoba, prospecting for minerals. Franklin suffered from TB and spent the last few years in a sanatorium until he died in Victoria, British Columbia on 26 July 1933. It has been said that his illness was contracted during his war service, although his mining may well have been the cause. Frances also died in Victoria, in 1982, and is buried alongside her husband. The whereabouts of Mabel Le Queux remains a complete mystery.

Before leaving for Canada, Le Queux gave Frances as a keepsake a number of Egyptian Faience amulets which he had collected when in Egypt. On her death the collection was donated to the Bead Center in Lake Placid.[396]

There is a poignant passage in a book written after the departure of Frances and Mabel. Describing Seton Darville in *Hidden Hands* as a popular novelist, clearly a reference to himself, Le Queux writes:

> Because of his awful loneliness amid the vortex of Society he had, years before, adopted as his daughter, Rene, a little girl left penniless and alone. Upon her the strong, self-willed man showered all his affections, and petted her as his own child. But now, ungrateful perhaps for all he had done for her, she had married, and left him again with that terrible loneliness which his friends never suspected.[397]

Despite all his wanderings Le Queux never once travelled across the Atlantic, even after his young charges had effectively emigrated. If indeed Mabel was his own child, it would be the second one he had been parted from. Despite his fame and fortune, love seems to have been the one 'thing' he desired most and the one 'thing' he was unable to hang on to.

---

396. Thebeadsite.com.
397. William Le Queux, *Hidden Hands*, pp 12–13.

Journey's End 1922–1927

In a short note to his American publishers, Macauley, which was returned with the signed contract, Le Queux mentions a second pseudonym:

> 93 Marina
> St Leonards-on-Sea
> England

I hereby grant to the Macauley Publishing Company, New York, the right to use as a pseudonym the name 'Varick Vanardy' upon my non-copyrightable books which they will publish in the United States of America.

William Le Queux

March 18. 1924

The name 'Varick Vanardy' appears to be a 'House Name' used by the Macauley Company. Another American publishing company who also used house names around this time was the Aldine Publishing Company. It gave the impression that they employed many more authors than they really had. The only known author to use the name 'Varick Vanardy' was Frederick van Rensselaer Dey.[398] Dey had been born in New York City in 1861 and trained to be a lawyer, only taking up writing following an illness. He helped to perpetuate the detective character, 'Nick Carter, Detective' for Street & Smith, and Dey went on to pen over one thousand tales. Despite his considerable output he died penniless in his hotel room at the Hotel Broztell in New York, when he shot himself in the head in April 1922.[399] It would appear that the publishers now turned to Le Queux in their quest to continue the 'Varick Vanardy' name. However, for whatever reason it now seems certain that Macauley finally abandoned any plans to reissue Le Queux's earlier work under the 'Varick Vanardy' pseudoym. But Dey, like Le Queux, was a bit of a dreamer.

---

398. Frederick van Rensselaer Dey (1861–1922).
399. *New York Times*, 27 April 1922.

Le Queux followed this letter up with a formal one to his American literary agents, Messrs Brandt & Brandt of New York City:

> 93 Marina
> St Leonards-on-Sea
> England
> April 2. 24
>
> Dear Mr Brandt,
>
> This is a formal letter to say that, in accordance with my agreement with the Macauley Company, I shall in future, submit to Mr Furman four books in order that he shall pick out two 'Le Queux' books each year. Perhaps you will kindly attach this to the agreement?
>
> Yours truly
> William Le Queux

In 1924 Le Queux began to contribute a number of short articles on real crime to the first two volumes of *The Great Stories of Real Life*, edited by Max Pemberton for George Newnes. Amongst Le Queux's subjects were Landru, the French Bluebeard; Dr Crippen; Mrs Maybrick; and Rasputin, the Mad Monk. Many years later some of these stories were reissued.

At around the same time Le Queux once again tried his hand as a playwright. The result was *The Proof*, a one-act play set in Italy. A typescript was discovered in the British Library containing a number of hand-written alterations. The play was premiered at the Grand Theatre, Birmingham on 28 April 1924,[400] where it was said to have been given a splendid reception. Unfortunately Le Queux was not present as he was still on his return from the continent. Despite his absence he was not pleased with the play and had decided to scrap it and set about revising

---

400. *Hastings & St Leonards Observer*, 3 May 1924.

it. Now with a fresh and more intense plot it was retitled *The Vendetta* before being transferred to London.[401] As far as we know Le Queux, perhaps rightly, never persisted with the experiment again.

Returning to what he knew best, in a talk given by Le Queux to his local Hastings Rotary Club he prophesied that there would be a new war with Germany within two years. His warning contained talk of chemical warfare and of guns which had a range of 120 miles.[402] Had it not been for the hyperinflation in the Weimar Republic during these times it may well have happened. In the end Le Queux was proved to be right, albeit not in his lifetime. Another Le Queux prophecy was made during a series of articles syndicated during 1925, under the series title of 'The World of Wireless'.

> In 1935, we shall have radio television. It will be possible to see, as well as to hear, by radio.[403]

It was a shame that Le Queux did not live long enough to see this come to fruition only a decade later when the BBC began their transmissions from Alexandra Palace. The first broadcasts were made by the BBC in 1934 and regular broadcasts began two years later in 1936.

At the turn of the year (1924) Le Queux was back in Switzerland where the winter sports season was in full swing. Amongst the new arrivals at Mürren in 1924 were Sir Claud and Lady Schuster and William Le Queux, although whether part of the same party is not known.[404] In a letter to the press sent from the Grand Hotel in Mürren, regarding the printed criticism by a Mr D. Henry Rees of Le Queux's recent outburst on Germany being bent on revenge in the near future, Le Queux said he felt it necessary to reply and again warn against the League of Nations' recent efforts and urging them not to repeat Herbert Asquith's policy of

---

401. *Hastings & St Leonards Observer*, 21 June 1924.
402. *Hastings & St Leonards Observer*, 22 November 1924.
403. *Herts Advertiser*, 2 May 1925.
404. *Aberdeen Journal*, 31 December 1924.

'wait and see'. Le Queux made the point that several continental papers also agreed with his views.[405] Today we know he was prefectly right, but at the time we can also surmise that most civilians had not the heart or strength to consider it.

It was whilst Le Queux was enjoying his winter holiday that his old friend George Beeforth died in Scarborough, in April 1924. I have no knowledge whether anyone wrote to Le Queux breaking the sad news.

The following year Le Queux is back on the ski slopes of Mürren in Switzerland where we find him writing from the Grand Hotel. In the letter, published in his local Hastings newspaper, he responds to criticism of his latest warnings of a future war with Germany. Yet again he dismisses the argument that the last war had put an end to any German thoughts of revenge. His new-found interest in winter sports extended to his writing and also to a new love interest. In 1926 Le Queux published *Hidden Hands* featuring:

> The thick-set Englishman, smiling and care-free, was one of the most popular of English novelists, whose name was known in every country throughout the world, Charles Seton Darville. In every bookshop and bookstall on the five continents his works were sold, for they were translated into many languages, even into Arabic and Chinese. In order to obtain the correct local colour for his books he was a constant wanderer to and fro across Europe, meeting many people and having adventures in all sorts of odd corners of the Continent.[406]

At the beginning of the story Seton Darville receives a letter from Edris Temperley in which she hopes he would be coming to Wengen for the season. We know that Le Queux had been to Wengen the previous year and to Mürren in 1926, for there is an association copy of this book,

---

405. *Hastings & St Leonards Observer*, 4 January 1925.
406. William Le Queux, *Hidden Hands*, p 11–12.

Journey's End 1922–1927

offered for sale back in 1980, which was inscribed to Mrs Agabeg of Peers Court:

> To my dear friend & hostess Mrs Agabeg of Peers Court – the 'Mrs Temperley' of this book – from her grateful guest William Le Queux. Peers Court. July 1926.[407]

In the same catalogue there were a number of books all inscribed to various members of the Agabeg family including one to Enid Edris Peers Agabeg[408] from 'Tuffy Le Queux', with memoirs of Mürren. It is the only occasion that I have come across where this nickname has been used.

If there lingers any doubt that Le Queux is describing himself in the character of Seton Darville then read on:

> The British Prime Minister had once said of him that he knew more of the underworld of Europe than any living Englishman. Certainly Seton Darville turned his unique knowledge of men and matters to good account, as witness the high pitch of excitement with which his books were always written and his descriptions of places and people. Hence they sold by the hundred thousand, and brought him in a very considerable income.
>
> He was, however, a very lonely man.[409]

If we go along with the idea that Le Queux is using the mask of Seton Darville to describe his own feelings, then in the same book comes this simple statement:

> Thank God I've never loved a woman in all my life; hence I've been spared the terrible pangs of jealousy. At least I've

---

407. *Ferret Fantasy* catalogue Q38, January 1980.
408. Enid Edris Peers Agabeg, Peers Court, Aspley Guise, Bedfordshire (1897–1977).
409. William Le Queux, *Hidden Hands*, p 12.

If You Can Walk With Kings

understood that that malady is a very common and extremely painful one.[410]

It had taken him two marriages and a long-term love affair to find out. Yet he seems to have learnt little as he had now set his sights on young Miss Enid Agabeg.

At the beginning of this book I disagreed with two eminent writers on Le Queux's prowess as a novelist. However, *Hidden Hands* is a dreadful read. It starts as a spy story until the spies are blown up trying to mine the Forth Bridge midway through the book. Then it switches to a love story in which an elderly man, Seton Darville, is in love with a much younger girl, Edris Temperley. After time they become affianced, only for her head to be turned by a Swiss ski instructor. Seton then decides to have British Intelligence engage his rival for a mission to Russia with the intention of informing upon him. We can forgive Le Queux for this novel as he clearly was a much-troubled man who had once again lost a loved one, albeit a decade earlier, and now his daughter had emigrated to Canada.

Le Queux's winter sports visits were always memorable, if not always for the right reasons, for on 14 August 1925 he nearly lost his life whilst crossing the the Eiger glacier. Fortunately he was attached to his Alpine guide when he slipped whilst traversing an ice-bridge, so he was saved from falling into a deep crevasse.[411] Le Queux was at the time staying in Wengen as a guest of Mr Liechi, a director of the Jungfrau Railway. Then early in the following year, whilst he was again staying in Mürren at the Hotel Grand, his room was trashed by a group of 'Hoorah Henrys'. It must have been a serious incident as the local court awarded Le Queux damages of £80 against a Mr MacKintosh of University College, Oxford, who was with a party from the Alpine Sports Club.[412] This was a considerable amount of money. This last incident may well be the same one described by John Betjeman, although he dates it as 1924.

---

410. Ibid., p 59.
411. *Derby Daily Telegraph*, 15 August 1925.
412. *Western Morning News*, 18 January 1926.

Journey's End 1922–1927

A group of undergraduates who were staying at the same hotel formed an 'Anti-Le Queux Club', resulting in them pouring ink over him and having him trussed up like a fowl.[413]

As a result of the incident at Mürren, Le Queux makes it quite clear in a letter to a Mr Dexter, sent from the Hotel du Lac at Interlaken, that they will not be going to Mürren any more. He goes on to say that he and Miss Agabeg will be staying at the Beau Rivage in Grindelwald for Christmas.[414] Le Queux would have been 62 years of age and his companion less than half his age at just thirty. Enid Agabeg was the only daughter of Lieutenant Colonel Frank Agabeg,[415] who had served with the Indian Army before retiring to Bedfordshire. Like her father, Enid had been born in Bengal, in about 1896. After her relationship with Le Queux, it seems that Enid never married and died a spinster in a nursing home in Folkestone, Kent in February 1977. A further letter from Interlaken dated 26 April 1927[416] strongly suggests that Le Queux stayed on in Switzerland through Christmas and until well past Easter. Clearly Le Queux had no intention of returning to England in the near future. It is very doubtful that he ever did whilst he was still alive.

There an interesting letter, of which I have only seen an extract, in which mention is made of a book, *Ilidor, the Mad Monk of Russia*, by Sergei Michailovich Trufanoff. A note from Le Queux says that this was the only copy extant, being the printer's proofs, as it was suppressed before being printed.[417]

Having turned sixty in 1926, Le Queux showed no let-up in his writing. The same year saw the arrival of six new titles and the following year the number reached double figures. Included amongst this last set of titles were three separate travel guides to Mürren, Wengen and Interlaken. In the booklet on *Wengen: The Giant's Gate*, there is a picture of The Crevasse, possibly the very one that Le Queux almost disappeared into.

---

413. John Betjeman, *The Sunday Times*, 22 May 1938.
414. WmLQ letter to Mr Dexter from Hotel du Lac, Interlaken, 4 November 1926.
415. Frank Joseph Agabeg (1861–24 February 1927).
416. WmLQ letter to Mr Channon (an autograph hunter) from Hotel du Lac, Interlaken, 26 April 1927.
417. WmLQ letter to Mr Baxter from unknown location, 9 October 1926.

If You Can Walk With Kings

On 15 April 1927, Le Queux was about to enter into a contract for seven mystery or detective-type full-length novels at the rate of one every nine months, again for the north American market. The contract was duly signed by both Le Queux and his business manager, Charles Terry.

Six of the selected novels were to be: *Poison Shadows* (also published in Britain as *The Chameleon*), *The Crime Code* (also published in Britain as *Double Nought*), *The Lawless Hand*, *The Sting*, *The Rat Trap* and *The Crinkled Crown*.

Then on 30 April 1927 a contract was drawn up for the purpose of publishing five books at the rate of one per year under a pseudoym as chosen by the Macauley Company for publication in the USA.

For the last few months of his life Le Queux was domiciled across the English Channel at Ostend. Why he chose to stay there rather than return to England is uncertain. Was it cheaper to live there or was there no real reason to return, or too many reasons to stay away? Almost the last public words we hear from Le Queux are from a couple of letters addressed to 'The Editor of *The Times*', on the riveting subject of the Belgian Post Office. The first is dated 5 August 1927 and his address is given as the Grand Hotel in Knocke. In it he warns the British public of having to queue for hours just for a postage stamp or the dangers of ever having been sent a registered letter and not being in! A second letter dated 22 August 1927 was following a visit from a representative of the Belgian Ministry of Posts and Telegraphs, who had reassured him that steps were being taken to update the system. Someone at the Belgian embassy must read *The Times*.

The last contract with Macauley was destined never to be completed, for William Tufnell Le Queux died on 13 October 1927, aged 63, in Knocke-sur-Mer in Belgium.

Loose Ends

In a life where William Le Queux knew everybody and everybody knew him, he seems to have died alone in a hotel room far from home. He was staying at the Hotel Links, Avenue du Zoute in Knocke-sur-Mer, situated on the Belgian coast close to Zeebrugge, when his death occurred at two in the morning. According to the death certificate, Le Queux was pronounced dead by a local doctor, Raymond de Beir, that morning, and his body was moved to a local church.

Although he was a well-known and popular novelist, there was no national outpouring of grief. Most of the obituaries which appeared in the British national press later that same day just mentioned the salient points which could be culled from any copy of *Who's Who*, plus an odd personal tit-bit. Although there were no major events taking place on that Thursday to banish his death from the front pages, he was just simply passed over. And so his star faded.

Le Queux had been ill for some weeks when his condition turned serious. According to Norman St Barbe Sladen, Le Queux sent a telegram to his old friend Alfred Praga asking him to come and visit. On arrival at the hotel, Praga was told that the patient was too ill to see him and by the next time he called Le Queux was dead. Futhermore, according to Sladen the coffin was placed in St George's Anglican Church adjacent to the hotel – although Sladen refers to the Grand Hotel and not the Links Hotel. Le Queux's business manager, Charles Terry, at the behest of Fred Le Queux, travelled to Belgium to supervise the removal of the body and to bring it back to England, The body was conveyed back to England on 18 October 1927.[418] It was believed that Le Queux had made his wishes known that he wanted to be cremated.

The family cremation took place at Golders Green Crematorium and Mausoleum on 19 October 1927, conducted by the Rev Francis Taylor, of Bedford. The ceremony took place in front of only a few friends. His ashes were placed in a white marble urn in a niche in the Ernest George Columbarium, with the following engraved inscription:

> IN EVER LOVING MEMORY
> OF
> COMMENDATORE
> WILLIAM LE QUEUX
> NOVELIST
> WHO ENTERED INTO REST
> OCTOBER 13TH 1927, AGED 63.
> "UNTIL THE DAY BREAK."

D I Chapman

According to information from the register held at the Golders Green Crematorium, it needed permission from the Home Office for the cremation to take place in the absence of the necessary forms resulting from his death occurring abroad.

The *Western Daily Press* was able to cover the cremation in only four lines, whereas the *Morning Post* condescendingly described Le Queux as:

> An amiable and placid little man, who looked as if he caught the 9.15 from Ealing to the city every morning. His whole aspect was so utterly unromantic that it was not easy to take his personal stories of murderous adventures as seriously as politeness demanded.[419]

---

418. *Hull Daily Mail*, 15 October 1927.
419. Roger T. Stearn, 'The Mysterious Mr Le Queux', p 10.

Loose Ends

Le Queux had managed to keep them guessing right up until the end. Not a bad effort for a boy from the mean streets of south London.

There were those who thought that there had to be a more sinister end to this 'Man of Mystery'. David Stafford believed, or was told by some of Le Queux's relations, that he had been murdered by the Bolsheviks whilst working as a secret agent in Russia.[420] Their 'cunning plan' was to wait ten years before doing away with their arch enemy, or even nearly the forty years it had been since the publication of his first novel involving the Russian leaders.

His various publishers were able to keep going on the manuscripts that Le Queux had left behind, bringing out five novels in 1928. In addition there was a collection of loosely connected short stories under the title of *The Peril of Helen Marklove and Other Stories*. The title character is a business girl who gets embroiled into aiding her crooked employers with a number of car thefts. These stories alone were not sufficient to warrant a collected edition so four other stories, all with a sporting theme, were added. The last of these stories had only just appeared in the April 1927 issue of the *Sovereign Magazine*. It is a very rare book in any edition and even the British Library does not hold a copyright edition. There was an announcement that his last novel was to be seralised as *The Great International Secret* and was spread over four issues of Hutchinson's *Adventure & Mystery Story Magazine* in the summer of 1928. The trickle of books finally stopped with the publication of *The Factotum and Other Stories* in 1931.

After a decade of waiting, and just a year before the advent of the Second World War with Germany which Le Queux had rightly surmised would be realised, the first biography of Le Queux appeared. Norman St Barbe Sladen's *The Real Le Queux* was published in May 1938. One question which remains is why he waited so long. And when it came it must have been an overwhelming disappointment to many, for Sladen did no new research, only succeeding in adding the death of Le Queux to that of the novelist's autobiography. On reading the many press reviews of Sladen's biography, it would seem that most reviewers had completely

---

420. David Stafford, *The Silent Game*. Atlanta: University of Georgia Press, 1989, p 20.

forgotten Le Queux's own autobiography, published many years earlier. However, one of the more interesting reviews came from a future poet laureate, John Betjeman, writing in *The Sunday Times*. After reading the Sladen biography Betjeman felt that Le Queux had no private life at all, with his entire life acted out in the spotlight. Mind you, Betjeman also made an admission that probably applied to many other critics, in that he himself had not read a word of any of Le Queux's books![421]

The dustwrapper from Norman St. Barbe Sladen's 1938 biography

---

421. John Betjeman, *The Sunday Times*, 22 May 1938.

Loose Ends

William's brother, Fred, was to make a number of house moves over the years ending up at 15 Hanger Lane, Ealing, where he died on 19 February 1941. His effects, which amounted to only £142, were left to his widow, Lilian. Lilian lived on till she was 97 years of age, dying in Torbay in 1985.

Over the years there have been a number of thoughtful articles on various aspects of Le Queux's life, but nothing in depth that completely covered his life and career. Eighty years were lost when people who knew him well were still alive, who would have been able to contribute so much that we now struggle to find, had a biographer appeared.

In the April 1996 edition of the *Book & Magazine Collector* there appeared a short notice to the effect that a society was in the process of being formed on behalf of the author William Tufnell Le Queux. Those who were interested should contact Yvonne Le Queux at an address in Suffolk. Yvonne was the granddaughter of Fred Le Queux, but even though she was 'family' this did not mean that Yvonne knew much more about her great-uncle than the rest of us. A small society was quickly formed. I have the list of the initial members before me now, some I already knew and some I fortunately got to know. In May 1996 the first issue of our magazine appeared under the imaginative title of *Le Queux Magazine*, edited by John Humphreys, who carried on for the first year. It was subsequently taken over by Donald Campbell in 1997. The magazine did have the effect of bringing together like-minded enthusiasts to exchange ideas. Donald would almost single-handedly hold the society together until 2004 when deteriorating sight and poor health made it impossible for him to carry on. The magazine finally stopped at issue thirty-one in the autumn of 2004. Sadly both Yvonne and Donald have since died.

One of those 'like-minded' enthusiasts was Stephen Baister, who together with Chris Patrick, wrote and privately printed their own biography, *William Le Queux, Master of Mystery*, in 2007. Chris and Stephen carried forward our knowledge and along the way uncovered a few skeletons in what was a rather large cupboard.

If You Can Walk With Kings

My own effort is far from being definitive, but I hope it may encourage others to investigate amongst other things Le Queux's undoubtedly important and secret role in Britain's fledgling secret service. Who knows what secrets remain hidden in the Ministry's files somewhere in the depths of Whitehall? However, some further records may well have been lost forever as, in 1956, a Gilbert Wakefield was employed by MI5 to destroy any records deemed not worth keeping. Some of the remaining files that I have used in this book only became available to researchers in 2010. Will we need to wait until the one hundred years rule allows us to see the release of dusty files covering the whole of the 'war to end all wars', the Great War.

William Le Queux was not completely forgotten or lost from view during these latter years, although it was only through the death of a more famous and destructive spy, Kim Philby, in 1988 that part of Alistair Cooke's weekly *Letter from America* reflected back to the work of Le Queux. Broadcast by the BBC on Friday 13 May 1988 it draws on an untransmitted broadcast with U Thant, the then Secretary General to the United Nations, some twenty years earlier. U Thant admitted to Cooke that during his schooldays in Burma he remembered being the only boy never to have read Le Queux. Cooke went on to give the usual potted biography of Le Queux, whose name he incorrectly pronounced any number of times. He also claimed that Le Queux could speak Spanish, but where that came from I do not recall. In recalling Le Queux's two most famous works, *The Invasion* and *The Spies of the Kaiser*, Cooke remarks how Le Queux's 'purple prose' and 'tubthumping' had Whitehall dismissing Le Queux as a 'crackpot'. Yet despite what Whitehall may have publicly said they had noticed how the public were reacting by the sales of the *Daily Mail* and of Le Queux's books. So much so that they did set up a committee which mushroomed into the MI5 we know today. With access to the internet we all have the chance to listen once again to the late Alistair Cooke's easy delivery.

So what of Le Queux's legacy? He left us a library of well over two hundred books and many many more short stories, any number of which have not been collected or even traced. Also there were magazine and newspaper articles which at the time were syndicated to a number of Britain's local papers and in commonwealth countries across the globe. Yet what I find almost unbelievable is that only two of his books have been reprinted in recent years – both with fresh introductions, the last a reprint of Le Queux's best-seller *The Invasion* under a new title of *If England were Invaded* and printed by the Bodleian Library in Oxford. Most surely this will change with the opportunists who have jumped onto the bandwagon to take advantage of his titles which have moved into the public domain. Some of these are faithful facsimiles and others print-on-demand which quite frankly are appalling – but they do allow access to titles which otherwise could be impossible to read.

To the best of my knowledge only one of his short stories has been considered for printing in an anthology and filmed. That was 'The Secret of the Fox Hunter' which had been selected by Hugh Carleton Greene in his well-regarded *The Rivals of Sherlock Holmes* in 1970. So successful was the book that it spawned a Thames Television series which was transmitted in 1973.[422] The original print was believed to have been lost, but thankfully it has been preserved and issued as part of the second series and is now available on DVD. *The Secret of the Foxhunter* was cast with Derek Jacobi playing William Drew of the Foreign Office. The change of name to William Drew from Duckworth Drew was not the only difference, as in the final scene Drew dies of poisoning in the Hotel Terminus St Lazare in Paris. A compelling performance from Derek Jacobi brings out what humour was available.

I now believe that with the passage of time Le Queux's vital contribution to the war effort will at last be recognised. He waved the flag for Britain at a time when the population did not want to hear of war and were turning a blind eye to events abroad. Fortunately his appeals were heard and these may well have resulted in the foundation of the British Secret Service. As Rudyard Kipling once wrote: 'if you can walk with Kings – nor lose the common touch'. I believe William Le Queux did just that.

---

422. Broadcast on ITV on 2 April 1973.

General Bibliography

Colomb, Rear Admiral P. et al., *The Great War of 189–*. William London: Heinemann, 1895

Cooper, Sir William Earnshaw, *Spiritual Science: Here and Hereafter*. Introduction by William Le Queux. London: L. N. Fowler & Co., 1911

Ffoulkes, Maude M. C., *My Own Past*. London: Cassell, 1915

Patrick, Chris and Stephen Baister, *William Le Queux, Master of Mystery*, privately printed c.2007

Sladen, Douglas, *Twenty Years of My Life*. London: Constable & Co., 1915

Sladen, Norman St Barbe, *The Real Le Queux: The official biography of William le Queux*. London: Nicholson and Watson, 1938

Stafford, David, *The Silent Game*. Atlanta: University of Georgia Press, 1989

Stafford, David A. T., 'Spies and Gentlemen: The Birth of the British Spy Novel 1893–1914'. *Victorian Studies* XXIV, 4 (1981)

Stearn, Roger T., 'The Mysterious Mr Le Queux: War Novelist, Defence Publicist and Counterspy', *Soldiers of the Queen* 70, September 1992, p 9

Treloar, Sir William Purdie, *A Lord Mayor's Diary 1906–7*. London: John Murray, 1920

West, Nigel, *MI5 in the Great War*. London: Biteback Publishing, 2014

Bibliography of works by William Le Queux in the order in which they were published

Books

Guilty Bonds. London: George Routledge & Sons, 1891, serialised in *Answers*

Strange Tales of a Nihilist. London: Ward, Lock & Co. 1892. Also published as *A Secret Service*, 1896

    A Crooked fate

    On Trackless Snows

    My Friend, the Princess

    The Burlesque of Death

    Sophie Zagarovna's Secret

    By a Vanished Hand

    The Judas-Kiss

    An Imperial Sugar Plum

    False Zero

    The Mystery of Lady Gladys

    An Ikon Oath

    The Tzar's Spy

The Great War in England in 1897.[423] Illustrated by Capt. C. Field & T. S. C. Crowther. London: Tower Publishing Company, 1894. Serialised in *Answers* as *The Poisoned Bullet*

Zoraida:[424] *A Romance of the Harem and the Great Sahara.* Illustrated by Harold Piffard. London: Tower Publishing Company, 1895

The Temptress. London: Tower Publishing Company, 1895

Stolen Souls. London: Tower Publishing Company, 1895

    The Soul of Princess Tchikhatzoff

    The Golden Hand

    The Masked Circe

    The Man with the Fatal Finger

    Santina

    The Woman with a Blemish

    The Sylph of the Terror

    One Woman's Sin

    Vogue La Galere! Also published as 'My Skeleton' in *In Town*, October 1894[425]

    Fortune's Fool

    Death-Kisses

    The City in the Sky

    The Blood-red Band

    A Child of the Sun

The Devil's Dice. London: F. V. White, 1896

A Secret Service: Being Strange Tales of a Nihilist. London: Ward, Lock & Co., 1896. Also published as *The Strange Tales of a Nihilist*, 1892

---

423. 'Dedicated To My Friend Alfred Charles Harmsworth – A generous editor and patriotic Englishman – I inscribe this forecast of the coming war.'
424. For translation of the dedication – see *Le Q Magazine*, issue 24, Summer/Autumn 2002.
425. The character Rose Henault originally Valerie Henault.

Bibliography

Why I became a Nihilist

On Trackless Snows

My Friend, the Princess

The Burlesque of Death

Sophie Zagarovna's Secret

By a Vanished Hand

A Romance of the Steppe

The Velvet Paw

The Judas-Kiss

An Imperial Sugar Plum

The Confession of Vassilii

False Zero

The Fate of the Traitor

An Ikon Oath

The Tzar's Spy

The Great White Queen: A Tale of Treasure and Treason.[426] Illustrated by Alfred Pearse. London: F. V. White, 1896

The Eye of Istar: A Romance of the Land of No Return. Illustrated by Alfred Pearse. London: F. V. White, 1897

Whoso Findeth a Wife.[427] London: F. V. White, 1897

A Madonna of the Music Halls: Being the Story of a Secret Sin. London: F. V. White, 1897. Also published as A Secret Sin, 1913

Scribes and Pharisees: A Story of Literary London. London: F. V. White, 1898

If Sinners Entice Thee. London: F. V. White, 1898.

England's Peril: a novel. London: F. V. White, 1899

---

426. 'Dedicated to my Friend, Hadj Hamoud Ben Abd El-Metkoub of Gelaa, Sheikh of the Oulad Aissa, in whose company I obtained my first sight of the Waterless Areg Region of the Sahara.'

427. Dated Viale Regina Margherita, Livorno, September 1897.

The Veiled Man, Being the account of the Risks and Adventures of Sidi Ahamadou, Sheikh of the Azjar Marauders of the Great Sahara. London: F. V. White, 1899

    The City of the Seven Shadows

    A Sappho of the Sand

    The Secret of Sa

    The Three Dwarfs of Lebo

    The Coming of Allah

    The Evil of the Thousand Eyes

    The Gate of Hell

    The Queen of the Silent Kingdom

    The Father of the Hundred Slaves

    The Mystery of Afo

    The Throne of the Great Torture (also published as 'The Throne of a Thousand Terrors' in *The Strand*, July 1896)

The Day of Temptation. A Story of Two Cities. London: F. V. White, 1899

The Bond of Black. London: F. V. White, 1899

The Secrets of Monte Carlo. London: F. V. White, 1899

    The Man with the Claws

    The Suicide's Table

    The Vengeance of Mother Viau

    An Entirely 'New System'

    The Cascade of Gold

    Their Serene Ugliness

    A King's Ransom

    Rosalie

    A Matter of Millions

    The Emperor

    Her Royal Highness's Secret

Bibliography

Wiles of the Wicked. London: F. V. White,[428] 1900. Syndicated in newspapers as *Purple and Fine Linen*

An Eye for an Eye. A Mystery. London: F. V. White, 1900. Serialised in *The Argosy*

In White Raiment. A novel. London: F. V. White, 1900

Of Royal Blood. A Story of the Secret Service. London: Hutchinson & Co., 1900

Her Majesty's Minister. London: Hodder & Stoughton, 1901. American Title: *The Shadow of the Throne.* Also published as *The Secret Struggle* nd (*c.*1930). Serialised in *Woman at Home*

The Gamblers. London: Hutchinson & Co., 1901

The Court of Honour. London: F. V. White, 1901

The Under-Secretary. London: Hutchinson & Co., 1902

The Unnamed. A Romance of Modern Italy. London: Hodder & Stoughton, 1902

The Tickencote Treasure: being the story of a silent man, a sealed script and a singular secret. London: George Newnes, 1903

The Seven Secrets. London: Hutchinson & Co., 1903

The Secrets of the Foreign Office: describing the doings of Duckworth Drew of the Secret Service. London: Hutchinson & Co., 1903

   The Secret of Dr Vaux's Intrigue

   The Secret of the Black Bag

   The Secret of the Princess's Love Affair

   The Secret of the Little Countess

   The Secret of the Redwitz Plot

   The Secret of the Submarine Boat

   The Secret of the Fashoda Settlement

   The Secret of the Smoked Spectacles (also published as 'The Man with the Black Spectacles' in *Cassell's Magazine*, December 1903)

   The Secret of Colonel Holtz's Disappearance

---

428. Edition published in Bells Indian & Colonial Library dated 1899.

The Secret of a Pair of Gloves

The Secret of the Gentleman from Paris

The Secret of the Fox Hunter

The Secret of Lieutenant Villar

The Secret of a Spy in London

The Three Glass Eyes: A Story of Today. London: Anthony Treherne, 1903

The Stella Polare. Translated by William Le Queux. Two volumes. London: Hutchinson & Co., 1903. *On the Polar Star in the Arctic Sea,* by Luigi Amedeo of Savoy, Duke of the Abruzzi

The Man from Downing Street. London: Hurst & Blackett, 1904

The Closed Book: Concerning the Secret of the Borgias. London: Methuen & Co., 1904. Serialised in *Chambers's Journal*

As We Forgive Them. Being the Story of a Man's Secret. London: F. V. White, 1904

The Hunchback of Westminster. London: Methuen & Co., 1904. Serialised in *The Hour Glass*

The Idol of the Town. London: F. V. White, 1904

The Sign of the Stranger. London: F. V. White, 1904

The Red Hat. Portrait of Cardinal Guilo – Known to the Trio of Assassins as 'The Red Hat'. London: *Daily Mail,* 1904

The Mask. London: John Long, 1905

Sins of the City: a story of craft, crime and capital. London: F. V. White, 1905

The Valley of the Shadow. Illustrated by Arthur H. Buckland. London: Methuen & Co., 1905

The Spider's Eye. London: Cassell & Co., 1905

Behind the Throne. London: Methuen & Co., 1905

Who Giveth This Woman? London: Hodder & Stoughton, 1905

The Czar's Spy: The Mystery of a Silent Love. London: Hodder & Stoughton, 1905

Bibliography

Confessions of a Ladies' Man. London: Hutchinson & Co., 1905. Being the Adventures of Cuthbert Croon, of His Majesty's Diplomatic Service

    Which Contains open Confession

    Divulges a Royal Scandal

    Concerns the Betrayers

    In Which a Finger is Missing

    Recounts the Mystery of a Front Door

    Lays Bear the Love of Narcisse

    Is About a White Frock

    Is in Strict Confidence

    'Because she Loved'

    Discloses an Emperor's Secret

    Is Mainly about a Red Cravat

    Tells a Mysterious Story

    Shows the Three Pins

    Relates a Grave Peril

    Concludes my Confessions

The Mystery of a Motor Car: being the secret of a woman's life. London: Hodder & Stoughton, 1906

The Invasion of 1910: With a Full Account of the Siege of London and the Great War in England in 1897. Naval chapter by H. W. Wilson. London: Eveleigh Nash, 1906. Serialised in the *Daily Mail*

The Woman at Kensington. With four illustrations by A. Bell. London: Cassell & Co., 1906

The House of the Wicked. London: Hurst & Blackett, 1906

The Mysterious Mr Miller. London: Hodder & Stoughton, 1906

Whatsoever a Man Soweth. London: F. V. White, 1906

The Great Court Scandal. London: F. V. White, 1907

Whosoever Loveth: Being the Secret of a Lady's Maid. London: Hutchinson & Co., 1907

An Observer in the Near East.[429] Illustrated with photographs by the author and Princess Xenia of Monténégro. London: Eveleigh Nash, 1907. American Title: *The Near East.* Also published as *The Balkan Trouble: or An Observer in the Near East,* 1912

The Secret of the Square. London: F. V. White, 1907

The Great Plot. London: Hodder & Stoughton, 1907

The Count's Chauffeur: Being the Confessions of George Ewart, Chauffeur to Count Bindo de Ferraris. Chronicled by William Le Queux. London: Eveleigh Nash, 1907

- A Move on the 'Forty'[430]
- A Sentimental Swindle
- A Story of a Secret
- A Run with Rosalie
- The Six New Novels
- The Gentleman from London
- The Lady of the Great North Road
- The Red Rooster
- Concerning the Other Fellow (also published as 'The Other Man', in *Holly Leaves,* Christmas 1906)
- The Lady in a Hurry
- The Peril of Pierrette

The Woman in the Way. London: Eveleigh Nash, 1908

The Crooked Way. London: Methuen & Co., 1908

Stolen Sweets. London: Eveleigh Nash, 1908

The Pauper of Park Lane. London: Cassell & Co., 1908

The Looker-On. London: F. V. White, 1908

---

429. Published anonymously.
430. In a later edition, Greenhill Books, London 1986, this is changed to *A Move of the Bentley.*

The Lady in the Car. In which the amours of a mysterious motorist are related, London: Eveleigh Nash, 1908
- His Highness's Love Affair
- The Prince and the Parson
- The Mysterious Sixty
- The Man with the Red Circle
- The Wicked Mr Wilkinson
- The Vengeance of the Vipers
- The Sign of the Cat's Paw
- Concerning a Woman's Honour
- A Double Game
- Love and the Outlaw
- Touching the Widow's Mite

The House of Whispers. London: Eveleigh Nash, 1909

Fatal Thirteen. Being the unpublished manuscript of Charles Cayler' Lord of the Manor of Stanbourne, in Worcestershire, sold by auction after his death. London: Stanley Paul (1909)
- In Which I Make a Purchase
- Tells of a Shabby Stranger
- Describes a Good Woman
- The Hermit of the Rue Madame
- Reveals the Secret of Don Pietro
- Golden Fingers
- The Cardinal's Eye
- The Chamber of Secrets
- The Silence of Monseigneur
- For a Mere Song
- The Sign of the Black Cravat
- The Man with Three Eyes

The Man in the Red Motor Car

Within the Circle

The Spies of the Kaiser: Plotting the Downfall of England. London: Hurst & Blackett, 1909. Serialised in the *Weekly News*

How the Plans of Rosyth were Stolen

The Secret of the Silent Submarine

The Back-door of England

How the Germans are Preparing for Invasion

The Secret of the New British Aeroplane

The Secret of the New Armour-plates

The Secret of the Improved 'Dreadnought'

The German Plot against England

The Secret of our New Gun

The Secret of the Clyde Defences

The Peril of London

How Germany Foments Strife

Our Wireless Secrets

Playing a Desperate game

The Red Room. London: Cassell & Co., 1909

Treasure of Israel.[431] London: Eveleigh Nash, 1910. American title: *The Great Gold God*

Lying Lips, London: Stanley Paul, 1910

Can We Win?[432] London, 1910

The Unknown Tomorrow: How the Rich Fare at the Hands of the Poor. The Horrors of a Socialist Revolution in England in 1935. London: F. V. White, 1910

---

431. Dated Devonshire Club, London 1910.
432. Claimed to have been written and published privately by Le Queux. The book was subsequently censored and withdrawn [Reginald Pound, *The Strand Magazine*, 1891–1950. London: Heinemann, 1966].

Bibliography

Hushed Up! A Mystery of London. London: Eveleigh Nash, 1911

The Money-Spider. London: Cassell & Co., 1911

Revelations of the Secret Service. London: F. V. White, 1911. Being the autobiography of Hugh Morrice, Chief Travelling Agent of the Confidential Department of His Britannic Majesty's Government

Reveals some Personal Secrets

Reveals the Tree Traitors

Concerns the Brass Butterfly

Reveals the Mystery of the King's Messenger

Reveals the Usborne Affair

Reveals the Black Boudoir

Reveals the Velvet Hand

Reveals the Spy Pierron (also published as 'The Kid Glove' in *The Story-Teller*, November 1909)

Reveals the Perfume of Mystery

Reveals the Secret of Stana

Reveals the Story of the Cipher

Reveals the Cotton Glove (also published as 'The White Apron' in *Chambers's Journal*, May 1911)

The Indiscretions of a Lady's Maid: being some strange stories related by Mademoiselle Mariette le Bas, Femme-de-Chambre. London: Eveleigh Nash, 1911

Madame's Gentleman Friend

The Wardrobe Drawer

Little Mrs Otway

The Noah's Ark

Guilty Bonds

The Mystery of Monsieur

The Chamber of Secrets

What was in the Strong Room

If You Can Walk With Kings

Concerns Two Visitors

Contains Some Revelations

A Queer Ménage

A Peer of the Realm

Concerning Madame's Luggage

Madame and the Butler

The People at Lancaster Gate

The Balkan Trouble or an Observer in the Near East. London: Eveleigh Nash, 1912. American title: *The Near East*. Also published as *An Observer in the Near East*, 1907

The Death Doctor. Being the remarkable confessions of Archibald More d'Escombe, M.D., of Kensington London, selected by Laurence Lanner-Brown M.D.[433] London: Cassell & Co., 1912

In which There is Open Confession

In which a Lady is Concerned

In which I Disclose a Secret

In which I Earn a Big Fee

In which My Love Affair is Explained

In which I Oblige a Lady

In which a Risky Coup is Described

In which a Problem is Presented (also published as 'Ousting a Rival' in Pearson's reprint)

In which I Attend an Eccentric Patient

In which I Silence an Enemy

In which I Attend a Strange Case

In which a Patient grows Confidential (also published as 'The Golden Hoard' in Pearson's reprint)[434]

---

433. Ghost written by Dr Richard Leonard Bealy Smith.
434. All the Contents titles have been changed in the Pearson's reprint. Where these bear no resemblance to the original the alternative title is shown.

    In which Mrs Anderson's Secret is Revealed (also published as 'Mrs Auberon's Secret' in Pearson's reprint)

    In which the Avenue Road Mystery is Explained

    In which I Make a Little Present

    In which a Red-haired Lady sheds Tears

    In which I am Discovered

Fatal Fingers. With a Frontispiece by A. Gilbert. London: Cassell & Co., 1912

Without Trace. London: Eveleigh Nash, 1912

The Mystery of Nine. London: Eveleigh Nash, 1912

The Price of Power: Being Chapters from the Secret History of the Imperial Court of Russia. London: Hurst & Blackett, 1913

Mysteries. London: Ward Lock & Co., 1913

    The Red Door

    The Third Cracker

    A Matter of Millions

    The Wizard of Warsaw

    A King's Ransom

    The Little Stocking

    The Corner House

    In the Name of the Tzar!

    The Dead Man's Christmas

    The Open Eye

    The Imperial Highness

    The Hand of the Doctor

    The Fourth Finger

    The Yellow Jasmine

    The Holly Wreath

A Secret Sin: or a Madonna of the Music Halls. London: A. M. Gardiner, 1913. Also published as *A Madonna of the Music Halls*, 1897

The Lost Million. London: Eveleigh Nash, 1913

The Room of Secrets. London: Ward Lock & Co., 1913

The Maker of Secrets. London: Ward Lock & Co., 1914

The Four Faces. A Mystery. London: Stanley Paul, 1914

Sons of Satan. The Whispered Word. London: F. V. White, 1914

The White Lie. London: Ward Lock & Co., 1914

The Hand of Allah. London: Cassell & Co., 1914. Also published as *The Riddle of the Ring*, 1927

Her Royal Highness: A Romance of the Chancelleries of Europe. London: Hodder & Stoughton, 1914

German atrocities: a record of shameless deeds. London: George Newnes, 1914

The German Spy: a present day story. London: George Newnes, 1914

The War of the Nations: A History of the Great European Conflict.[435] Volume 1, London: George Newnes, 1914. Remaining volumes by Edgar Wallace.

The German Spy System from Within. Preface by William Le Queux. London: Hodder & Stoughton, 1915.

German Spies in England; An Exposure. London: Stanley Paul, 1915

Britain's Deadly Peril: Are We Told the Truth? London: Stanley Paul, 1915

The Double Shadow. A Mystery. London: Hodder & Stoughton, 1915

The Mysterious Three. London: Ward Lock & Co., 1915

The Mystery of the Green Ray. London: Hodder & Stoughton, 1915. Also published as *The Green Ray*, 1934

The Sign of Silence. London: Ward Lock & Co., 1915

At the Sign of the Sword: a story of love and war in Belgium. London: T. C. & E. C. Jack, 1915

The White Glove. London: Eveleigh Nash, 1915

---

435. Part-work published weekly. Volume One written by William Le Queux.

Bibliography

The Devil's Spawn: how Italy will defeat them. London: Stanley Paul, 1915

The Way to Win. London: Simpkin Marshall, 1916

Number 70, Berlin: A Story of Britain's Peril. London: Hodder & Stoughton, 1916

'Cinders' of Harley Street, etc. London: Ward Lock & Co., 1916

    The Double Mask

    Bluebeard's Cupboard

    The Car with the Green Lights

    The Grey Plush Hat

    The Villa Jasmine

    The Silver Claw

    The Tower of Brass

    The Noughts and Crosses

    The Subtle Hand

    The Man with a Dimple

    The Riddle of Traquair

    The Missing Thumb

    The Three Threes

The Broken Thread. London: Ward Lock & Co., 1916

The Spy Hunter, etc. London: Ward Lock & Co., 1916

    The Green Blackbird

    The Mystery of the Two Circles

    The House of Suspicion

    The Mystery of the Five Beans

    Behind Locked Doors

    The Secret of the Lonely Farm

    The Red Rooster

    The Night of the Seventeenth

    The Glass Bombs

The Man About Town: A story of society and blackmail. London: John Long, 1916

Annette of the Argonne: A Story of the French Front. London: Hurst & Blackett, 1916

The Place of Dragons: a mystery. London: Ward Lock & Co., 1916

The Zeppelin Destroyer: Being some chapters of Secret History. London: Hodder & Stoughton, 1916

The Secrets of Potsdam. London: London Mail, 1917. Chronicled by William Le Queux

    The Tragedy of the Leutenbergs

    The Crown Prince's Revenge

    How the Kaiser Persecuted a Princess

    The Mysterious Frau Kleist

    The Girl who knew the Crown Prince's Secret

    The Affair of the Hunchbacked Countess

    The British Girl who Baulked the Kaiser

    How the Crown Prince was Blackmailed

    The Crown Prince's Escapade in London

    How the Kaiser Escaped Assassination

Further Secrets of Potsdam. London: London Mail, 1917. Chronicled by William Le Queux

    The Austrian Plot to Poison the Kaiser

    The Emperor Who Was a Thief

    Frederick William's Persecution of a Countess

    How the Crown Prince Tricked the Kaiser

    How the Crown Prince was Poisoned

    The Scandal concerning the Crown Princess

    The Story of an Unlucky Flirtation

    The Story of Isa Rosenberg

    The Uncrowned King of Germany

Bibliography

More Secrets of Potsdam: Startling Exposures of the Inner Life of the Courts of the Kaiser and Crown Prince. London: London Mail, 1917. Revealed for the first time by Count Ernst von Heltzendorff, Commander of the Black Eagle, etc. Late Personal Adjutant to the German Crown Prince. Chronicled by William Le Queux

The Secret Reason the Kaiser made War

The Crown Prince's Secret Wedding

The Plot to Poison a British General

How the Crown Prince Blackmailed the Kaiser

The Kaiser's Amazing Encounter with an Actress

Another Disgraceful Escapade of the Crown Prince

The Crown Princess Defies Her Husband

The Officer Who Struck the Kaiser

Hushed Up at German Headquarters.[436] London: London Mail, 1917 Amazing Confessions of Col. Lieut. Otto von Heynitz, 16th Uhlans, Principal Aide-de-Camp to his Imperial Highness the German Crown Prince in the Field, and now detained in Switzerland. Startling Revelations of the Crown Prince's Shameful Actions. Disclosed to and edited by William Le Queux

Shameful Life of the Crown Prince at the Front

The Unmasking of a Great German Plot

Why the Crown Prince Disappeared

The Secret Coronation of the Crown Prince

Kauffmann, The Kaiser's 'Double'

The Kaiser's Plot against a Cabinet Minister

The Crown Prince's Plan to Dethrone the Kaiser

Why the Monk Rasputin was Murdered

---

436. Dated Devonshire Club, London, August 1917.

Behind the German Lines.[437] London: London Mail, 1917. Amazing Confessions of Col. Lieut. Otto von Heynitz, 16th Uhlans, Principal Aide-de-Camp to his Imperial Highness the German Crown Prince in the Field, and now detained in Switzerland. Startling Revelations of the Crown Prince's Shameful Actions. Disclosed to and edited by William Le Queux

    The True Story of the Turkish Plot

    The Peril of the Hohenzollerns

    The Secret of the Emperor Carl

    The Plot to Invade Britain

    The von Lauenstein Scandal

    The Story of President Wilson's Despatch

    Von Bissing's Stolen Document

    The Kaiser's Secret Proclamation

    The Baroness who Betrayed Germany

    The Girl who saved Lille

The Bomb Makers. London: Jarrolds, 1917

    The Devil's Dice

    The Great Tunnel Plot

    The Hyde Park Plot

    The Explosive Needle

    The Brass Triangle

    The Silent Death

Beryl of the Biplane, etc. London: C. A. Pearson, 1917. Being the Romance of an Air-woman of To-day

    The Mysterious Number Seven

    Mr Mark Marx

    The Shabby Stranger

---

437. Dated Devonshire Club, London, November 1917.

    The Thursday Rendezvous

    Concerns the Hidden Hand

    The Price of Victory

Two in a Tangle. London: Hodder & Stoughton, 1917

The Devil's Carnival. London: Hurst & Blackett, 1917

Donovan of Whitehall. London: C. A. Pearson, 1917. Originally appeared in *Royal Magazine* as *Donovan of Downing Street*

    The Secret Dispatch

    Within Four Walls

    The Hundred Sous

    The Mysterious Mission

    The Coral Crown

    The Secret of the Wilhelmstrasse

    The Princess Feo

    The Yellow Tube

    The Two Mistletoe Berries

The Scandalmonger. London: Ward Lock & Co., 1917

    The Wardale Scandal

    The Urchfont Scandal

    The Aberleon Millions

    The Painted Pages

    The Siffleur

    At Downing Street

    The Triangle Tangle

    The Hidden Voice

    The Vanity Bag

    The Hundred Stones

No Greater Love. London: Ward Lock & Co., 1917

Rasputin the Rascal Monk: Disclosing the Secret Scandal of the Betrayal of Russia by the Mock-Monk 'Grichka', and the Consequent ruin of the Romanoffs. With Official documents revealed and disclosed for the first time by William Le Queux.[438] London: Hurst & Blackett, 1917.

The Rainbow Mystery: Chronicles of a Colour-Criminologist, etc. London: Hodder & Stoughton, 1917

    Green: The Man with the Cat's Eyes

    Yellow: The House with a Golden Door

    Red: The Mancroft Studio Murder

    Blue: The Song that was Never Sung

    Orange: The Broken Cup

    Purple: The Mystery of the Purple Binding

    Violet: The Hermit of Woldersmead

    Purple: The 'Unbound Book'

The Breath of Suspicion. London: John Long, 1917

The Secret Life of the Ex-Tsaritza. Edited by William Le Queux. London: Odhams, 1918

The Stolen Statesman: Being the Story of a Hushed-up Mystery. London: Skeffington & Son, 1918

Love Intrigues of the Kaiser's Sons. London: John Long, 1918

    The Exploits of the Blind Count

    Prince Adalbert and the Telephone Girl

    Prince August-Wilhelm's Escapade in Russia

    Prince Oscar and the Jew Banker's Daughter

    Prince Joachim and the Lady's Maid

    The Crown Prince and the Ironmaster's Daughter

    How Prince Adalbert paid his Gambling Debts

---

438. Dated Devonshire Club, London, November 1917.

The Closed House in Berlin

The Crown Prince's Judas Kiss

The Catspaw. London: Lloyds, 1918

The Little Blue Goddess. London: Ward Lock & Co., 1918

The Yellow Ribbon. London: Hodder & Stoughton, 1918

The Sister Disciple: a novel. London: Hurst & Blackett, 1918

The Minister of Evil: the secret history of Rasputin's betrayal of Russia.[439] London: Cassell & Co., 1918

Bolo, The Super-Spy. Edited by William Le Queux. London: Odhams, 1918

Sant of the Secret Service: Some Revelations of Spies and Spying.[440] London: Odhams, 1918

Espionage in Piccadilly

Spying on Spies

Berlin's Secret Code

The Hidden Hand in Britain

The Perfumed Card

In the 'Personal' Column

The Elusive Van Rosen

'One of the Naturalized'

The Secret of the Perfume

The Mystery of Blind Heinrich

An Air Raid on London

The Secret of the Ribbon

How Berlin Obtains Information

The Great Submarine Plot

The Real Mr Engstrom

---

439. Dated Devonshire Club, London, January 1918.
440. Dated Devonshire Club, London, 1918.

    In a Tight Corner

    The Plot Revealed

    The Mysterious Cylinders

    Spy's Letter Deciphered

    A Message from the Herrengasse

    The Admiral's Secret

The Life-Story of the Ex-Crown Princess of Saxony. London: Hurst & Blackett (1918). Told by Herself and Related by William Le Queux

Rasputinism in London, etc. London: Cassell & Co., 1919

The Lure of Love. London: Ward Lock & Co., 1919

Cipher Six: a mystery. London: Hodder & Stoughton, 1919.

The Forbidden Word. London: Odhams, 1919

The King's Incognito. London: Odhams, 1919

The Hotel X. London: Ward Lock & Co., 1919

    The Fatal Table

    A Bit of Iron

    The Missing Countess

    The Suicide's Room

    The Great Gas Gamble

    The Slice of Lemon

    The Mysterious Monsieur

    The Cat's Eye

    The Green Butterfly

    The Tin Box

    The Stolen Toothpick

    The Prayer Rug

The Doctor of Pimlico: being the disclosure of a great crime. London: Cassell & Co., 1919. Serialised (syndicated) as *Secrets of State*

Bibliography

The Secret Shame of the Kaiser: His dastardly plots at Amerongen, disclosed by Dr Franz Seeliger, late Director of the political section of the German Ministry of Foreign Affairs, and attached to the entourage of the Kaiser in his exile. Translated and edited by William Le Queux. London: Hurst & Blackett, 1919

The Secrets of the White Tzar: The truth revealed by His Majesty's Personal Attaché Colonel Vassili Grigorieff of the Preobrajenski whom the Provisional Government of Russia allowed to accompany him into exile, who was his constant companion from the day of his abdication to the moment of his death, and who has recently arrived in London. Translated and chronicled by William Le Queux. London: Odhams, 1919

The Red Widow; or, the Death Dealers of London. London: Cassell & Co., 1920

Society Intrigues I Have Known. Astounding facts concerning prominent people. Disclosed by Lady Betty G— and chronicled by William Le Queux. London: Odhams, 1920

    The Scandal of Carew-Burroughs

    The Scandal of the Swindled Husband

    The Scandal of the 'Pearl Woman'

    The Scandal of the Jewel-Hunger

    The Scandal of the Family Skeleton

    The Scandal of the Babbling Tongues

    The Scandal of the Girl in Black

    The Scandal of the Mystic Cross

    The Scandal of the Mystery People

    The Scandal of the Poison Cup

    The Scandal of the Shuttered House

    The Scandal of the Friend of the Family

The Heart of a Princess. A Romance of To-day. London: Ward Lock & Co., 1920

Mysteries of a Great City, etc. London: Hodder & Stoughton, 1920

    The Affair of the Blue Scarabs
    The Clue of the Newspaper Paragraph
    The Secret of the Gleboff Emerald
    The Affair of the Avenue Malakoff
    The Holes in the Wall
    The Mysterious Mademoiselle
    The Affair of the Rue Therese
    The Villa Jasmin
    The Death Dealers of Deauville
    The Chauffeur and the Little Lady
    The Lady in the Case
    The Black Satin Gloves

The Intriguers. London: Hodder & Stoughton, 1920

Whither Thou Goest. London: Lloyds, 1920

No. 7 Saville Square. London: Ward Lock & Co., 1920

The Terror of the Air. London: Lloyds, 1920

In Secret. London: Odhams, 1920. Originally entitled *Secrets I have Known*

    The Secret worth Half a Million
    The Secret of the Gloved Hands
    The Secret of a Hushed-up Affair
    The Secret of the Flame-Coloured Dress
    The Secret of the Jade Beads
    The Secret of a Ladies' Man
    The Secret of the Playful Princess
    The Secret which Concerned a Lady
    The Secret of the Death Doctor
    The Secret of the Great Black Pearl
    The Secret of a Girl's Indiscretions
    The Secret of the Missing Bride

Bibliography

This House To Let. London: Hodder & Stoughton, 1921

The Open Verdict. London: Hodder & Stoughton, 1921

The Lady-In-Waiting: A Royal Romance. London: Ward Lock & Co., 1921

The Secret Telephone, etc.[441] London: Jarrolds, 1921

    The Yellow Horror

    Spiders of Society

    The Girl with the Baby Eyes

    The Blackmailer's Decoy

    The House of Disgrace

    The Adventure of the Parrot's Eye

    Whispers Among Women

    The Lonely Little Lady

    The Little Lady from Japan

    The Curtained Room

    The Episode of the Russian Sisters

    The Web and the Spider

The Power of the Borgias: The Story of the Great Film. London: Odhams, 1921

The Luck of the Secret Service, etc. London: C. A. Pearson, 1921

    The City of Evil

    The Spotted Handkerchief

    Code Number Four

    The Folies Caprice (also published as 'The Dancer at the Folies Caprice' in *Royal Magazine*, February 1912)

    The Affair of the Avenue Louise

    A Page of Secret History

    The Brown Trunk

    The Copper Clock

---

441. Dated Devonshire Club, London, November 1921. Serialised in the *Sunday Post* as *My Two Years in a Night Club*, 15 August–31 October 1920.

The Fifth Finger. A Mystery. London: Stanley Paul, 1921

Mademoiselle of Monte Carlo, etc. London: Cassell & Co., 1921

The Elusive Four. London: Cassell & Co., 1921. The Exciting Exploits of Four Thieves
- The Strange Happenings at Froyle Park
- The Montefalco Venus
- Rasputin's Crucifix
- The Man who saw Red
- The Hunchback of Piccadilly
- The Crozier of Kresevo
- The Bolshevik's Black Beads
- The Brass Button
- The Sign on the Kerb
- The Millionaire's Secret
- The Lord of Glenfayne
- The Elephant's Eye

Tracked by Wireless, etc.[442] London: Stanley Paul, 1922
- The Secret Signal
- The Voice from the Void
- The Calico Glove
- The Devil's Oven
- The Mystery Widow
- The Cloven Hoof
- The Poison Factory
- The Great Intrigue
- The Three Bad Men
- The Mystery of Berenice

---

442. William Le Queux is shown as being a member of the Institute of Radio Engineers.

Bibliography

    The Marked Man

    The Crow's Cliff

The Young Archduchess. London: Ward Lock & Co., 1922

The Golden Face, etc. London: Cassell & Co., 1922

The Voice from the Void: The Great Wireless Mystery. London: Cassell & Co., 1922

The Gay Triangle, etc. London: Jarrolds, 1922

    The Mystery of Rasputin's Jewels

    A Race for the Throne

    The Seven Dots (also published as 'The Mystery of the Seven Dots' in *Royal Magazine*, February 1922)

    The Sorcerer of Soho

    The Master Atom

    The Horror of Lockie

    The Peril of the Préfet

    The Message for One Eye Only (also published as 'For One Eye Only' in *Royal Magazine*, February 1922)

Landru: His Secret Love Affairs. London: Stanley Paul, 1922

Three Knots. A Mystery. London: Ward Lock & Co., 1922

Things I Know About Kings, Celebrities and Crooks. London: Nash & Grayson 1923

Where the Desert Ends. London: Cassell & Co., 1923

The Bronze Face. London: Ward Lock & Co., 1923. American title: *Behind the Bronze Door*

Bleke, the Butler: being the exciting adventures of Robert Bleke during certain years of his service in various families. London: Jarrolds, 1923

    The Little Old Lady with Curls (also published as 'Bleke, the Butler' in *Royal Magazine*, July 1922)

    The Girl who rang Twice

    The Mystery of the Villa Poizat

If You Can Walk With Kings

The Red Pearls

The Indiscretions of Lady Bulverhythe

A Piece of Black Ribbon

The Folly of Lady Flavia

The Closed Chamber at Cruden

A Woman's Debt.[443] London: Ward Lock & Co., 1924

The Crystal Claw.[444] London: Hodder & Stoughton, 1924

The Stretton Street Affair. London: Cassell & Co., 1924. The strange story of Hugh Garfield, related by himself and set down by William Le Queux

Fine Feathers. London: Stanley Paul, 1924

Beautiful Switzerland. Introduction by William Le Queux. Geneva Édition des "Mille et une vues de la Suisse"; sole agents for Switzerland: Naville, (1925) By Christian Meisser

The Blue Bungalow. A Mystery. London: Hurst & Blackett, 1925

The Valrose Mystery. London: Ward Lock & Co., 1925

The Broadcast Mystery. London: R. Holden & Co., 1925

The Marked Man. London: Ward Lock & Co., 1925

The Black Owl. London: Ward Lock & Co., 1926

The Scarlet Sign. London: Ward Lock & Co., 1926

The Mystery of Mademoiselle. London: Hodder & Stoughton, 1926

The Letter 'E'. London: Cassell & Co., 1926. American title: *The Tattoo Mystery*

Hidden Hands. London: Hodder & Stoughton, 1926. American title: *The Dangerous Game*

Fatal Face. London: Hurst & Blackett, 1926

The Lawless Hand. London: Hurst & Blackett, 1927

---

443. Dedicated to Ruby Grayson.
444. Dedication: 'To all enthusiasts of winter sports in Switzerland. I dedicate this Mystery of the Great Silent World of the High Alps.'

Bibliography

Blackmailed. London: Eveleigh Nash & Grayson, 1927

The Chameleon. London: Hodder & Stoughton, 1927. American title: *Poison Shadows*

The Riddle of the Ring. London: Federation Press, 1927. Also published as *The Hand of Allah*, 1914

Double Nought. London: Hodder & Stoughton, 1927. American title: *The Crime Code*

The Office Secret. London: Ward Lock & Co., 1927

Interlaken, the Alpine Wonderland. A novelist's Jottings. London: Featherstone Press, 1927

Engelberg, the Crown Jewel of the Alps. London: Featherstone Press, 1927

Wengen, the Giant's Gate. London: Camelot Press, 1927

The House of Evil. London: Ward Lock & Co., 1927

The Crimes Club: a record of secret investigations into some amazing crimes, mostly withheld from the public. London: Eveleigh Nash & Grayson, 1927

    The Golden Grasshopper

    The Purple Death

    The Man with the Squint

    The Rogue of the Rue Royale

    The Crooked Sou

    The Cloche Hat (also published as 'The Affair of the Cloche Hat' in *Hutchinson's Magazine*, April 1926)

    The Affair of the Orange

    The House of Evil

    A Secret of the Underworld

    The Elusive Clue

    The Guinea Pig's Tail

    The Great Thames Mystery

The Rat Trap. London: Ward Lock & Co., 1928

Concerning This Woman. London: George Newnes, 1928

The Secret Formula. London: Ward Lock & Co., 1928

The Sting. London: Hodder & Stoughton, 1928

The Peril of Helen Marklove and Other Stories. London: Jarrolds, 1928

    The Peril of Helen Marklove

    I The Wizard of Westminster

    II The Knights of the Night

    III The Gripping Claw

    IV The Dangerous Game

    V The Sign of the Laughing Cat

    VI The Polite Monsieur

    Down Tack!

    The Duck's Egg

    Tally Ho!

    Love's Luck

Twice Tried. London: Hurst & Blackett, 1928. Serialised as *Tried Twice – The Great International Secret, Hutchinson's Adventure & Mystery Story Magazine,* June, July, August & September, 1928

The Crinkled Crown. London: Ward Lock & Co., 1929

The Amazing Count. London: Ward Lock & Co., 1929

The Golden Three. London: Ward Lock & Co., 1930

Scandals of Society. London: Modern Publishing, 1930

The Secret Struggle. London: Hurst & Blackett, 1930. Also published as *His Majesty's Minister,* 1901

The Foreign Spy. London: Hurst & Blackett, 1930

The Factotum and Other Stories. London: Ward Lock & Co., 1931

    The Factotum

    Secrets of State

    The Mystery Man

    The Barrier

Bibliography

    The Double Cross

    The Lost Key

Mysteries of a Great City. London: Mellifont Press, 1933. Previously published as *Mysteries of a Great City*, 1920

    The Affair of the Blue Scarabs

    The Clue of the Newspaper Paragraph

    The Secret of the Gleboff Emerald

    The Affair of the Avenue Malakoff

    The Holes in the Wall

More Mysteries of a Great City. London: Mellifont Press, 1934. Previously published as *Mysteries of a Great City*, 1920

    The Affair of the Rue Therese

    The Death Dealers of Deauville

    The Chauffeur and the Little Lady

    The Lady in the Case

    The Black Satin Gloves

The Battle of Royston. Royston: Ellisons' Editions, 1984. Taken from *The Invasion of 1910*

The Spies of the Kaiser. With introduction by Nicholas Hiley. London: Frank Cass, 1996

The Great War in England in 1897. With introduction by George Locke. London: Routledge Thoemmes, 1998

If England Were Invaded. With introduction by Mike Webb. Oxford: Bodleian Library, 2014. Previously published as *The Invasion of 1910*

Dubious Titles

A Demon's Shadow. Advertised to appear in *The Gossip* for 1888

The Idol of the Hour. Advertised in a newspaper as 'nearing completion' *c.*1893

A Woman's Enchantment. Title given to a story serialised in a newspaper, 1908

The Ambassador. Manuscript held by A. P. Watt.

A Child Expert. By Miss Edith M. Pegler & Miss C. E. Thornhill. An impression of the scenes by William Le Queux. Umpire Publishing. *c.*1915. Never seen – seems to be a view of 'The Brides in the Bath Murders'

The Hornet's Nest. Unpublished manuscript held by Denver Public Library

Short Stories

This list is by far the most extensive seen but is known to be far from complete. Even Le Queux himself once commented on having thirty short stories appearing in various magazines over one Christmas period. Some of those listed may have subsequently appeared under an alternative title when published as part of a collection.

Where an appearance in a provincial newspaper is indicated, this usually means the story has been syndicated to a group of papers. Earlier appearances may therefore eventually be established.

The author would like to hear from anyone who has knowledge of uncovered short stories or who can suggest an alternative appearance. Would they please contact him at dichapman9@ntlworld.com

La Pipe Casse,[445] *La Petit Journal*

Tracked, 1885

Cent Per Cent, 1885

A Temple of Justice, *Middlesex Chronicle,* 31 October 1885

An Alpine Flower, *Middlesex Chronicle,* 26 December 1885

Double Ruin, *Middlesex Chronicle,* 16 January 1886

Returned from the Dead, *Middlesex Chronicle,* 23 January 1886

---

445. William Le Queux, *Things I Know about Kings,* p 162.

Bibliography

The Ace of Trumps, *Middlesex Chronicle*, 30 January 1886

The Lake Mystery, *Middlesex Chronicle*, 15 May/5 June 1886

A Demon in Muslin, *Middlesex Chronicle*, 31 July 1886

Raising the Wind, *Middlesex Chronicle*, 21 August 1886

A Romantic Match, *Middlesex Chronicle*, 9 October 1886

Sinned Against, *Middlesex Chronicle*, 25 December 1886/5 February 1887

A Policeman's Story, *Middlesex Chronicle*, 9 April 1887

The Old Musician, *Penny Illustrated*, 31 December 1887

The Small Packet, *Every Week*, 20 June 1888

A Phantom Wife, *Nottinghamshire Guardian*, 24 December 1891

The Siren of St Petersburg, *Penny Illustrated*, 31 December 1892

The Man with the Fatal Finger, *Beeton's Christmas Annual*, 1892

Condemned to Silence, *Home Sweet Home*, circa May 1893

The Mystery of the Great Seal, *Answers*, 20 May 1893

A Perfect Adventuress, *Hull Daily Mail*, 17 June 1893

A Drama in Wax, *Piccadilly*, 28 September 1893

In Petticoat and Slippers, *Piccadilly*, 28 September 1893

Due North by Skyd, *Piccadilly*, 5 October 1893

Prince Orlovski's Secret, *Piccadilly*, 12 October 1893

In The Name of the Tzar!, *Cheshire Observer*, 12 May 1894

My Skeleton, *In Town*, October 1894

The Severed Hand, *Penny Illustrated*, 26 January 1895

The City in the Sky, *Windsor Magazine*, June 1895

The Sylph of the Terror, *The Wave*, 23 November 1895

The Throne of a Thousand Terrors, *Strand Magazine*, July 1896

The Accursed City, *Newcastle Courant*, 14 November 1896

The Wizard of Warsaw, *Canterbury Times*, December 1897

The City of the Seven Shadows, *The Idler*, October 1897

A Sappho of the Sand, *The Idler*, November 1897

If You Can Walk With Kings

The Secret of Sa, *The Idler*, December 1897

The Three Dwarfs of Lebo, *The Idler*, January 1898

The Coming of Allah, *The Idler*, February 1898

The Evil of the Thousand Eyes, *The Idler*, March 1898

The Secret of Two Emperors, *Pocket Magazine*, October 1898

The Man with the Claws, *Cassell's Magazine*, December 1898

The Vengeance of Mother Viau, *Cassell's Magazine*, January 1899

An Entirely 'New System', *Cassell's Magazine*, February 1899

The Cascade of Gold, *Cassell's Magazine*, March 1899

Their Serene Ugliness, *Cassell's Magazine*, April 1899

The Hermit of the Rue Madame, *Ainslee's Magazine*, April 1899

The Suicide's Table, *Cassell's Magazine*, May 1899

The Brothers of the Wolf, *Chambers's Journal*, 1 July 1899

The Prime Minister's Coup, *Pearson's Magazine*, July 1899

Under the White Ensign, *Penny Illustrated*, 2 September 1899

The Daughter of the Forty, *Harmsworth's Magazine*, October 1899

The Third Finger, *Sunderland Daily Echo*, 14 December 1899

A Matter of Millions, *Leeds Times*, 16 December 1899

Her Royal Highness's Secret, 1899

Chiffonette, *Ainslee's Magazine*, January 1900

The Nun of Moret, *Pearson's Magazine*, February 1900

The Man with Three Eyes, *Junior Munsey*, July 1900

The Shadow of the Throne, *Woman at Home*, July 1900,

The Emperor's Savoir, *Sunday Strand*, 1900

The Sign of the Seven Sins, *Lippincott's Magazine*, August 1900

The Kiss of Clo-Clo, *Evening Post*, 24 August 1900

The Game of Love, *Cassell's Magazine*, December 1900

The Three Pins, *The Woman at Home*, 1900

A Secret State, *The Woman at Home*, 1900

Bibliography

The Sign of the Black Cravat, *Sunday Strand*, February 1901

A Forest Tragedy, *Angus Evening Post*, 25 February 1901

The Image Maker, *Lippincott's Magazine*, July 1901

The Red Door, *Christmas Chronicle*, December 1901

Mr Theophilus Dixon Tells His Thrilling Adventure, *Peterborough Advertiser*, 21 December 1901

The Dead Man's Christmas, *Peterborough & Huntingdonshire Standard*, 7 December 1902

The Holly Wreath, *Peterborough & Huntingdonshire Standard*, 27 December 1902

A Man with the Black Spectacles, *Cassell's Magazine*, December 1903

The Cardinal's Eye: The Chamber of Secrets, *The Realm*, April 1904

The Cardinal's Eye: An Intrigue of the Countess, *The Realm*, May 1904

The Cardinal's Eye: The Silence of Monseigneur, *The Realm*, June 1904

The Avengers, *Cassell's Magazine*, June 1904

The Betrayer, *The Realm*, July 1904

The Lady of the Great North Road, *Cassell's Annual*, 1904

The Five Mistletoe Berries, *Christmas Chronicle*, December 1904

The Spider's Eye, *Popular Magazine*, December 1904

Fairest Among Women,[446] *Ideas*, 25 March 1905

The Silent Stranger, *The Graphic*, Summer 1905

The Secret of Friar Henry, *London Magazine*, August 1905

The Scarlet Motor, *Canterbury Times*, December 1905

A Move on the 'Forty', *Cassell's Magazine*, June 1906

A Sentimental Swindle, *Cassell's Magazine*, July 1906

The Fatal Finger, *Monthly Story Magazine*, July 1906

The Story of a Secret, *Cassell's Magazine*, August 1906

A Run with Rosalie, *Cassell's Magazine*, September 1906

---

446. Being the first two chapters.

If You Can Walk With Kings

The Six New Novels, *Cassell's Magazine,* October 1906

The Man of Secrets,[447] *Popular Magazine,* 6 October 1906

The Gentleman from London, *Cassell's Magazine,* November 1906

The Dragon's Snapdragon. *Canterbury Times,* December 1906

The Other Man, *Holly Leaves,* December 1906

A Diplomatic Secret, *Marlborough Express,* 24 December 1906

The Love Light, *Lady's World,* March 1907

Cheating the Avenger, *Penny Magazine,* 20 April 1907

The Genius of the Attic, *People's Magazine,* April 1907

The Peril of Pierrette, *The Story-Teller,* May 1907

The Trickster of No. 10,[448] *The Story-Teller,* July 1907

The Turk and the Temptress, *Pear's Annual,* 1907

The Red Circle, *Holly Leaves,* December 1907

The Prince and the Parson, *The Story-Teller,* January 1908

His Highness' Love Affair, *The Story-Teller,* May 1908

The Four Liqueur Glasses, *The Story-Teller,* September 1908

The Third Cracker, *Canterbury Times,* December 1908

The Count's Christmas Card, *Canterbury Times,* December 1908

The Black Boudoir, *The Story-Teller,* January 1909

The Princess's Escapade, *Cassell's Magazine,* January 1909

The Sign of the Cat's Paw, *Lancashire Daily Post,* 23 January 1909

The Mystery of the Fountain Pen, *Nash's Magazine,* April 1909

The Sultan's Sapphires, *Nash's Magazine,* July 1909

Within the Circle, *The Story-Teller,* July 1909

A Little Romance of 'PW', *Pearson's Weekly,* 9 September 1909

The Golden Fingers, *The Story-Teller,* October 1909

The Kid Glove, *The Story-Teller,* November 1909

---

447. First of seven instalments.
448. From a series entitled 'The Tenants of Toddington Terrace'. WmLQ contributed episode 3.

Bibliography

The Four Forget-Me-Nots, *The Story-Teller*, November 1909

The Mystery of Pierina, *The Story-Teller*, December 1909

Under Seal, *The Story-Teller*, January 1910

The Silence of His Excellency, *The Story-Teller*, February 1910

The Affair at Ashley Gardens, *Weekly Tale-Teller*, 2 April 1910

The Affair at Kensington, *Weekly Tale-Teller*, 28 March 1910

The Brass Butterfly, *The Story-Teller*, May 1910

Miserable Offenders, *Nash's Magazine*, October 1910

The Red Ring, *Adventure Magazine*, November 1910

The Mysterious Mistletoe, *Nash's Magazine*, December 1910

The Mystery of the Lean Englishman, *The New Magazine*, December 1910

The Third Cracker, *Hawera & Normanby Star*, December 1910

The Christmas Pudding, *Sunderland Daily Echo*, December 1910

The House with the Red Blinds, *The Story-Teller*, January 1911

The White Apron, *Chambers's Journal*, May 1911

Donna Elena, *Good Stories Magazine*, June 1911

The Affair at Kensington, *Weekly Tale-Teller*, 12 August 1911

The Christmas Tree, *Christmas Chronicle*, December 1911

The Crooked Hand, *The Story-Teller*, March 1912

The Frocks of Mademoiselle, *Young's Magazine*, May 1912

The Torn Card, *The Story-Teller*, December 1912

The Fur Motor Coat, *Marks & Spencer's Grand Annual*, Vol IV, Winter 1912–13

The Ducrocq Affair, *Weekly Tale-Teller*, 18 January 1913

The Christmas Candle, *Weekly Tale-Teller*, 6 December 1913

Rene Vidal's Last Christmas, *Short Stories*, December 1913

The Blood Orange, *Pear's Christmas Annual*, 1913

The Dark Spectacles, *Evening Post*, 1913

The Tide of Destiny, *Weekly Tale-Teller*, 6 June 1914

If You Can Walk With Kings

The Golden Mistletoe, *Western Gazette*, 26 December 1914
The Green Blackbird, *Royal Magazine*, June 1915
The Mystery of the Two Circles, *Royal Magazine*, July 1915
The House of Suspicion, *Royal Magazine*, August 1915
The Silk Purse, *The New Magazine*, September 1915
The Mystery of the Five Beans, *Royal Magazine*, September 1915
Behind Locked Doors, *Royal Magazine*, October 1915
The Secret of the Lonely Farm, *Royal Magazine*, November 1915
The Red Rooster, *Royal Magazine*, December 1915
The Blue Holly-Berry, *Teasdale Mercury*, 22 December 1915
The Night of the Seventeenth, *Royal Magazine*, January 1916
'Cinders' of Harley Street, *Christmas Premier Magazine*, January 1916
The Glass Bombs, *Royal Magazine*, February 1916
The Car with the Green Lights, *Premier Magazine*, February 1916
Secrets of State,[449] *Taunton Courier & Western Advertiser*, March 1916
The Secret Dispatch, *Royal Magazine*, April 1916
Within Four Walls, *Royal Magazine*, May 1916
The Hundred Sous, *Royal Magazine*, June 1916
The Mysterious Mission, *Royal Magazine*, July 1916
The Taint, *Cassell's Magazine*, July 1916
The Coral Crown, *Royal Magazine*, August 1916
The Secret of the Wilhelmstrasse, *Royal Magazine*, September 1916
The Yellow Tube, *Royal Magazine*, October 1916
The Great Tunnel Plot, *Grand Magazine*, October 1916
The Two Mistletoe Berries, *Royal Magazine*, November 1916
The Riddle of Traquair, *Red Magazine*, August 1916
The Traitress, *Cassell's Magazine*, February 1918

---

449. Serialised and published as *The Doctor of Pimlico*.

Bibliography

The Five Halfpennies, *Printer's Pie*, 1918

The Snare, *Royal Magazine*, January 1919

The Affair of the Rue Dauphine, *New Magazine*, June 1919

A Crooked Affair, *Blue Magazine*, July 1919

The Night Club Girl, *Blue Magazine*, August 1919

The Guest of the Embassy, *Hutchinson's Story Magazine*, October 1919

Twelve Days – and After, *Blue Magazine*, January 1920

Secrets of the Paris Sûreté: The Clue of the Newspaper Paragraph, *Premier Magazine*, 5 January 1920

Secrets of the Paris Sûreté: The Holes in the Wall, *Premier Magazine*, 16 January 1920

Secrets of the Paris Sûreté: The Secret of the Gleboff Emerald, *Premier Magazine*, 24 January 1920

Secrets of the Paris Sûreté: Affair of the Avenue Malakoff, *Premier Magazine*, 31 January 1920

Secrets of the Paris Sûreté: Mysterious Mademoiselle, *Premier Magazine*, 1 March 1920

Secrets of the Paris Sûreté: The Affair of the Rue Therese, *Premier Magazine*, 12 March 1920

Secrets of the Paris Sûreté: Villa Jasmin, *Premier Magazine*, 27 March 1920

Secrets of the Paris Sûreté: The Death Dealers of Deauville, *Premier Magazine*, 12 April 1920

Secrets of the Paris Sûreté: Black Satin Gloves, *Premier Magazine*, 23 April 1920

Secrets of the Paris Sûreté: The Chauffeur and the Little Lady, *Premier Magazine*, 26 April 1920

Secrets of the Paris Sûreté: The Hushed-Up Affair, *Premier Magazine*, 8 May 1920

The Silver Shadow: Strange Happenings at Froyle Park, *Premier Magazine*, 31 July 1920

The Stone Beetle, *The Story-Teller*, August 1920

If You Can Walk With Kings

The Silver Shadow: Montefalco Venus, *Premier Magazine*, 14 August 1920

The Silver Shadow: Hunchback of Piccadilly, *Premier Magazine*, 27 August 1920

The Silver Shadow: Rasputin's Crucifix, *Premier Magazine*, 30 August 1920

The City of Evil, *Royal Magazine*, September 1920

The Silver Shadow: Cupid and the Profiteer, *Premier Magazine*, 1 September 1920

The Silver Shadow: Crozier of Kresevo, *Premier Magazine*, 10 September 1920

The Silver Shadow: Bolshevik's Black Beads, *Premier Magazine*, 24 September 1920

The Silver Shadow: The Sign on the Kerb, *Premier Magazine*, 22 October 1920

Message of Mystery: The Cloven Hoof, *Premier Magazine*, 1919/21

The Elephant's Eye, *Premier Magazine*, 1919/21

The Priest of San Sisto, *Winter's Pie Magazine*, Christmas 1920

The Spotted Handkerchief, *Royal Magazine*, October 1920

Code Number Four, *Royal Magazine*, November 1920

The Dancer at the Folies Caprice, *Royal Magazine*, December 1920

The Affair of the Avenue Louise, *Royal Magazine*, January 1921

The Gems of Abdul Hamid,[450] *Royal Magazine*, January 1921

A Page of Secret History, *Royal Magazine*, February 1921

The Brown Trunk, *Royal Magazine*, March 1921

The Copper Clock, *Royal Magazine*, April 1921

The Left Hand Glove, *New Magazine*, September 1921

The Mystery of Rasputin's Jewels, *Royal Magazine*, December 1921

The Scarlet Kimono, *Grand Magazine*, January 1922

The Race for the Throne, *Royal Magazine*, January 1922

---

450. Also published as chapters 13 and 14 of *The Golden Face*.

Bibliography

The Little Old Lady with Curls, *Empire News*, 29 January 1922

The Mystery of the Seven Dots, *Royal Magazine*, January 1922

The Sorcerer of Soho, *Royal Magazine*, February 1922

The Master Atom, *Royal Magazine*, March 1922

For One Eye Only, *Royal Magazine*, May 1922

The Man in the Round Spectacles, *Grand Magazine*, July 1922

Bleke, the Butler, *Royal Magazine*, July 1922

The Girl Who Rang Twice, *Royal Magazine*, August 1922

The Mystery of Villa Poizat, *Royal Magazine*, September 1922

The Red Pearls, *Royal Magazine*, October 1922

The Indiscretions of Lady Bulverhythe, *Royal Magazine*, November 1922

The Closed Chamber at Cruden, *Royal Magazine*, December 1922

The Post Mark Code, *Cassell's Winter Annual*, 1922/3

A Round of Pleasure: The Lost Key, *Happy Magazine*, March 1923

A Round of Pleasure: The Man with the Golden Tooth, *Happy Magazine*, April 1923

A Round of Pleasure: The Secret of Enid Anderson, *Happy Magazine*, May 1923

The Hill of Winds, *Sovereign Magazine*, July 1923

The Factotum 1: The House of Silence, *Cassell's Magazine of Fiction*, September 1923

The Factotum 2: A Skeleton in the Cupboard, *Cassell's Magazine of Fiction*, October 1923

The Lure of Leonie, *The Story-Teller*, October 1923

The Golden Grasshopper, *Hutchinson's Magazine*, November 1925

The Factotum 3: A Slip of the Pen, *Cassell's Magazine of Fiction*, November 1923

The Factotum 4: A Wife from Nowhere, *Cassell's Magazine of Fiction*, December 1923

The Factotum 5: The Lost Pearl, *Cassell's Magazine of Fiction*, January

1924

The Factotum 6: A Woman's Sacrifice, *Cassell's Magazine of Fiction*, February 1924

The Enchanted Zero, *Sovereign Magazine*, December 1925

The Purple Death, *Hutchinson's Magazine*, December 1925

The Golden Ski, *Sovereign Magazine*, January 1926

The Man with the Squint, *Hutchinson's Magazine*, January 1926

The Rogue of the Rue Royale, *Hutchinson's Magazine*, February 1926

The Crooked Sou, *Hutchinson's Magazine*, March 1926

Tally Ho! *Sovereign Magazine*, April 1926

The Affair of the Cloche Hat, *Hutchinson's Magazine*, April 1926

The Tennis Alibi, *Sovereign Magazine*, May 1926

The House of Souls, *Hutchinson's Mystery Story Magazine*, May 1926

The Duck's Egg, *Sovereign Magazine*, August 1926

The Passport, *Hutchinson's Mystery Story Magazine*, August 1926

Down Tack!, *Sovereign Magazine*, September 1926

The Secret Worth a Million, *Sovereign Magazine*, October 1926

The House on Richmond Green, *Hutchinson's Mystery Story Magazine*, October 1926

The Affair of the Orange, *Hutchinson's Mystery Story Magazine*, November 1926

A Secret of the Underworld, *Hutchinson's Mystery Story Magazine*, December 1926

The Wizards of Westminster, *Sovereign Magazine*, January 1927

Chronicles of the Crimes Club, #1, *Hutchinson's Mystery Story Magazine*, January 1927

Knights of the Night, *Sovereign Magazine*, February 1927

Chronicles of the Crimes Club, #2, *Hutchinson's Mystery Story Magazine*, February 1927

The Gripping Claw, *Sovereign Magazine*, March 1927

Bibliography

Chronicles of the Crimes Club, #3, *Hutchinson's Mystery Story Magazine*, March 1927

The Dangerous Game, *Sovereign Magazine*, April 1927

The Peril of Helen Marklove, #1, *Hutchinson's Mystery Story Magazine*, July 1927

The Peril of Helen Marklove, #2, *Hutchinson's Mystery Story Magazine*, August 1927

The Stranger in Grey, November 1927. No publication details available

The Strange Case of the Phantom Fortune, *True Mystic Crimes*, April 1931

Marks on the Mirror, *Schoolboys' Adventure Book*, c.1931

The Secret of a Hushed-Up Affair, *The Book of a Thousand Thrills*, c.1935

The Secret of the Missing Bride, *The Book of a Thousand Thrills*, c.1935

Untraced Short Stories

Titles may have been changed before publication

A Mere Song

At the Last Judgement

The Affair in Pont Street

The Christmas Box

The Crooked Son (listed by his agent as The Crooked Son, but that could well have been a typographical error for The Crooked Sou)

The Curse of Abuhol

The Emperor's Son

The Golden Mistake

The House of Amen

The Lady in Grey

The Maid and the Motor

The Man at the Wheel

The Member for Hades

The Pilgrim of Piccadilly

The Purple Beast

The Red Rage

The Secrets of Yidiz

The Sherbourne Treasure, or The Treasure of the Sherbournes, or The Treasure of the Sherburns – destined at one time for *Royal Magazine*. A copy of the manuscript is in the safekeeping of the University of Texas.

Articles

Facts and Fancies: Loves, *Middlesex Chronicle*, 14 November 1885

An Italian Adventure, *Diprose's Annual*, 1889

An Escape from Siberia, *The Times*, 1 October 1890

The Mafiosi, Chambers's *Journal of Popular Literature, Science and Arts*, 18 June 1892. Published anonymously

Where Folly is God: Snap Shots at the Nice Carnival, *The Ludgate Magazine*, May 1898

Lazy Leghorn: The Brighton of Italy, *The Ludgate Magazine*, October 1898

From the Sunny South I: The Madonnas of Florence, The *Ludgate Magazine*, December 1898

From the Sunny South II: Pottering in Pisa, *The Ludgate Magazine*, January 1899.

From the Sunny South III: Rollicking on the Riviera, *The Ludgate Magazine*, February 1899

Mask and Domino: A Gossip about Carnivals, *Cassell's Magazine*, February 1899

Italics in Fiction: Inaccuracies in Foreign Background, *The Bookman*, February 1899

Bibliography

From the Sunny South IV: The Queen's Winter Home, *The Ludgate Magazine*, March 1899

From the Sunny South V: The Painted Hell, *The Ludgate Magazine*, April 1899

From the Sunny South VI: Over the Frontier, *The Ludgate Magazine*, May 1899

Snapshots in the Klondike, *The Ludgate Magazine*, December 1899

Italics in Fiction, *The Bookman*, March 1900

The Land of Liberty: San Marino and Its Wonders, *Cassell's Magazine*, March 1901

Further North Than Nansen, *English Illustrated*, April 1903

The Saviour of Italy, *Daily Mail*, 18 November 1904

A Master of Mystery, *Cassell's Magazine*, December 1905

Can England Be Invaded?, *Daily Mail*, 10 March 1906

If I Were a Millionaire, *Dundee Courier*, 8 January 1907

In the Days of My Youth, *Otago Witness*, 24 April 1907

Hoards of Treasure: Mysteries Hidden in the Earth, *Cassell's Magazine*, June 1909

Royalties I Have Met, *Cassell's Saturday Journal*, July 1910

King Peter, Diplomat, *Wanganui Chronicle*, 28 November 1912

The Story of the Chief of Police, *Canadian Magazine*, February 1915

Hotbeds of Alien Enemies and Spies in the Heart of the Metropolis, *The People*, 28 February 1915

The Spy Peril,[451] *Royal Magazine*, May 1915

The Silent Enemy, *The Post Sunday Special*, 27 August 1916

The Unknown To-Morrow, *The Post Sunday Special*, 24 September 1916

Germans in Scotland, *The Post Sunday Special*, 29 October 1916

Enemy Aliens in Scotland, *The Post Sunday Special*, 5 November 1916

---

451. Extract printed in the *Evening Telegraph* as 'Secret Agents of Germany'.

William Le Queux's Discoveries in Glasgow, *The Post Sunday Special*, 12 November 1916

Herr Burgdorff's Masonic Trip from Glasgow to Berlin, *The Post Sunday Special*, 19 November 1916

The Strange Case of Herr Kirchner, *The Post Sunday Special*, 26 November 1916

Prussian Sells Gramophones in Glasgow, *The Post Sunday Special*, 10 December 1916

The Four Fingers of the Hidden Hand in Scotland, *The Post Sunday Special*, 17 December 1916

Our Strangle-Hold on the German Spy System, *Canadian Magazine*, February 1917

Prussian Who Sold 'Blighty' Records, *The Post Sunday Special*, 8 April 1917

Rasputin, *Illustrated Sunday Herald*, June 1917

German's Hotel in Glasgow, *The Post Sunday Special*, 22 July 1917

Secret Life of Count de Borch, *The Post Sunday Special*, 16 September 1917

Von Kuhlmann: German Man of Mystery, *The Post Sunday Special*, 23 September 1917

Scandal of Escaping German Prisoners, *The Post Sunday Special*, 30 September 1917

Reprisals – But When? *The Post Sunday Special*, 7 October 1917

New Aliens at Large in Glasgow, *The Post Sunday Special*, 14 October 1917

Spies and Their Blunders, *Royal Magazine*, December 1917

From Behind the Curtain, *Everyweek*, 16 May 1918

All About Love, *Strand Magazine*, September 1918

The Secret History of the Kaiser's Shame, *Illustrated Sunday Herald*, 30 November 1918

How the Kaiser Went into Exile, *Illustrated Sunday Herald*, 21 December 1918

Who Stirs the Mud? *Royal Magazine*, October 1919

Bibliography

Foreign Listeners to British Wireless, *Popular Wireless Weekly*, 30 December 1922

Queer Company, *London Magazine*, July 1923

Early Adventures in Wireless. My Pioneer Experiments in Broadcasting, *Radio Times*, 21 December 1923

Why You Should Have a Set, *Popular Wireless Weekly*, 27 December 1923

Announcers as Teachers: The Scots Pictorial, *Radio Times*, 18 January 1924

The Tragic Love Story of an Emperor's Son, *Great Stories of Real Life*. Volume 1, part 1. London: George Newnes, 1924

Landru, the Bluebeard of France, *Great Stories of Real Life*. Volume 1, part 2. London: George Newnes, 1924

Dr Crippen – Lover or Poisoner, *Great Stories of Real Life*. Volume 1, part 3. London: George Newnes, 1924

The Mysterious Treasure of Madame Humbert, *Great Stories of Real Life*. Volume 1, part 5. London: George Newnes, 1924

Did Mrs Maybrook Kill Her Husband? *Great Stories of Real Life*. Volume 1, part 6. London: George Newnes, 1924

Rasputin the Mysterious, *Great Stories of Real Life*. Volume 1, part 7. London: George Newnes, 1924

Bela Kiss, the Mystery Man of Europe, *Great Stories of Real Life*. London: George Newnes, date unavailable

The World of Wireless: For VOI Coils, *Herts Advertiser*, 17 January 1925

The World of Wireless: Amateurs' Aerials, *Herts Advertiser*, 31 January 1925

The World of Wireless: The History of Wireless, *Herts Advertiser*, 7 February 1925

The World of Wireless: Our Earth, *Herts Advertiser*, 14 February 1925

The World of Wireless: Are We Safe? *Herts Advertiser*, 21 February 1925

The World of Wireless: The Present Licensing Position, *Herts Advertiser*, 28 February 1925

The World of Wireless: About Spark Interference, *Herts Advertiser*, 7 March 1925

The World of Wireless: Television in the Future, *Herts Advertiser*, May 1925

The World of Wireless: What About the Amateur, *Herts Advertiser*, 9 May 1925

The World of Wireless: Will Radio Last? *Herts Advertiser*, 13 June 1925

The World of Wireless: Wireless on Tap, *Herts Advertiser*, 4 July 1925

The World of Wireless: Poison by Wireless, *Herts Advertiser*, 18 July 1925

The World of Wireless: The Daventry Station, *Herts Advertiser*, 8 August 1925

An Aerial Swoop on London, *Empire News*, 6 September 1925

The World of Wireless: Wireless for the Invalid, *Herts Advertiser*, 24 October 1925

The World of Wireless: Wireless and the Next War, *Herts Advertiser*, 31 October 1925

The World of Wireless: Freaks of Crystal, *Herts Advertiser*, 12 December 1925

The Cleverest Murder: In Fact or Fiction, *Strand Magazine*, December 1926

A Bomb for the Winter Palace, *Secret Service Stories*, August 1928

The Wreck of the Royal Train, *Secret Service Stories*, September 1928

The Girl, the Doctor and the Missing Wife, *True Detective Mysteries*, May 1930

Untraced Articles

A London Sensation

His Country and His Queen

Lonely Lapland

Modern Greece

The German Death Factory

The Greatest Invasion

The Invasion of England

The Mysterious East

The Police of Europe

The War Secret

Sunshine and Snow 1924

What I Saw in the Balkans

When War Breaks Out

Index

Abingdon Mansions, Warwick Street, Kensington, 27, 35
Abruzzi, Duke of, 53
Agabeg, Enid Edris Peers, 229–231
Agabeg, Mrs of Peers Court, 229
Albania, Mission to, 67–97
Alderson, Frederick Cecil, 55
d'Angleterre, Hotel, Copenhagen, Denmark, 116

Baird, John Logie, 221
Beach's Theatre of Varieties, Brentford, 19
Beacon Place, Littleham, Devon, 30
Beau Rivage Hotel, Grindelwald, 251
Beckett, Arthur, 17
Beeforth, Beatrice May Crawford, xi, 60, 88, 119, 147
Beeforth, Elizabeth, 99
Beeforth, Gabrielle Marie Louise, xi, 99

Beeforth, George Lord, xi, 11 *passim*
du Boulevard, Hotel, Bucharest, Roumania, 86
Boyson Road, Southwark, 7, 11, 24
Brentford Gas Company, 196
Brighton, Sussex, 109
British Ski Association, 221
Buchanan, Sir George William, 86
Bunstow, Ann Ellen, 172
Buxton Opera House, 195–198

Café Vachette, Boul' Mich, Paris, 13
Campbell-Bannerman, Sir Henry, 61–62
Cardigan and Lancastre, Countess of, 147–148
Carmichael, Montgomery (Monty), 40, 49, 141, 162
Castor, Cambridgeshire, 43, 49
Cecil Hotel, Strand, 64–65, 70, 96–97, 103–105, 110, 112, 127, 130–132, 139

Cedars, The, Castor, nr Peterborough, 43–44, 50, 98

Chatfield, Ada (partner) (see also Emily Elizabeth Kelly) 120, 219–223

Chatfield, Alfred, 210

Chatfield, Frances Elizabeth (adopted daughter) (see also Emily Elizabeth Kelly) 210–211, 219, 222–224

Chatfield, Mabel Elizabeth (possible daughter) (see also Gertrude Miriam Kelly) 210–211, 219, 222–224

Cioni, Luisa Gemma (second wife), 45, 55, 66, 97–98, 115, 129, 137

Clifton Hotel, Welbeck Street, 56, 98

Colwyn Bay Hotel, Colwyn Bay, 205–206

Cooper, Sir William Earnshaw, 106, 136, 220

Croydon Road, Penge, 11, 26

Cromer, Norfolk, 178, 214–215

Dack, Charles, 52

Daily Mail, x, 38–39, 58, 60, 63

Dane's Inn, Strand, 27

Deene Park, Wansford, Northamptonshire, 147–149

Devonshire Club, St James's, 135, 138, 140, 143, 150, 182

Dey, Frederick van Rensselaer, 225

Doncaster Air Show, 149–150

Dorsett, Afred Thomas (father-in-law), 20, 24

Dorsett, Florence Alice (first wife), 19–20, 24, 42

Dorsett, Maria (mother-in-law) (see Maria Ann Wright)

East Harding Street, Fleet Street, 24

Eastbourne Gazette, 17

Edmonds, James Edward, 155–156

Edwards, G. H., 189–190

Elgin Avenue, Maida Vale, 142

Evans, Stanley (solicitor), 98, 168

Field, W. T., 19

Florence, 32

Foskett, Julia Amelia (sister-in-law), 36, 108

Fraulein, see Ernestina Kloss

Genoa, 10

Gilks, Louise (maternal grandmother), 6

Globe, The, x, 26, 29, 39

Golders Green Crematorium, 254

Index

Golding-Bird, Dr Cuthbert Hilton, 45, 92, 131
Goodrick, Charles, 2
Goodrick, Isaac, 2
Grand Hotel, Belgrade, Servia, 77
Grand Hotel Bulgarie, Sofia, Bulgaria, 68, 84, 87
Grand Hotel, Cettigne, Montenegro, 68, 72–73
Grand Hotel, Mürren, Switzerland, 227–231
Grand Hotel, Stockholm, Sweden, 117, 120
des Graz, Charles, 72, 74, 76
Greene, Conyngham, 89
Greville, Sir Sidney Robert, 65
Grey, Sir Edward, 97, 104, 110–111

HMS *Antrim*, 158–165
Haldane, Richard Burdon, 101
Hambledon, nr Henley-on-Thames, 194
Hammerfest, Norway, 114, 122
Harmsworth, Alfred, 34, 38
Hawson Court, Buckfastleigh, Devon, 156–157, 161–172
Henry, Sir Edward Richard, 190
Henson, Henrietta Maria (mother), 4, 11
Henson, Thomas (maternal grandfather), 6, 9
Hermitage, The, Guildown, Guildford, 194–199
Hill House School, Downham Market, 2
Holdsworth, Jack, 109, 125, 127, 194
Hounslow, 17, 24–26
Howes, Benjamin, 3–4
Hume Towers, Bournemouth, 106–107, 158
Husbands, Frederick Newton, 64, 110, 158–159, 165

Invercauld House, nr Braemar, 206

Johore, Crown Prince of, 209

Kabylia, 33
Karadodević, Peter, King of Servia 78, 83
'Kelly, Emily Elizabeth', 163, 210
'Kelly, Gertrude Miriam', 163, 210
'Kelly, William', 153–172
Kincardine Castle, nr Auchterarder 100–101, 146
Kings Cliffe, Northamptonshire, 3, 5, 8–10
Kings Somborne, 140

Kloss, Ernestina (Fraulein), xii, 38, 144
Knocke-sur-Links, Belgium, 252–253

du Lac, Hotel, Interlaken, Switzerland, 231
Lambton, Arthur, 190
Latin Quarter, Paris, 13–14
Lavender Cottage, Mount Street, Guildford, 208–209, 217–218
Le Queux, Frederick Henson (brother)
  birth, 10
  first wife, see Julia Amelia Foskett
  second wife, see Hylda Sophia Weston
  third wife, see Lillian Mary Norris
  death, 257
Le Queux, Vera Gladys Alice (daughter), 30
Le Queux, William Tufnell
  Who's Who, x, 182, 221
  birth, 6
  father, see William Lequeux
  mother, see Henrietta Henson
  education, 10
  Rue St Severin, Paris, 14–15
  first wife, see Florence Alice Dorsett
  marriage to first wife, 19
  daughter, see Vera Gladys Alice Le Queux
  death of first wife, 42
  second wife, see Luisa Gemma Cioni
  divorce, 66, 97–98, 115, 129, 135–141
  Cross of Chevalier, 51
  mission to Albania, 61–97
  offer of knighthood, 110
  De Windt–Le Queux Expedition, 103, 109, 112–124
  Order of the Cross of Italy, 151
  1911 National Census, 163
  River Nile accident, 170–171
  Egyptian artefacts, 175–177
  German spies shot at Aldershot, 187
  relationship with Ada Chatfield, 210
  'stepdaughters', 210
  wireless experiments, 214, 217
  'Uncle William' (BBC), 217
  skiing Accident in Bernese Oberland, 221
  relationship with Enid Agabeg, 229–231
  accident crossing the Eiger Glacier, 231

death in Ostend, 252
funeral, 254
Le Queux Magazine, 153
Leghorn (Livorno), 42, 216
Lemaire, M., 16
Lequeux, William Tufnell (father)
  birth, 2
  education, 2
  marriage to Henrietta Henson, 4
  French army, 7
  Norman Cross, 8
  death, 11, 26
Links Hotel, Knocke-sur-Mer, 253
Lodge, Mabelle (secretary), 208, 217
Lyon, 10–11, 16

Marashi, Vatt, 76
Marconi, Guglielmo, 216
Marina, St Leonards-on-Sea, Sussex, 219, 225–226
Methley Street, Lambeth, 42
Metropole Hotel, Folkestone, 144
Metropolitan Police, 183–191
Middlesex Chronicle, 17
Mina Road, Southwark, 4–6
Montenegro, 55
Montignoso, Countess of, 125–129

Mürren Ski Club, 221
Nicholas, Crown Prince, 6
Norman Cross, Cambridgeshire, see William Tufnell Le Queux
Norris, Lillian Mary (sister-in-law) 108, 257

Paris Morning News, 16
Pasha, Ahmed Tewfik, 91–92
Pegli, nr Genoa, x, 10, 13
Pera Palace & Summer Palace, Constantinople, 68, 90, 92–93
Peterborough Museum, 8, 50, 53, 176
Piazza Della Stazione, Milan, 40
Piccadilly, The, 33
Praga, Alfred, 253

Queen Anne's Mansions, London, 57, 60, 62, 98
Quinn, Superintendent Patrick, 190–191

Raven, William (uncle), 9–10
Reed, Major A. J., 96, 100, 107
Roberts, Earl, 35, 58–61
Rosebank, off Wales Farm Road, Acton, 108
Royal Oak Hotel, Bettws-y-Coed, 145

Rue St Severin, Paris, see William Tuffnell Le Queux
St Clement Danes Grammar School, Houghton Street, 10, 27
St Stephen's Road, Hounslow, 25
Sala, George Augustus, 29
San Remo, Republic of, x, 41, 51
Scarborough, xi, 57, 77, 141, 167, 195, 200, 228
Scutari, 68, 74–76
Sedan, Battle of, 7–8
Sladen, Douglas, ix, 38, 42, 152, 194, 209
Sladen, Norman St Barbe, xi, 17, 221, 253, 255
Smith, Dr Richard Leonard Bealy, 177–178
Stafford, Holland Road, Hove, Sussex, 109
Sunbury Cottage, Upper Halliford, 183–192, 214, 216
Sunny Bank, Godalming, Surrey, 41
Swiss Alpine Club, 221
Sydenham, 17

Talbot House, St Martin's Lane, 35, 38
Taylor, Rev. Francis, 254
Terry, Charles (business manager) 252–253

Thomson, David Coupar, 154
Times, The, 28, 39, 41, 62, 151–152, 186, 189, 196, 252
Toselli, Enrico, 125–126
Tomsk, 40–41
Tower Publishing Company, 14, 36–37
Tower, Reginald Thomas, 64
Tucker, Alexander, 84
'Traill, Tufnel', 222
Treloar, William, 106

Upper Phillimore Place, Kensington, 38

'Vanardy, Varick', 225
Via Babuino, Rome, 137
Villa Le Queux, Lastra a Signa, nr Florence, 53, 56, 98
Villa Renata, Florence, 97–98
Villa Teresa, Ardenza, 39, 41–42

Wansey Street, Southwark, 7, 9–10
Warnham, nr Horsham, Sussex, 31, 38
Warwick Gardens, Kensington, 46
Watt, A. P. (literary agent), 41, 59
West Mount, see Lavender Cottage
Weston, Hylda Sophia (sister-in-law), 108

Index

Whitehead, James Beethorn, 104

Willsie, Franklin Stanley, 222–224

de Windt, Harry Willes Darell, x, 112,–124, 130

Wright, Maria Ann (mother-in-law), 20

Zola, Emile, 17